T0383090

Turkish Accession to the EU

Is Turkey on the way to meeting the economic Copenhagen criteria?

The enlargement process that the European Union faced in the last decade stirred the debate again about the role Turkey has to play and whether or not Turkey should be part of the European Union. While the enlargement with the Central and Eastern European countries was a logical process, given the strong trade relationships and the political and historical context of these countries, the potential enlargement with Turkey is much more complex and controversial.

The main innovation of the present study is that it unravels the complexity of the Turkish case by approaching the problem from different angles in a comprehensive way. In particular, by tuning in on the historic, political and economic processes, new insights are obtained about the feasibility of Turkish accession to the EU. By combining lessons from the existing literature, the use of new data and the analysis of the political economic processes, a new perspective on the enlargement question – with the key Copenhagen criteria used as a cornerstone – is offered.

From an enlightened and liberal European perspective, and using empirical data throughout, *Turkish Accession to the EU* fills an important gap in the recent literature on EU–Turkey relations. Its well organized and accessible analytical format makes it a valuable contribution to students in political, social, economic, management and European studies as well as providing a framework for journalists, civil servants, managers, politicians and the general public unfamiliar with the topic.

Eric Faucompret is Professor of International Relations, University of Antwerp, Belgium.
Jozef Konings is Professor of Economics at the Catholic University of Leuven (KUL), Belgium.

Routledge Studies in Middle Eastern Economies

This series provides up to date overviews and analysis of the region's economies. The approaches taken are not confined to a particular approach and include analysis of growth and future development, individual country studies, oil, multinational enterprises, government policy, financial markets and the region's role in the world economy.

The Egyptian Economy
Performance policies and issues
Khalid Ikram

The Turkish Economy
The real economy, corporate governance and reform
Edited by Sumru G. Altug and Alpay Filiztekin

Economic Co-Operation in the Gulf
Issues in the economies of the Arab Gulf co-operation council states
Badr El Din A. Ibrahim

Turkish Accession to the EU
Satisfying the Copenhagen criteria
Eric Faucompret and Jozef Konings

Turkish Accession to the EU

Satisfying the Copenhagen criteria

**Eric Faucompret and
Jozef Konings**

Routledge
Taylor & Francis Group

LONDON AND NEW YORK

First published 2008
by Routledge
2 Park Square, Milton Park, Abingdon, Oxon, OX14 4RN

Simultaneously published in the USA and Canada
by Routledge
270 Madison Ave, New York NY 10016

Routledge is an imprint of the Taylor & Francis Group, an informa business

Transferred to Digital Printing 2009

© 2008 Eric Faucompret and Jozef Konings

Typeset in Times New Roman by Bookcraft Ltd,
Stroud, Gloucestershire

British Library Cataloguing in Publication Data
A catalogue record for this book is available
from the British Library

Library of Congress Cataloging in Publication Data
Faucompret, Eric.
 Turkish accession to the EU: satisfying the Copenhagen criteria / Eric
 Faucompret and Jozef Konings
 p. cm. – (Routledge studies in Middle Eastern economies; 4)
 Includes bibliographical references and index.
 1. European Union–Turkey. 2. European Union–Membership.
 I. Konings, Jozef. II. Title.
 HC240.25.T8F38 2008
 341.242'2–dc22
 2007039106

ISBN10: 0-415-45713-0 (hbk)
ISBN10: 0-203-92896-2 (ebk)
ISBN13: 978-0-415-45713-2 (hbk)
ISBN13: 978-0-203-92896-7 (ebk)

Contents

Figures

Tables

Acknowledgements

Many scholars, colleagues and friends have contributed ideas that influence this book. The book owes a special debt to Drs. Italo Colantone, who helped us with data research, and Drs. Stijn Vanormelingen, who helped us with the layout. We would also like to thank three anonymous referees who provided us with valuable information on an earlier manuscript. The management of LICOS, the Centre for Institutions and Economic Performance at the Katholieke Universiteit Leuven, provided us with a comfortable working climate and with logistical support. Finally, we are grateful to our home universities – the Katholieke Universiteit Leuven (Department of Economics and Applied Economics) and the Universiteit Antwerpen (Department of International Management and Diplomacy) – for having given us the opportunity to work on this book. The errors, of course, remain our own responsibility.

We are grateful to the following authors, institutions, journals and publishers for permission to make use of tables, reports or quotations in this publication:

- CABI Publishers for A. Burrell, 'Turkey's Foreign Trade Position' and 'Opportunities, Threats and Challenges', in A. M. Burrell and A. J. Oskam (eds), *Turkey in the European Union: Implications for Agriculture, Food and Structural Policy*.
- Cengage Learning Services Ltd on behalf of Taylor and Francis Books (UK) and Prof. Dr M. Uğur for M. Uğur, 'Economic Mismanagement and Turkey's Troubled Relations with the EU: Is there a Link?', in M. Uğur and N. Canefe (eds), *Turkey and European Integration: Accession Projects and Issues*.
- Centre for European Policy Studies (CEPS) for EU–Turkey Working Papers 2, 6 and 13.
- COFACE Belgium for @ratings EU and Turkey, *http://www.coface.be*.
- CPB Netherlands Bureau for Economic Policy Analysis for A. M. Lejour, R. A. de Mooij and C. H. Capel, 'Assessing the Economic Implications of Turkish Accession to the EU'.
- *The Economist* Intelligence Unit for *Country Report Turkey*.
- *The Economist* Newspaper Limited for *The Economist* (7 September 2000; 21 December 2000; 11 April 2002; 11 March 2004; 9 September 2004; 11 November 2004; 17 March 2005; 15 September 2005; 11 February 2006; 12 April 2006; 6 July 2006; 27 July 2006; 24 August 2006; 19 October 2006; 30 November 2 December 2006; 15 March 2007; 29 March 2007; 19 April 2007; 14 June 2007; 19 July 2007; 27 July 2007; 24 August 2007).

- Elsevier Limited for Y. Akyüz and K. Boratav, 'The Making of the Turkish Financial Crisis', *World Development*, and A. Mãné-Estrada, 'European Energy Security: Towards the Creation of the Geo-energy space', *Energy Policy*.
- EU Institute for Security Studies for K. Kirişçi, *Turkey's Foreign Policy in Turbulent Times* (Chaillot Paper No. 92).
- European Commission Directorate-General Enlargement for Commission of the European Communities, *Commission Regular Reports on Turkey (1998–2006)*, and Commission of the European Communities, *Issues Arising from Turkey's Membership Perspective.*
- Federal Trust for Education and Research for N. B. Gültekin and K. Yilmaz, 'The Turkish Economy before the EU Accession Talks', in M. Lake (ed.), *The EU and Turkey: A Glittering Prize or a Milestone?*
- *Foreign Affairs* for E. Aydinli, N. A. Özcan and D. Akyaz, 'The Turkish Military's March toward Europe', and E. Rouleau, 'Turkey's Dream of Democracy'.
- Foreign Policy Association for K. A. Wilkens, *Turkey Today: Troubled Ally's Search for Identity.*
- The ISIS Press for S. Deringil, *The Ottomans, the Turks, and World Power Politics.*
- Journals Rights for L. M. McLaren, 'Turkey's Eventual Membership of the EU: Turkish Elite Perspectives on the Issue', *Journal of Common Market Studies.*
- Koninklijke Brill NV for K. H. Karpat, 'Structural Change, Historical Stages of Modernization, and the Role of Social Groups in Turkish Politics', in K. H. Karpat (ed.), *Social Change and Politics in Turkey: A Structural Historical Analysis.*
- The Middle East Institute for Z. Önis and S. Yilmaz, 'The Turkey–EU–US Triangle in Perspective: Transformation or Continuity? *Middle East Journal.*
- Publications World Trade Organization for C. Hartler and S. Laird, 'The EU Model and Turkey: A Case for Thanksgiving?', World Trade Organization Staff Working Paper.
- Rand Corporation for S. F. Larrabee and I. O. Lesser, *Turkish Foreign Policy in an Age of Uncertainty.*
- I. B. Tauris & Co. Ltd and Prof. Dr E. J. Zürcher for E. J. Zürcher, *Turkey. A Modern History.*
- Taylor and Francis Journals (UK) for Z. Önis, 'Varieties and Crises of Neoliberal Globalization: Argentina, Turkey and the IMF', *Third World Quarterly.*
- Prof. Dr Hans Vollaard for R. T. Griffiths, 'Turks Lidmaatschap: Implicaties voor de Begroting', in R. T. Griffiths and D. Özdemir (eds), *Turkije in Europa: Turkije en Lidmaatschap van de Europese Unie.*
- Westview Press, a member of Perseus Books Group, for E. Özbudun, 'Constitution Making and Democratic Consolidation in Turkey', in M. Heper, A. Kazancigil and B. A. Rockman, *Institutions and Democratic Statecraft.*

Every effort has been made to contact copyright holders for their permission to reprint material in this book. The publishers would be grateful to hear from any copyright holder who is not here acknowledged and will undertake to rectify any errors or omissions in future editions of this book.

Abbreviations

ACP	Africa, Caribbean and Pacific
AKP	Justice and Development Party
BSRA	Banking Regulation and Supervisory Agency
CAP	Common Agricultural Policy
CEC	Commission of the European Communities
CEEC	Central and Eastern European Countries
CEN	Comité Européen de Normalisation
CENELEC	Comité Européen de Normalisation Electrotechnique
CENTO	Central Treaty Organization
CFSP	Common Foreign and Security Policy
CIS	Commonwealth of Independent States
CPI	Corruption Perceptions Index
DP	Democratic Party
EAEC	European Atomic Energy Community
EBRD	European Bank for Reconstruction and Development
EC	European Community
ECO	Economic Cooperation Organisation
ECSC	European Coal and Steel Community
EDC	European Defence Community
EDSP	European Defence and Security Policy
EEA	European Economic Area
EEC	European Economic Community
EFTA	European Free Trade Association
EMU	Economic and Monetary Union
ERDF	European Regional Development Fund
ESF	European Social Fund
ETSI	European Telecommunications Standards Institute
FAO	Food and Agricultural Organization
FDI	foreign direct investment
FPÖ	Freiheitliche Partei Österreichs (Austrian Freedom Party)
GA	General Assembly
GCI	Global Competitiveness Index
HDI	Human Development Index

HS	Harmonized Commodity Description and Coding System
IMF	International Monetary Fund
IPA	Instrument for Pre-Accession Assistance
IPARD	Instrument for Pre-Accession Assistance for Rural Development
KDP	Kurdish Democratic Party
MP	Motherland Party
NACE	Nomenclature Générale des Activités Économiques dans les Communautés Européennes
NATO	North Atlantic Treaty Organization
NGOs	Non-governmental organizations
NSC	National Security Council
NUC	National Unity Committee
OEEC	Organization for European Economic Cooperation
OSCE	Organization for Security and Cooperation in Europe
PECS	Pan-European Cumulating System
PKK	Kurdish Workers' Party
PPS	Purchasing Power Standards
PUK	People's Union of Kurdistan
RCA	Revealed Comparative Advantages
RPP	Republican People's Party
SDIF	Saving and Developing Insurance Fund
SMEs	Small and Medium-sized Enterprises
TRIPs	Trade-Related Intellectual Property Rights
UNIDO	United Nations Industrial Development Organization
UNRISD	United Nations Research Institute for Social Development
WEU	Western European Union

Map of Turkey, 2008

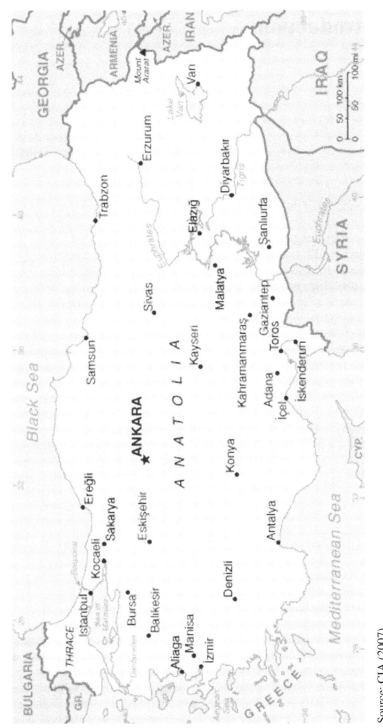

Source: CIA (2007).

Introduction

Since the fall of the Berlin Wall in 1989 we have seen a wave of countries wanting to join the European Union. The most controversial of these candidates is Turkey. Many interesting books and articles have been published on the relationship between the EU and Turkey, from either an economic or a political point of view. However, works with a global approach have been missing from this literature. This book tries to fill this gap in that it focuses on political, cultural, historical and economic constraints typifying the relationship between the EU and Turkey. Turkey–EU relations have always been difficult because of the very nature of Turkey's history and political, economic and societal structure. The problem is nicely illustrated in Samuel Huntington's *The Clash of Civilizations*. Huntington (1996: 148–9) calls Turkey a 'torn country' with a modernizing pro-Western elite and a population that clings to traditional Islamic values.

In order to find the answer to the question 'Does Turkey satisfy the Copenhagen criteria?', we will start with a short survey of the political history of Turkey. Is Turkey comparable with the Ottoman Empire? What can we tell about political parties and the corresponding class structure? Is the European interest in Turkey a recent phenomenon? In the second chapter we will discuss the evolution of the EU in conjunction with different stages of Turkey–EC/EU relations. What were the objectives of the EEC? How did it evolve over time? How did it cope with enlargement and the deepening of the integration process? How did it react to Turkey's attempts at rapprochement? We will see that the 1993 Copenhagen European Council marked a watershed in EU–Turkey relations. The Copenhagen criteria are the focus of this publication.

In the accession process, the EU has several instruments at its disposal, including gatekeeping, benchmarking and monitoring (Aydin and Keyman 2004: 14). Once the European Council has approved the accession partnership, candidate countries get privileged access to trade and financial aid,[1] while the Commission reports annually to the European Council on the progress the candidates have made towards fulfilling the Copenhagen criteria. At the end of each chapter in the Commission report, a list of recommendations is published. These reports guide the European Council in the decision whether to carry on with the negotiations. The first regular report for Turkey was published in 1998. Candidate states are expected to submit national programmes, indicating in detail how they envisage implementing the partnership priorities in the short and the medium term. Turkey submitted its first national programme to the Commission in 2001. In March 2003 the Commission published a revised accession partnership for Turkey, and Turkey prepared its complementary national programme at the end of 2003.

There is a strict Negotiation Framework. Negotiations are taking place – outside the EU framework – in an intergovernmental conference in which all member states and Turkey are participating. Building on the Commission's regular reports, the European Council, acting by unanimity, lays down benchmarks for the provisional closure and for the opening of each chapter. Chapters can be reopened if there are new EU rules or if Turkey has failed to meet its commitments. Each member state can use its veto twice. If agreement is reached between Turkey and all EU member states on each of the thirty-five chapters, the European Council can decide to recommend that the Commission signs the Accession Treaty. Only upon ratification by the European Parliament and by each of the twenty-eight parties can the Treaty enter into effect. The Negotiating Framework encompasses three formal chapters:

- the economic Copenhagen criteria;
- the political Copenhagen criteria;
- Turkey's unequivocal commitment to good neighbourly relations; Turkey's efforts to achieve a settlement of the Cyprus problem; the extension of the association agreement to Cyprus.

We will deal with the economic Copenhagen criteria in Chapter 3. Chapter 4 analyses the political Copenhagen criteria. In Chapter 5 we will deal with the remaining issues in the negotiating framework. Chapter 6 offers some concluding remarks.

We will try to answer the following questions. If the bottom line of the Copenhagen criteria is that the EU does not change and that the candidate country has to make the necessary adjustments, where does that leave Turkey? Has Turkey narrowed the discrepancies between its economic and political levels and those of EU member states? Is Turkey's entry going to cause unmanageable economic and political problems in the EU? How significant is the risk for existing EU member states and institutions of integrating Turkey? Is it not condescending for a great nation like Turkey to comply with EU requests? Does the EU not benefit from its position of strength? Can the Copenhagen criteria be used by the candidate state to overcome domestic resistance to economic and political reform?[2] Does the EU lose all influence on the candidate once it has joined? (See also Long 1997: 8; Harun 2003: 32; Uğur 2004: 96).

In order to answer our basic questions we will use the following working assumptions:

- We think that the Copenhagen criteria have raised the barrier for membership by adding political criteria that the EU did not invoke in past enlargements. Indeed, in Turkey, many observers have the impression that these criteria

were invented to make it easier for the Central and Eastern European countries to join the EU, while making it more difficult for Turkey to do so (see
also Larrabee and Lesser 2003: 50).

- We think that it is in the interest of the Turkish government to comply as
  much as possible with these criteria 'if it wants to realize a more democratic,
  tolerant, and civilian-ruled country' (see also Khan and Yavuz 2003: 122).
- We think that the Copenhagen criteria are considerably open to interpretation
  and thus the applicant's readiness for EU membership depends heavily on the
  view of the Commission as expressed in the *Progress Reports*.

We will try to summarize the results for each negotiating chapter of the different
Progress Reports and we will start each of our chapters with a short summary
of conclusions drawn by the Commission in the 2006 *Progress Report* based on
the Negotiation Framework and the Accession Partnership. In the accompanying
tables, we will indicate whether there was 'progress', 'no progress' or 'limited
progress' according to the Commission. We will give Turkey the benefit of doubt.
When it is not so clear whether there was progress or limited progress, then we
opt for progress. When it was not clear whether there was limited progress or
no progress at all, we opt for limited progress. However, in general it was clear
from the text of the *Progress Reports* which category we had to tick. Next, we
will elaborate on these conclusions by confronting them with primary data and
findings from distinguished scholars who have published on this topic. We will
pay most attention to the sensitive issues in the negotiations: free movement of
workers, common agricultural policy, structural policy, human rights and foreign
and security policy.

We hope we have written an objective unbiased report on Turkey–EU relations
that will appeal both to undergraduate students and to professionals whose work
requires knowledge of economic and political developments in Turkey and its
relations with the EU. Subsidiary interest may arise among postgraduate students
searching for possible research topics and lay readers who are interested in this
topic of current interest.

1 Short survey of the history of Turkey

We will open this chapter with a brief discussion about the Ottoman Empire, before focusing on the establishment of modern Turkey. We will then deal with the events that have been important in the further evolution of Turkey, using a chronological approach to outline events, and basing our analysis in essence on the publications of Kemal H. Karpat and Erik J. Zürcher.

The end of the Ottoman Empire

Diplomatically, Turkey has been part of the European state system since the nineteenth century, when the Ottoman Empire was included in the Concert of Europe. Throughout the nineteenth century, the Ottoman Empire fought to survive. It was threatened by outside powers (France, Russia and Austria), while its ally, the UK, wanted to be paid for its protection. Russia, in particular, tried to expand its territory at the expense of the Ottoman Empire. It created satellite states (Serbia, Montenegro, Romania and Albania) in Ottoman territory in the Balkans, and it tried to establish its hold on the strategically important sea lanes of the Bosporus and the Dardanelles. The sultan feared for the survival of the Empire. As the Ottoman Empire lost its military superiority, the Ottoman elite began to look to Europe as a model and to import European ideas (Larrabee and Lesser 2003: 45). Like Japan's Meiji restoration in 1868, Ottoman modernization was going to be a top-down project, where citizens were not directly involved. The Tanzimat edict of 1839 was the turning point in the sultan's modernization efforts. Reforms covered the army, the central bureaucracy, the provincial administration, taxation, education, communication and judiciary (Karpat 1973a: 43; Zürcher 1997: 59). New penal, commercial and maritime trade law codes were adopted, and the Shari'a was restricted to family law (Zürcher 1997: 64). The period of the Tanzimat also represented a cultural revolution, albeit a limited one. Leading civil servants – having acquired knowledge of the French language – became acquainted with the ideas of nationalism and liberalism. However, the 'Young Ottomans' – a small group within the elite – were opposed to the Tanzimat regime, which they considered authoritarian and out of date (Zürcher 1997: 71).

Instead, the Young Ottomans wanted to introduce Western concepts, such as a constitution, a parliament, freedom and equality, without giving up traditional

Islamic values. Under sultan Abdülhamit 2 (1876–1909) – though he himself was a tyrant – administrative centralization went further on. More than any of his predecessors, Abdülhamit called upon Islam to unite the people. However, he did not succeed in making the new generation of civil servants and military more loyal to the regime, let alone the people. The new generations were seduced by the liberal ideas as well as the Ottoman patriotism of the Young Ottomans (Zürcher 1997: 90). In Paris those who had been forced to flee the Ottoman Empire set up secret societies. These emigrants attacked the sultan in pamphlets and periodicals.[1] They called themselves 'Young Turks' (Zürcher 1997: 91). The re-emigration of Young Turks back to the Empire rejuvenated the domestic opposition. The Young Turks' uprising of 1908 against the sultan caught the regime by surprise (Karpat 1973a: 47). The Young Turks replaced the sultan with his more progressive brother. The Union and Progress Committee, the Young Turks' former secret organization, won elections. That committee soon became a mass organization from which Turkey's future leaders emerged. One of them was Mustafa Kemal (Deringil 2000: 184). In international relations, military defeats are often followed by a change of regime. It was no different in the Ottoman Empire.

Following the defeat of the Ottoman Empire by Bulgaria, Greece and Serbia in the Balkans Wars and the subsequent loss of Macedonia and Adrianople (1912–13), the army staged a coup in January 1913. The sultan was not officially deposed at this time, but from then on the Union and Progress Committee exercised real domestic power in the country (Zürcher 1997: 115). Barely a year after the end of the second Balkans War, the Ottoman Empire joined Germany and Austria-Hungary in the First World War. The German emperor, William II, had pricked the sultan's imagination by his megalomaniac ideas on world politics. In particular, his project to build a railway linking Berlin, Byzantium and Bagdad convinced the sultan that he should join the German war effort. For Germany, the entry into the war of the Ottoman Empire was of vital importance: it meant it could block Russia's access to the Bosporus and the Dardanelles and it could call on the Arabs to rise up against their Western oppressors.[2] The Empire had apparently been desperate for allies, and negotiations with both France and the UK had led nowhere. The sultan – impressed by the boasting of the German emperor – greatly overestimated Germany's war capacity. Moreover, like many, he had assumed that the war would be limited to the Balkans and would not turn into a world war. He had never expected the UK to join in the war (Zürcher 1997: 116–17). Public opinion as well as the army was unprepared for war. After four years of intensive war effort, the army was finally defeated. In accordance with the Moudros ceasefire agreement (1918), the Ottoman Empire had to accept the inevitable: the Bosporus and the Dardanelles were occupied by an inter-allied force, led by Great Britain. The European part of the country was going to be occupied by France, Italy and Greece. After the war had ended, the sultan had to accept the humiliating Peace Treaty of Sèvres (1919). The Ottoman Empire lost its Arab territories. It retained Anatolia, but was to grant autonomy to Kurdistan, pending a referendum on independence. Armenia became a separate republic under international guarantees, and Smyrna (now İzmir) and its environment were placed under Greek administration pending a plebiscite to determine its permanent status. In Europe, the Empire had to give up parts of Eastern Thrace and certain Aegean islands to Greece, and the Dodecanese and Rhodes to Italy, retaining only a small strip of land on the European continent: Constantinople and its surroundings, including the Zone of the Straits, which was neutralized and internationalized. The treaty was accepted by the government of Sultan Muhammad VI at Constantinople but was rejected by the rival nationalist government of Kemal Atatürk at Ankara. The First World War brought the end of four absolute monarchies: the house of Habsburg in Austria, the Hohenzollerns in Prussia, the Romanovs in Russia –and the Ottomans in Turkey. It heralded a new time, also, for Turkey.

The establishment of modern Turkey

Unlike many other states, Turkey has never been a colony. It has always been able to exercise a certain amount of autonomy and form a local intelligentsia, which explains the proud nature of its people (Kazancigil 1986: 132–3). Modern Turkey owes a lot to the Ottoman intelligentsia. This intelligentsia knew everything about law, checks and balances, political rights, the free press and the way to govern a country. It was also middle-class oriented. For the Ottoman scholars, a modern state could come into being only if it had a sound democratic and industrial basis. They knew the principles of modern political and economic thought. Modern Turkey's first generation of leaders was raised in schools set up by the Ottomans and they were taught how to rule a modern state. Moreover, from time to time, the Ottoman Empire itself had had experience with institutions such as a parliament, political parties and the press. Some Ottoman statesmen-historians even favoured a kind of Turkish nationalism (Karpat 1974: 97; Deringil 2000: 178–9). Mustafa Kemal was a product of the Ottoman intelligentsia. He combined a splendid intellect with a far-sighted vision and shrewd diplomatic skills. In the aftermath of the First World War, he saw his chance to unite his people. He succeeded in canalizing the anger of the army and public opinion incensed by the unjust Treaty of Sèvres. When the Greek, helped by British officers, tried to occupy Smyrna, Turkey declared war on Greece.

The War of Liberation (1919–22) created national unity in Turkey, for it brought together notables, intelligentsia and lower sections of civil servants and the military as well as the population, for the first time since the early days of the Ottoman Empire (Karpat 1973a: 47). In that war, both sides committed many atrocities. Yet the result was more important: under Mustafa Kemal, Atatürk, the Turkish army stood fast, and it drove the Greeks out of Smyrna. This was the military's finest hour, and it greatly enhanced Atatürk's reputation. Thanks to Atatürk, the humiliating Sèvres Treaty was repudiated and replaced by the very favourable Lausanne Treaty (1922). Turkey recovered Eastern Thrace, several Aegean islands, a strip along the Syrian border, the Smyrna (İzmir) district and the internationalized Zone of the Straits, which, however, was to remain demilitarized and remain subject to an international convention. In return, Turkey renounced all claims on Arab territories outside its new boundaries. Armenian and Kurdish independence were no longer mentioned. All wartime reparations were renounced. Turkey declared itself ready to protect its minorities, but there was no supervision of this (Zürcher 1997: 170). The remainder of the Greek orthodox population of Anatolia was exchanged against the Muslims from Greece. The League of Nations[3] tried to soften the impact of this human tragedy.

A republican regime established in 1923 replaced the monarchy. The decentralization and self-rule that had been typical of the Ottoman Empire were abolished. Geographic regions and minorities were put under one centralized Turkish government, and national political identity was emphasized. This was a clear break with the past if one looks back at the multicultural and Islamic nature of the Ottoman Empire, where the sultan had also been the caliph of the Muslims' world community. However, this was how modern Turkey would be governed (Karpat 1973a: 48; 1973b: 320).

In Atatürk's view, moreover, Turkey had to be ruled in accordance with the following principles (Zürcher 1997: 189; Rill 2006: 137):

- The sultanate and the caliphate had to be abolished (1 November 1922 and 3 March 1924) and the republic proclaimed (23 April 1923); the decline of the Ottoman Empire was attributed to the autocratic rule of the sultan and the rule of Islam.
- Religion had to be removed from public life and controlled by the government.
- Modern Turkey had to be a homogeneous state.[4]
- The interest of the people had to be the main concern of the ruling party.
- The state had to be distinct from the person of the leader, and there had to be cooperation between the private and the public sector.
- The state had to be pre-eminent in the economic field and it had to be continuously adapted to the requests of modernization.
- There had to be national solidarity, and the interests of the whole nation had to be put before those of any group or class.

The concept of national sovereignty that inspired modern Turkey was no different from that of nineteenth-century Europe. Many new European states saw the light. Nations felt united because of common race, religion, language, culture, geography and economic interests. Leaders like Cavour in Piemont or Bismarck in Prussia, and intellectual movements like the *Burschenschaften* in Germany or the *Carbonari* in Italy, encouraged the rise of nations against oppressors. This was also the case in Turkey. Events like the dismantling of the Ottoman Empire, the loss of territory in the Balkans and the Middle East (85 per cent of Ottoman territory and 75 per cent of population) and the attempts by Kurds and Armenians to carve out a separate state on Ottoman territory accentuated Turkish nationalism (*The Economist* 2007e). Out of these experiences came a strong desire for unity, with modernization and Westernization as key elements (Larrabee and Lesser 2003: 22). For Atatürk, Westernization and modernization were synonyms: 'We cannot shut ourselves in within our boundaries and ignore the outside world. We shall live as an advanced and civilized nation in the midst of contemporary civilization' (Waxman 1998: 3).

The first Grand National Assembly was elected in 1923, and, one year later, the first republican constitution was passed. Elections were strongly controlled by Kemal's Republican People's Party (RPP). The constitution was of an authoritarian nature: it did not provide for a check and balances system and it put a lot of power in the hands of the executive (Özbudun 1998: 230). Under Atatürk, Turkey was a strong one-party state. The event that was used by the president to put an end to political opposition was the Kurdish rebellion in February 1925 (Zürcher 1997: 176). The RPP was made up of the middle-class Muslim bourgeoisie. It governed the state. The elite were made up of the intelligentsia, land nobility and military. Workers and peasants were left out of the system – even if there was some class mobility (Karpat 1973a: 48; Deringil 2000: 180).

The Republicans

Kemalism was a top-down modernization project. The state took charge of cultural and socio-economic development. It had, therefore, to be modernized, which meant it had to import cultural and socio-economic concepts of Western civilization (Rumford 2003: 379). Yet elements of the Western political system were not introduced straight away: representative government, pluralism and freedom of thought and expression lagged behind (Zürcher 1997: 197; McLaren 2000: 118; Yavuz and Khan 2004: 389). Atatürk's view of Westernization clashed with Turkey's Ottoman and Middle Eastern Islamic traditions. Turkey adopted the Swiss civil code, Mussolini's Italy penal code and the Latin alphabet.[5] The Islamic dressing style and courtesy titles (except in the army) were abolished. Shari'a rules leading to the discrimination of women or prohibiting conversion were no longer valid.[6] However, in rejecting part of the Ottoman past and in turning against popular religion and against minorities, the Kemalists created unnecessarily opposition, particularly in the religious countryside and in the south-east, where the Kurdish minority lived. Whereas the Ottoman Empire had favoured a religious and multicultural society, Kemalism was opposed to the Islamic past and defended a strictly national identity (Zürcher 1997: 200; Waxman 1998: 7; Rumford 2002: 262).

During the first years after independence, Turkey's economy was in bad shape. Greek and Armenian traders were no longer there; Turkish industry was very weak. Only the recovery of the agricultural sector in those early years was spectacular (Zürcher 1997: 205). At the Economic Congress of İzmir in 1923, Turkey favoured rapid industrialization based on private entrepreneurship (Karpat 1968: 330; Lejour *et al.* 2004: 17). Before the 1929 economic crisis, things went relatively well. The Anatolian new bourgeoisie found common ground with the old bourgeoisie in the West (civil servants, officers, teachers, doctors, lawyers and entrepreneurs of larger commercial enterprises). They both dominated the RPP (Zürcher 1997: 203; Boratav and Özugurlu 2006: 159). But with the 1929 economic crisis, 'statism' was enforced as the government's official economic policy. In Atatürk's view, 'statism' was neither collectivism nor economic liberalism:

> The statism that we are implementing is a system peculiar to Turkey, engendered by its own needs. It means that while recognizing private entrepreneurship as the main basis, but realizing that many activities are not undertaken, the state must be given the control of the economy to face all the needs of a large country and of a great nation ... (Karpat 1968: 330–1)

In reality, after 1929 Kemalism became a policy of protectionism and import substitution. The first investments were in basic consumer goods, previously imported from the West. When, in 1932, a Soviet delegation visited Turkey and the Soviet Union made available a loan to aid the Turkish industrialization programme, the involvement of the state in the economic life became stronger. Yet private ownership remained intact. The state established industries in which the private sector was not interested. The economic policy was liberal in the sense that it was based on private ownership and initiative. But it was not liberal in the sense of non-interference on the part of the state. The state bought out railroad companies, created state monopolies and took interest in banks (Zürcher 1997: 204–6; Boratav and Özugurlu 2006: 163). Soon statism became state capitalism, and state economic enterprises became an economic asset in the hands of private interest groups that controlled the government (Karpat 1968: 332). (This is a still a problem besetting today's Turkey.) During the second half of the 1930s, there was a steady increase in Turkey's GDP. Living standards of workers improved and industry profits boomed. There was room for some tepid social legislation, but surprisingly the government implemented it only in foreign-owned firms employing large numbers of workers (Boratav and Özugurlu 2006: 166). The industrialization process brought wealth for new classes, like the captains of industry and skilled workers (Karpat 1973a: 52–6). Yet it hardly influenced the life of villagers, who made up the bulk of Turkey's population. The Kemalist state sided with the industrial elite. The Labour Law of 1936 was a copy of that of Fascist Italy, prohibiting strikes and the formation of trade unions (Zürcher 1997: 209).

The Democrats

In 1940 the liberal Mustafa İsmet İnönü succeeded Atatürk as president of the republic. Under his influence and in part as a result of pressure from the USA and the new economic middle class, Turkey introduced a multi-party democracy (Karpat 1973a: 53). At the same time, the state capitalist system remained intact. Turkey learned from the past mistakes of the Ottoman Empire: it remained neutral in the Second World War until June 1944. It concluded a Treaty of Mutual Assistance with the UK and France (19 October 1939) as well as a Treaty of Friendship and Non-Aggression with Germany (18 June 1941) (Deringil 2000: 219). On the one hand, the war increased Turkey's foreign reserves: it got a large gold loan from the allies in 1939 and it exported strategic commodities to both sides. On the other hand, during the Second World War Turkish GNP dropped sharply. It did not reach its 1939 level again until 1950 (Zürcher 1997: 208). The state deficit reached alarming proportions. The government introduced all kinds of taxes and other draconian measures to finance it. This hurt the bourgeoisie in particular.

There were both internal and external causes for the political and economic changes in Turkey after 1945. Domestically there was widespread discontent. Farmers and industrial workers had suffered severe income losses (Zürcher 1997: 215–17), and reforms were needed to save the system. Moreover, whereas throughout the 1920s and 1930s a close relationship with the USSR (which had helped Atatürk in the struggle against Greece) had been the cornerstone of Turkey's foreign policy, this changed after the Second World War. Turkey identified itself with the American ideals of multi-party democracy and liberal capitalism (Zürcher 1997: 218–19; Deringil 2000: 245). So Turkey moved to a multi-party system, but it did not take long before all left-wing parties were banned and their leaders prosecuted (Boratav and Özugurlu 2006: 171). The USA did not seem to object to this.

There were two rival factions in the RPP: the so-called revolutionaries favouring statism and planning and the 'moderates' favouring liberal capitalism (Boratav and Özugurlu 2006: 169–70). Formal opposition to the RPP first came from within its own ranks over the question of land reform (Karpat 1973b: 320). The Democratic Party (DP) was founded in 1946 mainly to unseat the ruling RPP. Whereas the civil servants and the military led the RPP, landowners, industrialists and the free professions assumed the leadership of the DP. Even so, the ideological differences between the DP and the RPP should not be exaggerated. Both parties represented the interests of the economically dominant classes, not the workers or the peasants. More than the Republicans, the DP favoured individual rights, respect for private property and freedom of economic enterprise (Karpat 1973b: 321; Boratav and Özugurlu 2006: 171). In the first multi-party elections (July 1946), it won only 62 of the 465 seats in the Assembly (Zürcher 1997: 222). In 1950, with the electoral victory of the DP, it was clear that a significantly different section of Turkey's elite had come to power (Karpat 1973a: 58; Zürcher 1997: 231). In the 1954 elections, the DP increased its majority in Parliament.

In order to stay in power, the Democrats favoured populist policies. Their measures included new infrastructure, cheap credits and high prices for farmers, municipal services for the urban poor, legislation on industrial relations and social security, and free education and health services. Agriculture was modernized and large-scale industrial firms were set up that are today still dominating the Turkish economy. All these measures cost a lot of money. Domestic savings were too small and foreign investors did not come to Turkey – a perennial problem in Turkey – so the government had to contract loans. Despite the liberal economic ideology of the DP, the state's role in the economy increased. Between 40 and 50 per cent of investment came from the state and privatization of large state-owned enterprises proved impossible. Successive democratic governments had to take the demands of the lower classes of society into account. All kinds of interest groups brought pressure to bear on the government to reap economic benefits (Karpat 1973a: 59;

1973b: 322; Zürcher 1997: 234–6; Deringil 2000: 247; Boratav and Özugurlu 2006: 172). The new middle class enjoyed its wealth. Yet, at the same time, it seemed to feel the need for some kind of counterweight, which it found in Islam (Karpat 1973b: 324). For the DP, Islam could go hand in hand with economic development. Thus in the 1950s there was a religious revival in Turkey, one that had always been there, but that had not dared to show its true face under the RPP's reign. The prayer call became legal again; religious education was expanded; the number of preacher schools was increased. Religious brotherhoods (which Atatürk had outlawed) were re-established. Pilgrimages to Mecca were even subsidized (Zürcher 1997: 245; Liel 2001: 10). Both the RPP and the army felt that the government infringed upon Kemalism.

In the mid-1950s things went wrong for the Democrats. The government had created expectations it could no longer honour. Living standards started to deteriorate and support dwindled because of the authoritarian style of government (Zürcher 1997: 234, 241). Civil servants were fired. Journalists were taken to court. After the September 1955 riots martial law was declared in three big cities (Istanbul, Ankara and İzmir). Controls on prices and supplies were reintroduced. The government ran out of money. It could have taxed the big landowners, but they were part of their electorate. Seeing no other way out, the Menderes government went to the IMF, which imposed budget cuts and a devaluation of the lira (Zürcher 1997: 239–40). The old intellectual bureaucratic elites felt threatened by the DP and the rising middle class. As rulers of the RPP, they had not cared for social reform; now they were in opposition, they declared themselves in favour, for it was their ticket to power again (Karpat 1968: 300–1). In the 1958 national elections the Democratic Party lost its absolute majority, but it remained the largest party thanks to the division in the opposition and vote rigging (Zürcher 1997: 243).

The second republic

On 27 May 1960 middle-rank officers – grouped together in the National Unity Committee (NUC) – removed the DP from government (Karpat 1973a: 61). The two precipitating causes that prompted the military to intervene were the activities of a parliamentary investigatory commission and the use of troops to suppress students' demonstrations (Zürcher 1997: 251). The intermediate causes were related to the fact that the founding principles of the Turkish Republic were being eroded, and that, because of this, there was growing public dissatisfaction with the government's intolerance of criticism. The deep cause for the military intervention has to be found in the fact that the junta wanted to end party strife and to bring new social classes to power. Indeed, the coup was directed against those who had acquired economic and political power under the Democrats (Karpat 1973b: 325). The Democrats' policy had alienated part of the elite and thus had jeopardized national unity, one of the basic tenets of Kemalism. The military could no longer stand on the sidelines. This explains why the NUC was not just satisfied with a change of government. It also purged the army and the universities of DP supporters (Zürcher 1997: 255). Most importantly of all, it wanted to lay the foundation for the second Turkish republic and to substitute a new more liberal constitution for the one of 1924. It set up a bicameral constituent assembly. The NUC constituted one of its chambers. The second chamber was made up of elected members (one-third) and members appointed by the opposition parties, the president and institutions like the judiciary, universities, bar associations, chambers of commerce and so on. Members of the outlawed DP were excluded (Özbudun 1998: 230). Behind the scenes, the NUC saw to it that a constitution emerged in line with its wishes. On 9 June 1961 it was approved by popular referendum, with 61.7 per cent in favour.

The 1961 Constitution of Turkey was the most liberal Turkey had ever had and ever would have. The following was explicitly stated:

- The Turkish Republic is a nationalistic, democratic, secular and social state, governed by the rule of law, based on human rights and fundamental tenets set forth in the preamble (art. 2).
- The Turkish State is an indivisible whole comprising its territory and people. Its official language is Turkish. Its capital is the city of Ankara (art. 3).
- Sovereignty is vested in the nation without reservation and condition. The nation shall exercise its sovereignty through the authorized agencies as prescribed by the principles laid down in the Constitution. The right to exercise such sovereignty shall not be delegated to any one person, group or class. No person or agency shall exercise any state authority that does not drive its origin from the Constitution (art. 5).
- The fundamental rights and freedoms shall be restricted by law and only in conformity with the letter and spirit of the constitution. The law shall not infringe upon the essence of any right or liberty not even when it is applied for the purpose of upholding public interest, morals and order, social justice as well as national security (art. 11).
- All individuals are equal before the law, irrespective of language, race, sex, political opinion, philosophical views, or religion or religious sect. No privileges shall be granted to any individual, family, group or class (art. 11).
- The state is entrusted with the tasks of economic, social and cultural planning; carrying out land reform; providing health care and housing; creating social security organizations; helping to ensure full employment and the like. The state is also empowered to take measures to force private enterprises to act 'in accordance with the requirements of national economy and with social objectives' (art. 49).
- The political use of religion is prohibited (art. 19).

Moreover, the 1961 constitution introduced a bicameral system and a president to be elected by both houses for a term of seven years. The president had limited veto power and could dissolve the Parliament. The constitution also had an extensive chapter on political, individual, economic and social rights. It introduced proportional representation, thus making it less likely for one party to hold an overwhelming majority in the Assembly. Workers got the right to strike and to engage in collective bargaining, and trade unions were recognized. The constitution provided the basis for the establishment of Western-type industrial relations based on tripartite representation.

This constitution brought Turkey in line with progressive Western countries. The new electoral system brought workers and peasants into the political system (Boratav and Özugurlu 2006: 174). The military also favoured economic and social institutions to encourage economic development and social justice. The State Planning Organization was one of these institutions (Karpat 1973a: 61). Its aim was to advise the government when it had to made decisions on resources, economic and social objectives, economic cooperation and planning (Karpat 1973b: 353).

Both radical and moderate junior officers sat on the NUC. The radicals wanted the NUC to keep power for as long as necessary, most certainly until the time had come for competent and social-minded politicians to take over. The moderates wanted a quick return to parliamentary democracy. As the moderates gained the upper hand, the military returned power to civilians seventeen months later (Karpat 1973a: 90). To put it into perspective, the 1960 coup was very important. It proved that the military were concerned about democracy. In the power struggle between the bureaucratic elite of the early days of the republic and a new group involved in economic occupations and liberal professions, the army had to step in. It supported the labour class and the farmers (Karpat 1973b: 317), and also favoured the secularists in their power struggle with the Islamists. Since the 1960s, the prestige of the generals has been further enhanced because it became very clear that they alone could safeguard Atatürk's state system (Karpat 1973b: 334).

In the 1960s ideology entered Turkish politics. Whereas before then it was self-evident that the elites ruled the country and that the lower classes were in a position to bring either of two elites to power, now it was possible – at least in theory – for workers and farmers to get elected and for themselves to become part of the elite. Thus, new political parties were set up: the Justice Party (successor to the DP), the New Turkey Party, the National Action Party and the Labour Party (Karpat 1968: 302; 1973b: 355; Zürcher 1997: 259). Even when the 1961 national elections were disappointing for the military – for they were won by the Justice Party – the highest-ranking generals resisted the demand of officers and university professors to intervene. Yet General Cemal Gürsel was nominated as the presidential candidate (Karpat 1973b: 354; 1973c: 250). Thanks to the new constitution, it was possible for the military – through the presidency – to check the activities of the government. It took some time for the political situation to stabilize. Two new military coups failed (1962 and 1963). There were hot ideological debates on the State Planning Organization, with the RPP advocating state planning and the Justice Party rejecting it (Karpat 1968: 302).

Religion did not yet manifest itself as a separate political ideology. At that time, there were no independent Islamic parties that could upset the political balance. Both the RPP and the Justice Party appealed to religion feelings to win elections. A modern rationalist version of Islam was propagated, very different from the one professed in villages (Karpat 1968: 304; Zürcher 1997: 259). New mosques were built and religious education in schools was expanded. The directorate for religious affairs started publication of sermons and the Koran was published in Turkish translation. The new constitution provided for greater freedom of assembly. This led – perhaps unintentionally – to the establishment of hundreds of religious organizations (Liel 2001: 10). In 1963 the state security organization issued a report on the confused ideological atmosphere with 'extremist' currents such as communism, Islamism and Kurdish nationalism (Karpat 1973b: 357).

The 1960s

In the golden 1960s Turkey went through a period of economic boom that made social reforms possible. For entrepreneurs this was the golden age of industrial capital, benefiting from low interest rates and cheap loans, cheap inputs and expanding domestic markets shielded from foreign competition (Boratav and Özugurlu 2006: 177). From 1961 to 1965 weak coalition governments ruled Turkey. Workers regularly took to the streets, asking for the implementation of the constitutional rights to strike and to engage in collective bargaining (Karpat 1973c: 275). Bülent Ecevit's RPP (the traditional party of bureaucratic elites), shifting to a policy of 'left of centre' after 1965, intended to attract the left-oriented younger intelligentsia. At the same time, it became a party of self-made men from the countryside and provincial towns (Karpat1973a: 82; Zürcher 1997: 263). Süleyman Demirels's Justice Party (a very heterogeneous coalition of industrialists, small traders and artisans, peasants and large landowners, religious reactionaries and Western-oriented liberals) catered for the business vote and the 'right of centre' and still had its base in the more developed part of the country (Karpat 1973c: 279). One of Demirel's most important achievements was to reconcile the army with a party that was the successor to the DP that had been removed from power by the military only a couple of years before. There was a price to be paid for that: the complete autonomy of the armed forces (Zürcher 1997: 263). The 1965 elections created one small group from the extreme left (Labour Party: 2 seats), one small one from the extreme right (National Action Party: 11 seats) and a large number of middle-class groups (Justice: 239 seats; Republican: 134; National: 31; New Turkey: 19) (Karpat 1973b: 363; Karpat 1973c: 262). In Parliament, the middle class was overrepresented, and workers and peasants were still underrepresented. Yet, thanks to social-minded lobbies that cared for the poor, the ruling politicians were going to take into account their needs (Karpat 1973c: 280).

In the second half of the 1960s Turkey was heading for a new crisis. Once again there was a growing proliferation in the political landscape. Right-wing hardliners left the Justice Party to create a party of their own, the Democratic Party. Those who thought the RPP was pursuing a too left-wing policy left the party and established another one: the Reliance Party (Zürcher 1997: 263–6). On the extreme right, the National Action Party had established a youth organization: the Grey Wolves. Their mission was to crush the left (Zürcher 1997: 269–70). At the end of the 1960s all kinds of left-wing groups – inspired by the demonstrations in the

USA and France – started campaigns of terrorism and guerrilla warfare in order to destabilize the country. The Demirel government was unable to act and stop the violence.

The 1970 coup

After the general elections of 1969, Turkey was in the grip of violence. The chief of the general staff presented a letter of memorandum to President Cevdet Sunay requesting a strong and credible government (12 March 1971). Upon the warning of the civilian officers that, unless the Demirel government stepped down, the army could take over the rule of the country, Demirel resigned, and Nihat Erim, a university professor and a member of the RPP, replaced him. Parliament was not dissolved, but, after new clashes, martial law was declared (27 April 1971). Following the coup, the Labour Party and many leftist organizations were outlawed. Leftist militants were arrested and left-wing officers in the army were fired. The constitution was twice amended (1971 and 1973). Civil liberties were curtailed; the autonomy of universities and of radio and television was ended; the Executive received more power and the institutional autonomy of the military was increased (Zürcher 1997: 273; Özbudun 1998: 234). The rule of Erim was not very successful. He was unable to implement his main reform programme (land reform, land tax, nationalization of the mineral industry and measures to protect Turkish industry) by demanding that joint ventures be at least 51 per cent Turkish-owned (Zürcher 1997: 271).

Again the military kept word: they did not keep power for a long time. In October 1973 the first free national elections after the coup were held. Ecevit's RPP and Demirel's Justice Party were the winning parties, but neither of them had an absolute majority. This pattern was to repeat itself during the 1970s. There were weak coalition governments led either by the Justice Party or by the RPP with smaller parties or minority governments. A coalition of both the Justice Party and the RPP proved impossible.

The polarization was due to ideological factors and to the personal rivalry between Demirel and Ecevit (Zürcher 1997: 276). No government was able to deal with two major problems: the economic crisis and political violence. In the 1970s Turkey continued its import substitution policy. It protected its industry by imposing high tariffs on imports, by keeping the exchange rate of the Turkish lira very high, by supporting inefficient state-owned industries and by helping Turkish firms in subsidizing imports. After 1973 inflation ran out of hand, Central Bank Reserves were depleted and a booming black market came into existence. Foreign-exchange constraints pulled industrial output and productivity downwards, and inflation started to rise (Boratav and Özugurlu 2006: 177). Workers requiring wage increases went on strike or occupied factories. Seeing no way out, the government negotiated a new standby agreement with the IMF, but trade unions made it impossible to implement it (Zürcher 1997: 278–82; Aydin and Keyman 2004: 4–6). The number of victims of political violence increased quickly: from around 230 in 1977 to between 1,200 and 1,500 two years later.

Whole neighbourhoods, especially in the squatter towns, came under the control of gangs and were declared liberated territory. To make matters worse, in 1978 Abdullah Öcalan founded the neo-Marxist Kurdish Workers Party (PKK), whose aim was to establish a socialist Kurdish state in the south-east of the country (Zürcher 1997: 277).

In this confusing economic and political climate, religion manifested itself for the first time as an independent ideological factor. Necmettin Erbakan's National Salvation Party accused the major parties of corruption and offered a solution to Turkey's economic and political crisis: a return to Islam. It won his party a growing number of votes. Because of the political stalemate between the two big parties, the National Salvation Party became an indispensable coalition partner, which in turn enabled the party to get more votes in new elections. Erbakan's agenda was openly religious: he emphasized Islamic virtues, the criminalization of offences against Islam and larger budgets for Islamic affairs. His party fought against alcohol consumption, 'obscene' magazines and women in official positions wearing 'indecent' clothes. Under his influence, Turkey became in 1976 a full member of the Islamic Conference. Erbakan's support grew because of the 1979 Islamic Revolution in Iran. On the eve of the 1980 coup, the National Salvation Party organised a mass demonstration requesting the reinstatement of the Islamic state in Turkey and the Shari'a, to be a substitute for the Turkish constitution (Zürcher 1997: 282; Liel 2001: 12).

The 1980 coup

There were several factors explaining the new coup – this time carried out by the hierarchy of the army and supported by the business organizations – on 12 September 1980 (Boratav and Özugurlu 2006: 179):

- the economic crisis worsened by the second oil crisis;[7]
- the lack of discipline in the labour market and the demands of trade unions;
- the political violence;
- the PKK separatism and the inability of politicians to do something about it;
- the threat of Islamic fundamentalism.

Right from the start the generals made it clear that they intended to return power to politicians. Yet first Turkey's house had to be put in order. Repression was going to be much harsher than it had been in 1960 or 1971. All political parties were dissolved and their possessions confiscated; newspapers were closed; politicians (including Erbakan, Ecevit and Demirel) and journalists were arrested. Academics were fired (Zürcher 1997: 292–4).

The generals wanted to draw a new constitution, in their own words 'aimed at a major restructuring of Turkish democracy' (Özbudun 1998: 234). To reach this aim they set up a bicameral structure: one chamber was the NSC itself and the other one was entirely made up of members appointed by the NSC. In the new constitution (which was much less liberal than the previous one) the president was given important powers, like the right to appoint judges and rectors of universities, the two areas considered sensitive by the military. The freedom of association was severely restricted. The electoral system was changed, establishing a 10 per cent threshold of the total popular vote, thus preventing political party proliferation. The senate was abolished. Industrial relations were covered in fine detail. Conditions were imposed on membership of trade unions; political involvement of trade unions was forbidden. Religious education was reintroduced into schools. The constitution also provided for an extensive judicial system. State Security Courts were to deal with offences against the integrity of the state. The high court system included a Constitutional Court responsible for judicial review of legislation, a Court of Cassation (or Supreme Court of Appeals), a Council of State serving as the high administrative and appeals court, a Court of Accounts and a Military Court of Appeals. The High Council of Judges and Prosecutors, appointed by the president, supervised the judiciary (Özbudun 1998: 236; Wilkens 1998: 55; Liel 2001: 13; Tocci 2001: 9–10; Bonner 2005: 50; Boratav and Özugurlu 2006: 179).

Turgut Özal

Again the military kept word: elections were held in 1983. However, only three (new) parties could take part: the Party of Nationalist Democracy, which had been set up by the army; the Populist Party, which came closest to the RPP, and the Motherland Party (MP) of Turgut Özal. His party was a rainbow coalition of technocrats, religious conservatives, and supporters of the centre right. It scored an overwhelming victory by appealing to the supporters of the old Justice Party, the fundamentalist National Salvation Party and the extreme right-wing National Action Party (Zürcher 1997: 297; Waxman 1998: 10). In the 1987 elections, the Motherland Party even increased its votes. Turkey was going to enjoy a decade of successful leadership under Turgut Özal, first as prime minister (1983–9) then as president (1989–93). Özal believed in a bottom-up revolution: he wanted the people to engage in the modernization process. Modernization led to more wealth. Therefore, Turkish industry had to become more competitive by opening up to the world. The goal of industrialization was shifted from import substitution to export promotion. Özal was very much in favour of EU membership, cooperation with the Balkans (he launched the Black Sea Economic Cooperation initiative[8]) and special relations with the 'external Turks' in the former Soviet Union. Özal believed in the benefits of capitalism and free markets: his economic policy created a new class of businesspersons (Boratav and Özugurlu 2006: 180). An entrepreneurial spirit emerged. For the first time, genuine efforts were made to attract foreign investors and to invest in tourism.

Özal was a shrewd politician: he kept the confidence of the military, gradually enabled other political parties to take part in elections and at the same time played off one faction in his own party against the other. He also broadened the power basis of the Motherland Party by attracting the Muslim vote. The party used an Islamic discourse to beat left-wing ideologies and to create unity in the political system (Waxman 1998: 9; Cizre and Çinar 2003: 312; Aydin and Keyman 2004: 8).

According to Özal, there was not necessarily a contradiction between Kemalism and Islam. Love for the state and for the army was religious duty (Zürcher 1997: 303; Waxman 1998: 11; Wilkens 1998: 55; Kazancigil 2004: 19). Part of Özal's new entrepreneurial class was close to the Islamic movement.

Unfortunately – like the sorcerer's apprentice – Özal set in motion forces that, in the end, he could no longer control. Unbridled consumption led to high inflation and a substantial decline in income of workers and farmers. Accusations of nepotism and corruption undermined the prestige of the Motherland Party. Political Islam resurfaced. Once again there was growing polarization in Turkish society, this time between secularists and Islamists. Debates were centred on the wearing of the headscarf in public places, the rights of graduates from 'imam-hatip' (Koran) schools and the religious content of schoolbooks (Boratav and Özugurlu 2006: 180).

The bloodless 1997 coup

The 1990s were for Turkey 'a lost decade' (Kazancigil 2004: 19). Özal left behind a deeply divided party system. Economic growth stagnated; there were two major financial crises in 1994 and 2001; immigration from the south-east increased and created tensions in overcrowded cities. Kurdish nationalists and fundamentalist Islamists became very vociferous. The old political parties came back under different names. Weak coalition governments that could not cope with economic, social, let alone political problems paralysed the political system. In 1991 Demirel returned to the political scene. However, his government could not realize any of its electoral promises. This was partially due to obstruction by President Özal. After Özal's sudden death in 1993, Demirel became the ninth president of Turkey. Tansu Çiller was elected leader of the True Path Party and thus automatically became prime minister. She did not enjoy the prestige of her predecessor. Her coalition was constantly in danger of falling apart. Ecevit's Democratic Left Party attacked her for huge unemployment rates and restrictive labour legislation (Zürcher 1997: 310). Under her term of office, the National Security Council gained even more power and the military almost determined on their own security issues (Wilkens 1998: 57).

The generals focused in essence on Kurdish and religious issues. However, they underestimated the electoral support of the Islamists, now grouped together in the Welfare Party of Necmettin Erbakan, the successor of the banned National Order Party. Like the leopard, Erbakan had not changed his spots. He continued to attack secularity, led anti-Israel demonstrations and warned against Turkey joining the EU, which could make it a 'province of Israel' (Liel 2001: 13). In the December 1995 elections, Welfare became the largest party. There were several reasons for this: the Welfare Party was a grassroots movement; it was not tainted by corruption, like the other parties; it used computerized, high-tech voting rolls and data banks; it had governed well at the local level; it combined a pro-Islamic and Turkish nationalist agenda. Most of all: it was a populist party (Wilkens 1998: 59). Its voters were mainly found among the religious people from the countryside who had immigrated to the cities and who had kept their traditional religious values ('Black Turks') (Waxman 1998: 11). When in June 1996 a coalition between the Motherland Party and the True Path Party fell apart only four months after its inauguration, Erbakan became the first openly Islamic prime minister in the history of Turkey. His Welfare Party joined Çiller's True Path Party in a coalition (Zürcher 1997: 314).

Right from the start, it was clear that the generals wanted to bring down this government – and Erbakan gave them every reason to do so. He interpreted in a very lenient way constitutional restrictions on religion (including the right to wear headscarves in public places), he met in public with members of banned Sufi brotherhoods; he recruited Islamists for government jobs and he paid an official visit to Libya (Wilkens 1998: 7, 60). On 28 February 1997 the National Security Council called on the government to enforce constitutional bans on Islamic dress codes, close newspapers that followed an anti-secular line, prohibit the civil service from hiring officers who had been discharged for fundamentalist activities and regulate enrolment in Islamic schools. After a few months of escalating tensions, Erbakan's government collapsed as a result of this 'bloodless coup' by the army (Wilkens 1998: 8). The next government was led by Ahmet Mesut Yilmaz, co-founder of the Motherland Party. It carried out an anti-Islamic agenda. It curbed the influence of Islamic schools, and many national and local leaders of the Welfare Party were prosecuted (Wilkens 1998: 58). The coalition that emerged after the 1999 elections, comprising Prime Minister Bülent Ecevit's Democratic Left Party, the centre-right Motherland Party and the right-wing Nationalist Action Party was too heterogeneous to govern. In order to keep this mothballed coalition together and to curry favour with the Nationalist Action Party, the weak Ecevit pursued a nationalistic and populist policy, criticizing the IMF and the EU and vowing to combat corruption (Larrabee and Lesser 2003: 11). It was clear that things were once again going in the wrong direction.

Erdoğan

The result of the November 2002 elections sent shock waves throughout Turkish society. The traditional centrist parties – tainted by alleged corruption, incompetence and continuing infighting – were swept away by a new party, the Justice and Development Party (AKP). This party – a loose coalition of Islamists, nationals and liberals – got two-thirds of the seats at the National Assembly, while all other parties but the RPP disappeared. The AKP had been established in 2001 and was an offspring from the outlawed Welfare Party. Its leader, Recep Tayyip Erdoğan, was a former disciple of Erbakan, who broke with him after the 1997 coup. In 1998 he was jailed for reading an Islamist poem in public, and he once described democracy 'as a train we could get off before we reach our destination' (*The Economist*, 2007e). Therefore relations between the AKP government and the army were bad right from the start. In January 2003 the chief of general staff issued a stiff warning to the government. Concerns were raised as to the party's commitment to secularism and its attitude with respect to Cyprus and EU membership

(Kirişçi 2006: 44). When suicide bombers attacked two synagogues and a British bank and consulate-general in Istanbul (November 2003), the military blamed the government for being too lax on Islamists. The AKP called itself not Islamic but conservative democratic. Its leaders toned down the Islamic rhetoric. In foreign policy, the AKP was wary about globalization, and it was more nationalistic in tone than other parties (Larrabee and Lesser 2003: 10). However, it believed in the benefits of EU membership and in cooperation with the IMF to stabilize the economy. Only a stable and prosperous Turkey could guarantee religious freedom. Since 2002 no other Turkish government has implemented that many constitutional reforms as the AKP government. This has impressed public opinion in both Turkey and the EU.

In the face of stiff opposition from the army, the urban middle class, trade unions and employers' associations, civil movements and religious minorities, the AKP government had to walk a fine thread. Its electoral base was – similar to that of the earlier Welfare Party – in the religious countryside and with the religious city-dwellers. It had developed a strong presence in civil society. Religious foundations provided support in education, housing and health for those the state did not help (Waxman 1998: 11). The AKP was also supported by the Anatolian middle class, who had suffered from the past high rates of inflation and devaluation, and by secular workers, who had to live with minimum social services. Therefore, if the AKP government wanted to be re-elected, it had to pursue a progressive social-economic policy and it had to satisfy at least part of the demands from its religious electorate. It put party members on key administrative posts. It tried to lift the ban on women wearing headscarves in public places. It tried to enable graduates from 'imam hatip' (Koran) schools to go to university without an entry exam. It tried to criminalize adultery. It tried to appoint an Islamist as head of the Central Bank. It recruited, as teachers, hundred of graduates from Koran schools. Its controversial education minister, Huseyin Çelik, ordered a revision of textbooks to remove Darwin and introduce creationism (Kazancigil 2004: 33; *The Economist*, 2007e).

Most of the time the president – in close collaboration with the army – stepped in and vetoed laws. That is why the AKP government seized the opportunity when President Ahmet Necdet Sezer's seven-year term was about to end. Under the 1982 constitution, the president has significant powers: the power to veto a bill and to choose judges, rectors and chief of general staff. On 27 April 2007 the AKP majority in the National Assembly nominated Abdullah Gül (foreign minister and founder of the party, whose wife wears a headscarf) to succeed Sezer. This prompted a threat of the generals to intervene. As the message was posted on the general staff website, this action was dubbed as an 'electronic coup'. In reaction to the meddlesome generals, the defiant AKP passed a law to allow a direct election of the president by the people. In that case, the AKP would dominate the legislative, executive and judicial powers of the state, thus enabling it to implement an Islamic agenda. As was to be expected, President Sezer vetoed the law on the direct election of the president. In May 2007 the Constitutional Court struck down the Assembly's attempt to elect Gül and thus stopped the government's candidate from taking office.

Seeing no other way out, Erdogan called for early national elections. In view of its impressive economic record and the start of negotiations with the EU, the AKP could hardly lose the elections.

Through its economic policy the AKP government has created a new religious middle class in the west of the country that opposes the old secular elite and the industrial class in the east. Yet the opposition has blamed Erdogan for refusing a cross-border operation by the army against PKK bases in northern Iraq, for covering up the corruption some of its ministers were accused of and for the lack of progress in negotiations with the EU (*The Economist*, 2007b, c, d). Moreover, the AKP has not made good on its social promises: income inequality as well as unemployment have further increased (Kazangicil 2004: 41).

On 5 June 2007 – to the surprise of many – Turkey's Constitutional Court ruled (six to five) that the disputed constitutional reforms package passed by the government was valid. This was a blow for the secular opposition as well as for the military. As expected, the July elections were won by the AKP and on 28 August 2007 Abdullah Gül was sworn in as president. The military stayed away from the inauguration ceremony. The domestic political situation in Turkey will remain tense in the future.

Conclusion

From the preceding, we draw the following conclusions:

- Turks are a proud people for whom national unity and territorial integrity are essential. Atatürk taught them to love their fatherland. He also wanted his nation to copy the West and to remove Islam from public life.
- Kemalism was a top-down modernization project. At first Turkey was ruled by urban and rural elite. Gradually but slowly new classes were incorporated into the political system.
- After 1946 a multi-party democratic system was established, but it has never worked properly. Big elitarian parties dominated the political scene without caring too much for the interests of the people.
- Even if they differed sometimes among themselves on some themes (e.g. the organization of the economy), until the 1960s there was a common ideology among elites (civil officers, military, landowners, bourgeoisie and industrialists) that could be characterized as authoritarian paternalism.
- After the 1960s the ideological consensus disappeared: new classes – such as workers and peasants who professed a new class ideology and Turkish nationalists – established their own parties and joined the old elites. The political system accommodated the newcomers without giving up its elitist nature.
- In the 1970s religion became a separate political ideology, as it was embodied first in the Welfare Party and later on in the AKP. Because of the 10 per cent threshold in the national parliament – one of the highest in the world - the ethnic ideological factor was absent in Turkish national politics until the July

2007 elections. By running as independent candidates, Kurdish politicians could get around the 10 per cent threshold.

- Political parties are coalitions themselves between different factions. Corruption and political infighting often paralysed efficient ruling. That is why governments in Turkey have always been very unstable.
- Turkey did not have many politicians who could appeal to the nation at large. Demirel, Özal and Erdoğan are the exceptions to the rule.
- The military establishment wants to keep Atatürk's inheritance intact. Therefore, it steps into the political arena each time it feels that politicians are heading in the wrong direction. Until now, it has always propagated a quick return to democracy when conditions have allowed for this.
- The position of Islam in Turkish society is an unsolved problem. Secularists and Islamists are continuously engaged in a test of wills. In times of economic prosperity, the problem seems to move to the background. In times of economic crisis, the problem comes back with more vigour.

2 History of Turkey–EU relations

In this chapter, we will deal both with the history of the EU and with the place of Turkey within this. Again, we will do so in the form of a chronological outline of events. The European Community was not very accommodating towards Turkey. Its attitude has not changed. Even when negotiations finally started in 2005, the EU was less than enthusiastic about the outcome.

The Cold War

After the Second World War, Western Europe felt threatened by the Soviet Union. The Soviet army did not demobilize; there were strong communist parties in the West benefiting from economic misery; Eastern Europe disappeared behind the iron curtain. Moreover, there were crises in countries where the spheres of influence between East and West were not yet fixed: in Iran, Greece and Turkey. As far as Turkey was concerned, Stalin did not want to renew the 1925 Neutrality and Non-Belligerence Treaty. Instead, he made some territorial requests and wanted a joint Soviet–Turkish defence of the sea lanes.[1] Fearing for loss of territory, Turkey asked for help from the UK and the USA. As the UK announced it could no longer defend these countries, the American president wrote history by proclaiming his famous doctrine. Truman – renouncing the 1923 Monroe doctrine – said that the USA was going to defend every country in the world against Soviet interference, be it militarily or by means of communist parties (Faucompret 2001a: 22; Van de Meerssche 2006: 32). This American initiative was at the dawn of European integration. Two organizations were the direct result of the Truman doctrine: the Organization for European Economic Cooperation (OEEC) and the North Atlantic Treaty Organization (NATO). West European countries had to unite in order to qualify for American help. The economies of Western Europe recovered quickly thanks to Marshall Aid. Markets were opened so as to promote exports among the member states of the OEEC. The European Payments Union made full convertibility of currencies possible. The West European economic recovery damaged the strength of the communist parties (they had benefited from the misery of the workers, which had undermined their beliefs in the capitalist system). Because of its geopolitical position and its geographical proximity to the USSR, Turkey played a prominent role in the US containment policy (Zürcher 1997: 246; Wilkens

1998: 17). The USA encircled the USSR with regional alliances in which Turkey played a major part. Turkey was one of the main beneficiaries of Marshall Aid (even if it did not have a deficit on its balance of payments); it joined the OEEC, was one of the few countries that immediately sent troops to Korea and in 1952 became a member of NATO[2] and the ill-fated pro-western Baghdad and Balkan pacts.[3] US military bases were established on Turkish territory, the Turkish army was equipped with US material and Turkish officers were trained in the USA.

The ECSC and the EDC

The first attempt to create an independent European organization dated from May 1948. At the Congress of The Hague, European federalists favoured the establishment of a United States of Europe. Unfortunately, governments decided otherwise: they set up the Council of Europe, which would not have supranational powers. One of the most remarkable achievements of this international organization was the Convention on the Protection of Human Rights and Fundamental Freedoms. That convention not only set a common standard for human rights in Europe but also provided a framework for judicial remedy. Turkey joined the Council of Europe but (until 1989) did not recognize the right of citizens to appeal to the Court of Human Rights.

European federalists were disappointed. It was clear that the initiative for a united Europe had to be taken elsewhere (Van de Meerssche 2006: 91–2). On 9 May 1950 French Foreign Minister Robert Schuman made a daring proposal: the French and German coal and steel industries were to be placed under a common authority with supranational competencies, in an international organization that other European countries could also join. Why did France launch such a proposal? France feared German rearmament: some sort of control over German industry would help. France also wanted to play a key role in post-war Europe, thereby denying both the USA and the UK the opportunity to do so. Schuman also succeeded in uniting both the government and the opposition: they all rallied behind the plan. The radical left-wing French trade unions would be influenced by their moderate German counterparts, which would soften their stance on issues such as nationalization and price controls. The Schuman proposal was a product of the cold war and thus was supported by the USA: it was necessary to keep the French communists and socialists from power. It was also going to prevent nationalizations by the French government and would create a strong European pillar within NATO. Western Germany, Italy and the Benelux countries reacted favourably to the proposal, which led to the creation of the European Coal and Steel Community (ECSC) on 18 April 1951. For Western Germany it was a means for reconciliation with the rest of Western Europe. It would also enable Western Germany to get rid of all kinds of restrictions still imposed on it by the victors of the Second World War. Last but not least, it would make German reunification possible in the long run. A rich Western Germany would act like a magnet on the poor Eastern Germany, which was going to be exploited by the USSR. The Benelux countries did not want to stay out of this organization. Their coal and steel sectors needed subsidies, and foreign trade was important for their economies.

The ECSC was not much more than a free-trade zone with harmonized external tariffs and a common policy on price, production, competition and social affairs. Yet the institutions that were set up were innovative in international relations: the High Authority (predecessor of the European Commission), a European Assembly (predecessor of the European Parliament) and the European Court of Justice. The Council of Ministers had only coordinating responsibilities. The six ECSC member states did not like to see Western Germany rearmed. For that reason, in 1950 they launched a plan for a European Defence Community (EDC). That organization was to supervise a European army, with German contingents. But the treaty that the six countries signed in 1952 did not go as far as the original plan. There were no supranational institutions and no common defence budget. Weapons industries remained national. Unfortunately, the EDC plan was never put into effect. Again, there was a link with the cold war. After 1953, when Stalin had died and Khrushchev had entered the Kremlin, it seemed that the cold war had come to an early end. The West European countries no longer saw a need to substitute a European army for their own armies. Nationalism was on the rise. France was fighting a colonial war in Indo-China. Opponents of the EDC argued that politicians were stabbing the French army in the back, while that same army was fighting for the honour of the French nation. In the end France asked for the treaty to be renegotiated. Yet the governments of Germany and the Benelux countries – which had already gone through a lot of trouble putting the treaty to the vote in their national assemblies – refused. In the end the EDC treaty was not ratified by France and Italy (Van de Meerssche 2006: 95–100). Paradoxically, it was then decided to establish the Western European Union (WEU) encompassing the six ECSC member states and the UK. As a member state of NATO, Germany could now rearm much more independently than would have been the case in the EDC. The UK was ready to join, while it had continuously rejected the EDC. Perhaps UK readiness to join the EDC could have saved the organization. Apparently West European countries put more trust in NATO and the USA than in their own defence capacities (Faucompret 2001a: 25). Not much has changed since 1954.

The EEC

In the course of 1954, the foreign ministers of the ECSC countries discussed a Benelux proposal on further stages in the European integration process. At the Conference of Venice (May 1956), the ministers expressed support for two projects: the establishment of a customs union and cooperation in the atomic energy sector. Again, the cold war affected progress in the European integration process. Both the Suez crisis and the repression of the Hungarian uprising in October 1956 made ECSC member states feel the need for further cooperation. On 25 March 1957 the Treaty of Rome was signed; it provided for the establishment of the European Economic Community (EEC) and the European Atomic Energy Community (EAEC). The EEC treaty agreed on the customs union and the unification of trade, competition, agriculture and transport policies. The EAEC treaty was about a common supply policy, a common research and development policy, and a common investment policy in the nuclear sector. New institutions were created, but they were less supranational than the ones in the ECSC treaty. The Council of Ministers became the main decision-making body, but the European Commission had the exclusive power of making proposals. The European Parliament had only advisory power. The EEC and the EAEC treaties were a pragmatic compromise between France and Western Germany. France wanted Western Germany to subsidize its farmers, while Western Germany wanted new outlets for its industry. At the same time, cartels and mergers would have to be strictly supervised. France was a politically centralized and economically backward country with poor farmers, uncompetitive industry and burdensome overseas territories. Its economy was state led, with powerful trade unions which believed in Marxist class struggle, while its income distribution was very unequal. The French government adhered to Keynesian policies to stimulate economic growth and employment. It pursued an anti-American foreign policy and it believed in close cooperation between EEC member states without them giving up national independence. Thus in the end France favoured a European political confederation with economies closely monitored by Brussels. Western Germany, on the other hand, was a politically decentralized country whose economy quickly recovered after the Second World War thanks to its raw materials, skilled and unskilled labour[4] and Marshall Aid. Western Germany believed in free initiative and in liberal economics. Its workers rejected class struggle and were even represented on the boards of companies, while the government believed in strict monetary policy to keep the value of the Deutschmark as strong as possible. Western Germany owed the USA a lot, so it favoured close relations with Washington. As far as the EEC and the EAEC were concerned, Western Germany believed in a European federation without too much control over economic policies by European or national institutions.

In contrast with the ECSC treaty, the EEC treaty gave non-member states the opportunity of 'associate' membership in the organization (article 238). No sooner had the EEC treaty come into effect than three Mediterranean countries applied for association: Spain, Greece and Turkey. The European Parliament gave its reaction through the voice of its reporter Willy Birkelbach. Birkelbach's report defined the position of the Parliament on relations between the EEC and countries with political systems and economic orders that were deemed incompatible with those in EEC member states. For Birkelbach the simple desire of a European state to join the EEC was not enough if some precise political conditions were missing – that is to say, if there was not a democratic state system guaranteeing a free political order. Birkelbach wanted EEC membership to be limited to democratic states with a western military and political alignment. Moreover, the economies of these states should be strong enough to sustain the European economic integration process and they should display the political will to take part in the European integration process. Associated states should not undermine the integration process between existing member states. Associated states should not receive special advantages without having to bear membership burdens.[5] This could result in the gradual dismantling of the EEC. Association was not to be definitive: it was only a transition stage for countries that for the time being were not economically ready for full membership (Faucompret 1979: 146). The Birkelbach report became the semi-official enlargement doctrine of the EEC, a kind of Copenhagen doctrine *avant la lettre*. It was with reference to the Birkelbach report that Spain's request for association was rejected while those of Greece and Turkey were considered favourably.

Turkey had seen immediately the many economic and political opportunities association of the EEC would bring. It was in line with Atatürk's doctrine; it would modify the influence of nationalists, Islamists and populists, it would reduce dependence on the USA and it would consolidate Turkish democracy. The EEC would be a powerful economic partner that could help Turkey to overcome its economic problems. Moreover, it was not a supranational organization, so Turkey would be able to keep its national political system intact (Uğur 1999: 2). During the negotiations for the General Agreement on Tariffs and Trade (GATT) (January–November 1958) Turkey had asked to take part in the future Common Agricultural Policy (CAP), a request that was turned down by the six. In June 1959 Greece applied for association. Two months later Turkey did the same. In a memorandum, Turkey referred to the unbalanced structure of trade existing between the six and Turkey and to the political situation resulting from the cold war (Faucompret 1979: 46).

In a show of goodwill and to fend off the UK – which, in the meantime had set up its own competing organization: the European Free Trade Association (EFTA) – the EEC declared itself ready to sign Association Agreements with both NATO member states, invaluable partners in Western security against the Soviet bloc with a strategic position in the Mediterranean (December 1959) (Tekin 2005: 287). Yet negotiations with Turkey were going to be tough. In March 1960 Turkey requested the following (Faucompret 1979: 47):

- investment aid from the EEC;
- harmonization of its economic policy with that of the EEC;
- unlimited market access for its farming exports;
- tariff reductions without reciprocity;
- conclusion of supply contracts in the farming sector;
- EEC commitment not to import from third countries if Turkey could supply the product;
- increase of the common external tariff on tobacco for third countries;
- free emigration of Turkish workers to the EEC;
- annual development aid of $100 million.

It was clear from these requests that Turkey was taking the EEC at its word. If association meant preparing a country for membership, then the EEC should offer maximum assistance. Unfortunately, the EEC did not want to go that far. It wanted to negotiate only on trade, financial aid and the establishment of an association council. In addition, the EEC wanted to sign a simple commercial agreement.

This was because of the unstable political and economic situation in Turkey and the problems the EEC was experiencing in negotiations with Greece. Moreover, the EEC was concerned about possible reactions from European farmers and did not want to set precedents for the eight other Mediterranean countries that were planning to apply for association. So negotiations with Turkey were not easy for the EEC. After the 1960 coup, members of the negotiating team were arrested and some were even executed. For some member states the coup made it quite clear that Turkey did not satisfy one of the Birkelbach criteria: being a democracy with respect for human rights. In other words, the signing of the Association Agreement would be premature. Other member states thought that signing the Association Agreement would strengthen the democratic forces in Turkey. Internal bickering over Turkey went on for quite some time. In the end, the EEC did sign an Associa-tion Agreement in 1963. It wanted to put Greece and Turkey on an equal footing and it wanted to circumvent possible Greek intervention as regards the common external tariff.[6] Turkey agreed only on condition that, in the not too distant future, the Association Council would deal with issues like the free movement of workers and the establishment of a customs union. The Ankara Agreement did not go as far as the Athens Agreement signed two years earlier. Yet it did stipulate that at the appropriate time the possibility of full membership was to be examined (art. 28). The Ankara Agreement provided for the establishment of a customs union in three stages. During the first (preparatory) phase of five years, Turkey would enjoy duty-free quotas on its four most important export products (tobacco, raisins, figs and nuts) and it would get financial aid (175 million European Currency Units phased out over five years). During the second (transitional) phase of twelve years, both parties would grant tariff concessions on a reciprocal basis. During the third (final) phase, the customs union would be set up and economic policies would be harmonized. According to Feridun Cemal Erkin, Minister of Foreign Affairs: 'By signing the Association Agreement, Turkey opened up a new chapter in its relations with Europe. This would bring major accomplishments and confirmed, for good, Turkey's European vocation' (Faucompret 1979: 48). Walter Hallstein, the President of the European Commission, added: 'Europe and Turkey pursue common political, economic and military objectives, which can only lead to full EEC membership of Turkey' (Faucompret 1979: 48).

The EEC in the 1960s and 1970s

Three important moments of political crisis characterized the first decade of the EEC. The de Gaulle plan on European political cooperation came to nothing because of Benelux resistance (1962). France took its revenge and opposed UK membership (1963). The third crisis broke out in the middle of 1965 when France decided to boycott all EEC meetings because it opposed the Commission proposals on financing the CAP. Fortunately, during that decade there were also positive achievements. The customs union for industrial products was realized earlier than expected and the CAP provided farmers with a decent income. In 1965 the exec-utives of the three communities (ECSC, EEC and EAEC) were merged. In the so-called Kennedy Round the EEC spoke with a single voice during important trade negotiations in the GATT. The two British membership applications and the applications for association and trade agreements by a lot of countries can also be regarded as further proof of the success of the European integration process (Van de Meerssche 2006: 107–13, 163–70).

In 1969 the new French president Georges Pompidou and the new German chancellor Willy Brandt organized an EEC summit in The Hague. Important decisions were made concerning EEC completion, enlargement and deepening. As far as completion was concerned: on 1 January 1970 the customs union was solemnly proclaimed, even though, in reality, it had already come into being a year and a half earlier. As far as enlargement was concerned, on 1 January 1973 the UK, Denmark and Ireland entered the European Community (EC). Some of the problems raised during enlargement negotiations, like the financing of the budget, were put off. As far as deepening was concerned, two decisions were made. First, the European Political Cooperation Process was launched. Member states were to coordinate their foreign policies, but this process was to take place outside the framework of the EEC. Secondly, the monetary union was to be set up. Fluctuations in exchange rates had to be reduced and member states had to aim at more macroeconomic convergence. However, the American decision to suspend the convertibility of the dollar spelt the end of the Bretton Woods system of fixed exchange rates (August 1971). In contrast with earlier crisis moments (but related to the cold war), EC member states did not act in unison. Fluctuations in member states' exchange rates increased rather than decreased. And the worst had yet to come. In October 1973 the EC went through one of the most serious crises in its existence. The Arab oil-producing countries decided to impose an embargo on exports of oil to EC members, like the Netherlands, that sympathized with Israel. Instead of formulating a common policy, the EC member states tried to conclude bilateral deals with Arab oil-producing states. The Copenhagen summit (December 1973) tried to realign the nine member states. Their unity was again broken when France refused to enter the International Energy Agency, which was established by the OECD (February 1974). Whereas France wanted to set up privileged relationships between the EC and the Arab world, other member states did not favour this. Moreover, they feared negative US reactions to the so-called Euro-Arabian dialogue (Faucompret 2001a: 27–8).

The crisis in the EC adversely affected relations between the EC and Turkey. Since the Association Council of May 1967, relations with Turkey had deteriorated. At that time Turkey made three requests (Faucompret 1979: 48):

- reductions of the common external tariff on industrial products that were considered 'sensitive' by the EC (such as textiles or shoes);
- reductions of the common external tariff on new farming products;
- free emigration of Turkish workers to the EC.

Because of the EC's refusal to negotiate on these issues, Turkey asked that the second phase of the Association Agreement should start on the day the Ankara Agreement had stipulated (1 January 1969). When Turkey refused to extend the first stage of the Ankara Agreement by ten years, negotiations started between Turkey and the Commission on the content of the twelve-year transition period. On 23 November 1970 the two sides reached agreement on the Additional Protocol. It provided for the following (Faucompret 1979: 49–50):

- the EC would immediately abolish all import duties on industrial imports from Turkey with the exception of the 'sensitive' products;
- all EC tariffs would be abolished on imports of Turkish raisins and tobacco;
- Turkey itself had twenty-two years to abolish its industrial tariffs on imports from the EEC and to harmonize its external tariffs with those of the EEC;
- Turkey would get new financial aid (195 million European Currency Units phased out over five years).

The Turkish government was not satisfied with this protocol. In Istanbul, left-wing students held protest demonstrations against the association with the EC (29 January 1971). In September 1971 Turkey asked for a complete revision of the agreement. There were several reasons for this:

- tariff concessions granted to the EC ran counter to its import substitution policy;
- Turkey wanted to sign an agreement that led to full EC membership;
- the accession of the UK to the EC could possibly reduce Turkish farming exports to the British markets;
- in addition, the EC had plans to launch a global Mediterranean policy, which would further erode Turkish preferences.

Whereas negotiations on extending the Additional Protocol to the three new EC member states finally succeeded, there remained fundamental differences of mind on the EC Mediterranean policy. On 16 September 1974 the Turkish government submitted the following memorandum (Faucompret 1979: 50):

- Turkey is one of the few democracies in the Mediterranean area; therefore, it wants to take part in the European Political Cooperation.
- Turkey still considers itself as a candidate for joining the EC.
- The Association Agreement should not harm the interests of Turkish industry.
- Turkey upholds its commitments taken in the Ankara Agreement, but the terms of this treaty should be amended in the near future.

Upon EC refusal to negotiate this memorandum and pressured by its domestic industrialists, Turkey put off tariff reductions unilaterally. The EC did not retaliate, but it decided to freeze relations. No new tariff concessions were given and no new financial aid was granted. The EC exempted Turkey from certain tariff reductions, and Turkey was allowed to sign preferential trade agreements with neighbouring countries. Nevertheless, relations between Turkey and the EC deteriorated further for the following reasons (Faucompret 1979: 51; Uğur 1999: 123):

- The Turkish army invaded Northern Cyprus (July 1974), and the EC condemned the occupation.
- Turkey felt disfavoured when the EU signed agreements with other Mediterranean countries. Moreover, the EU system of general preferences – one of the most generous among developed countries – in favour of developing countries further eroded Turkey's preference margins.
- Turkey made new requests that were rejected by the EC: further tariff reductions on its farming exports, better access to the EC market for its textiles and clothing products, financial aid of $8 billion and a five-year freeze on Turkey's own commitments under the Additional Protocol. Under the influence of France and Italy, the EC did not give in to Turkey's requests for preferences, when Turkey itself reneged on its obligations. After all, Turkey did benefit from EC concessions that were more generous than the reciprocity principle of the Additional Protocol would have implied.

In the second half of the 1970s trust was re-established between EC member states, and the European integration process was making progress again. At the Paris summit (December 1974), it was decided to set up the European Council. This was a limited body that operated outside the framework of the EC and that grouped together leaders of the executives (the French president and the prime ministers of the other member states). In 1975 the EC signed the Lomé Convention with the so-called ACP countries (Africa, Caribbean and Pacific), which are former colonies or territories of member states. It was the first convention in its kind: it was signed within the framework of a new economic arrangement between a group of developing countries and a group of industrialized countries. In 1976 the Tindemans report was published. Three years later two important recommendations of his report were implemented: direct elections for the European Parliament and the Exchange Rate Mechanism. In the meantime, democracy had been restored in Greece, Spain and Portugal. In contrast with Turkey, these countries had opted for an export promotion policy and Europeanized their foreign policy. Having shaken off the yoke of dictatorship, they hoped to consolidate their democracy via EC membership. At first the European Commission did not come out in favour of EC membership for these countries. In its view, it would have been better to extend the existing Association Agreement with Greece and the preferential trade agreements with Spain and Portugal in order to make them better prepared for membership. Yet the Council of Ministers decided to brush aside these economic objections and gave priority to political considerations (stabilization of democracy and security interests in the Mediterranean) (Larrabee and Lesser 2003: 48–9). Negotiations dragged on for a long time because the Mediterranean countries were in stages of economic development that differed from EC member states. Greece eventually entered the EC on 1 January 1981. For Spain and Portugal, it would take another four years before they were able to join. For Greece, there was a general five-year transition stage and one of seven years for the so-called sensitive sectors (essentially the CAP, free movement of workers and social policy). For Spain and Portugal, transition stages were even longer: seven years and ten for sensitive sectors (essentially fisheries policy, free movement of workers, the CAP and social policy). Not to be outdone by Greece, Spain and Portugal and at the same time fearing a military coup, the Turkish government in turn asked for EC membership (February 1980). The EC stalled. On the one hand, it did not want to alienate or discriminate against Turkey or upset the USA during a period of new tension in East–West relations (Uğur 1999: 97). On the other hand, it deemed Turkey not ready for membership for economic as well as for political reasons. The September 1980 military coup offered the EC a welcome alibi not to react to the Turkish application for membership. After the restoration of democracy three years later, relations between Turkey and the EC remained strained because of the political situation in Turkey.

The EC in the 1980s

In June 1984 an important European Council was held at Fontainebleau. EC member states compromised on three bottlenecks that had been impeding the further progress of the European economic integration process in the previous decade. The European Regional Fund gained more scope. The CAP was thoroughly reformed. A solution was reached for the British contribution (Van de Meerssche 2006: 230). At the same time, it was found that the importance of the EC on the geopolitical stage had dramatically decreased. The EC felt threatened by the newly industrialized world. There was an increase in scale of production processes, and Europe was lagging behind in data processing, materials technology, biotechnology, telecommunications and other modern industrial sectors. The public was not exactly burning with enthusiasm for European integration. The European integration process stagnated because of the lack of a legal basis in the treaties. Therefore, at the European Council of Milan (June 1985) EC member states decided to call an intergovernmental conference in order to amend the treaties. Here agreement was reached on the Single European Act (February 1986), which took force on 1 July 1987 (Faucompret 2001a: 29). A brief summary gives the following:

- the internal market (free movement of goods, persons, services and capital) would be realized no later than 31 December 1992;
- the EC was given competence over regional policy, research and development;
- the system of qualified majority voting was extended to certain items: the implementation of the internal market (except social and fiscal policies and the free movement of persons) and the implementation of the three new policies;
- many decisions had to be made by the Council of Ministers in cooperation with the European Parliament;
- the principle of the Economic and Monetary Union (EMU) was put forward;
- the European Political Cooperation was legally institutionalized.

The Single European Act was criticized for several reasons. It did not bring anything substantially new to European economic integration. The creation of the internal market had already been implicitly mentioned in the treaty establishing the EEC. In fact, by creating a new transition stage, it undid part of the European adjudication in the field of the internal market. It made things unnecessarily complicated. Where did basic formulation of policy end and implementation of policy start? When would the Council of Ministers have to vote by qualified majority and when did it have to cooperate with the European Parliament? On the other hand, the Single European Act put an end to the so-called European scleroses of the previous years by providing a fresh impetus to European economic integration (Faucompret 2001a: 29; Van de Meerssche 2006: 232).

The Single European Act had important consequences for Turkey. From now on, the Council needed the European Parliament in many policy fields and the Parliament had proven in the past that it cared a lot for human rights. During the cold war the EC had subordinated strategic interests to human rights. Now that the cold war had become less intensive, Turkey found its Western credentials challenged. The Europeans, who seemed to distinguish Turkey from other European Mediterranean countries, questioned Turkey's democracy, the role of the military, its secular nature and its ethnic problems. If Turkey's membership application were serious, the EC would have to enquire into its human-rights record, the more so because a growing number of Turkish asylum-seekers were knocking on the EC's door. In its resolution of 23 October 1985, the European Parliament put forward five conditions for restoring EC relations with Turkey and for releasing the Fourth Financial Protocol[7] (Waxman 1998: 4; Uğur 1999: 215–16, 224):

• abolishing the death penalty;
• putting an end to torture and prosecution of torturers;
• ending mass trials;
• granting Turkish citizens the right to petition to the European Court of Human Rights;
• removing all restrictions on the freedom of opinion.

Meanwhile, the EC wanted to make a second attempt at establishing a monetary union. The European Council of Hanover (June 1988) put Jacques Delors, the President of the European Commission, in charge of a report on the EMU. The European Council of Strasbourg carried this report six months later. The first stage of the EMU was to take effect on 1 July 1990, the day when the free movement on capital would go ahead in most member states. The second stage, which mainly implied the establishment of the European Monetary Institute, would start on 1 January 1994, while the third stage would start on 1 January 1999.

Fearing the growing economic integration process in the EC was going to make Turkish membership even more problematic and with very outspoken domestic political objectives, Turkey's prime minister, Turgut Özal, decided to press the EC's hand (Wilkens 1998: 18). Confronted with the increasing erosion of its preferences on EC markets and haunted by the spectre of second-class status, Turkey decided against revitalizing the Additional Protocol and instead asked again for full EC membership. As a token of goodwill, it was ready to speed up the process of tariff dismantlement. Taken by surprise, the EC took two years to react officially. The answer was again negative: the EC was still in the process of absorbing three Mediterranean countries and it wanted to focus on the process of deepening instead of enlarging. The Turkish application for membership could not be considered for the following reasons (CEC 1989):

- the political and economic situation in Turkey;
- the access of Turkish labour to the EC labour market, which gave rise to fear, particularly while unemployment remained at high levels within the EC;
- the Cyprus problem, which affected relations with Turkey in a negative sense; Turkey would have to recognize the (Greek) Cypriot government if it wanted closer relations with the EC.

The Commission suggested that it would be premature for Turkey to become a full member. Turkey was not ready to fulfil the obligations arising from EC membership, particularly since the adoption of the Single European Act (European Communities 1987), a new step in the European economic and political integration process. If negotiations could not be concluded successfully, then it was better not to start with the negotiation process. To sugar-coat the pill, in June 1990 the Commission presented a comprehensive package of economic, trade and political measures – the so-called Matutes package[8] – designed to improve Turkish–EU relations (Larrabee and Lesser 2003: 50). These proposals provided for the completion of the customs union with Turkey, the resumption and intensification of financial cooperation, the promotion of industrial and technological cooperation and the strengthening of political and cultural ties. Unfortunately, the Matutes package was vetoed in the Council by Greece.

The EC in the 1990s: the Maastricht treaty

The 1989 revolutionary changes in East and Central Europe took the EC by surprise. Free elections were held in Poland and Hungary. The Berlin Wall was pulled down in November 1989. Germany was reunified in October 1990, and one year later the Soviet Union collapsed. Though the EC had fought communism during the cold war, its reaction was rather hesitant. Emergency aid was granted to the Central and Eastern European Countries (CEEC) under the so-called PHARE programme. In 1991 and 1992 the Europe agreements were signed. The aim was to set up free trade areas for industrial products between the EC and each of the CEEC, with a ten-year transition period. Yet these agreements did not carry many trade privileges for the CEEC. About 80 per cent of EC industrial imports from third countries entered duty free anyhow. That is why, one after another, the CEEC applied for membership (Faucompret *et al.* 1999: 123–4). The EC did not consider itself ready for such a major event. That is why it wanted to focus first on strengthening its domestic cohesion. To this end, it decided at the European Council of

Dublin to organize a new intergovernmental conference with a view to amending the treaties (June 1990). Out of this came the notorious Maastricht treaty, signed in February 1992 but only entering into effect on 1 November 1993. In summary, the Treaty on the European Union[9] contained the following stipulations (EU 1992; Faucompret 2001: 30):

- Dates were fixed for the start of the EMU. The decision about which countries were ready to enter the EMU would be based on five criteria for convergence.
- New policy fields came under the competence of the EC, but under the subsidiarity[10] principle.
- The possibility to make majority decisions by the Council of Ministers was extended.
- The European Parliament was granted more competencies. In certain policy fields it had to co-decide with the Council of Ministers;
- A Committee of Regions – with only advisory power – was set up.
- A Cohesion Fund was to complement the existing Structural Funds.
- A European citizenship was established, which meant among other things that EC citizens could take part in local and European elections.
- Member states would try to pursue a common foreign and security policy.
- Member states would try to coordinate their policies on home affairs and domestic security.
- A social protocol was added to the treaty.

In contrast with earlier treaties, the Maastricht treaty was very controversial, and it moved public opinion. European federalists thought the treaty did not go far enough. Sensitive policy areas (such as taxation and social policy, domestic security, foreign policy) were left out of majority voting, and there was still a 'democracy deficit' in the sense that many policy areas were transferred from the national to the European level, while there was no corresponding shift of power from national parliaments to the European Parliament. Opponents of Maastricht took advantage of the extremist right-wing propaganda, which held out the prospect of uncontrolled immigration flows, money laundering, environmental damage, international crime and dominance by the Brussels bureaucracy.

The EU in the 1990s: the enlargement with the CEEC

In 1993 the European Council decided to start enlargement negotiations with four EFTA countries: Norway, Finland, Austria and Sweden. This was an easy nut to crack. The four were part of the European Economic Area Agreement.[11] They were rich countries with strong economies, a balanced industrial structure and attractive import markets that would not cause budgetary problems for the EU. Apart from Finland, they would become net contributors to the EU budget, thereby alleviating the burden for countries such as Germany and the Netherlands who had been net payers to the EU budget. They had left-wing

governments with a strong administrative capacity that favoured high environmental and social standards. For member states with European federalist aspirations there were only two disadvantages attached to the future membership
of Austria, Finland and Sweden. These countries were very much in favour of
their national sovereignty, and they were not ready to give up decision-making
power in the fields of foreign and defence policy. Moreover, they were closely
allied with the UK and thus indirectly with the USA. This might reduce the
power of the Franco-German axis in the future EU. Anyhow, member states
decided that the pros outweighed the cons. Austria, Finland and Sweden entered
the EU on 1 January 1995.

The situation was completely different for the CEEC. These were poor countries with weak economies, an overcapacity in some industrial sectors compared
to insufficient domestic demand and an average income of about 30 per cent of the
EU average. Their economies were biased towards agriculture and the so-called
sensitive sectors like textiles. Thus, they would all become net receivers from
the EU budget. Moreover, most of them had right-wing governments with poor
administrative capacity, which favoured loose social and environmental standards
in order to create a competitive environment for firms to export. The CEEC did
not want to give up sovereignty either. To top it all: they were even closer allies of
the USA than the Scandinavians and Austria. At face value, most member states
did not want the CEEC to join the EU. However, they felt a kind of moral duty to
welcome countries that had been occupied by the Soviet Union after the Second
World War. Moreover, one member state in particular insisted on their accession: Germany. Right from the start, Germany – wanting stability on its eastern
borders – championed the case of Poland and the Czech Republic. At the same
time, member states thought that the existing criteria for countries to join the EU
as defined by the treaty establishing the EEC and the Birkelbach report needed
further clarification and elaboration. Because of this, the European Council in
Copenhagen (June 1993) decided the following:

> The European Council today agreed that the associated countries in Central
> and Eastern Europe that so desire should become members of the European
> Union. Accession will take place as soon as an associated country is able
> to assume the obligations of membership by satisfying the economic and
> political conditions required. Membership requires that the candidate country
> has achieved stability of institutions guaranteeing democracy, the rule of law,
> human rights and respect for and protection of minorities, the existence of a
> functioning market economy as well as the capacity to cope with competi-
> tive pressure and market forces within the Union. Membership presupposes
> the candidate's ability to take on the obligations of membership including
> adherence to the aims of political, economic and monetary union. The
> Union's capacity to absorb new members, while maintaining the momentum
> of European integration, is also an important consideration in the general
> interest of both the Union and the candidate countries. The European Council
> will continue to follow closely progress in each associated country towards

fulfilling the conditions of accession to the Union and draw the appropriate conclusions. (Conclusions of the Presidency 1993: 6)

Turkey was also briefly mentioned in the Conclusions of the Presidency. In order not to send the Turks away empty-handed, the Commission tried to revitalize the Association Agreement:

> With regard to Turkey, the European Council asked the Council to ensure that there is an effective implementation of the guidelines laid down by the European Council in Lisbon on intensified cooperation and development of relations with Turkey in line with the prospect laid down in the association agreement of 1964 and the protocol of 1970, as far as it relates to the establishment of a customs union. (Conclusions of the Presidency 1993: 6)

One year later at the European Council of Corfu a so-called pre-accession strategy was defined in favour of the CEEC:

> The European Council invites the Commission to make specific proposals as soon as possible for the further implementation of the Europe Agreements and the decisions taken by the European Council in Copenhagen. The European Council also asks the Presidency and the Commission to report to it for its next meeting on progress made on this basis, on the process of alignment since the Copenhagen European Council, and on the strategy to be followed with a view to preparing for accession. (Conclusions of the Presidency 1994a: 9–10)

Again, Turkey was mentioned only briefly in the Conclusions of the Presidency. The Commission wanted to start implementing the third stage of the Association Agreement: 'Concerning Turkey, the European Council notes the convening of the EC–Turkey Association Council to deal in particular with the achievement of the Customs Union foreseen in the Association Agreement of 1964' (Conclusions of the Presidency 1994a: 9).

Half a year later, at the European Council of Essen (October 1994), the EU backtracked. Before entering in enlargement negotiations with the CEEC, it wanted to wait for the results of the 1996 Intergovernmental Conference, which for that reason had to take place before accession negotiations with the CEEC began. It also asked the Commission for yet another detailed analysis of the effects of enlargement in the context of EU policies. Finally it called on the Commission to complete the customs union with Turkey (Conclusions of the Presidency 1994b: 8–9). At the Cannes European Council (June 1995) the heads of state and of government and ministers of foreign affairs of the CEEC, including the Baltic states, as well as Cyprus and Malta, were invited, though not the prime minister of Turkey. The vague language in the final communiqué showed that the EU was still waiting for the results of the Intergovernmental Conference before accession negotiations could start: 'There was a wide-ranging exchange of views on various topical matters. They also made an initial favourable assessment of the progress in implementing the pre-accession strategy' (Conclusions of the Presidency 1995: 4).

With the Amsterdam Treaty (signed in October 1997) it became clear that a lot of time had been wasted. Indeed, this treaty did not modify the decision-making process, as had initially been hoped. The 'leftovers' were referred to a new intergovernmental conference, to be held not later than one year before the twentieth member state joined. This does not mean that the Amsterdam Treaty did not have certain merits. The treaty was made up of four chapters and progress was made in the first three of them:

- to place employment and citizen's rights at the heart of the EU;
- to sweep away the last remaining obstacles to freedom of movement and to strengthen security;
- to give Europe a stronger voice in world affairs;
- to make EU institutional structure more efficient with a view to enlarging the EU.

Turkey and the EU in the 1990s

Whereas the CEEC were still waiting for the result of the Intergovernmental Conference, Turkey decided to take the bull by the horns. At the beginning of 1995 the Turkish government of Prime Minister Çiller decided to go along with the European Council's proposal on implementing the third stage of the Association Agreement. Although it would have preferred to be immediately included, like the CEEC, in the group of countries qualifying for negotiations on membership, Turkey decided to focus its European policy on the short-term goal of achieving a customs union. This EU–Turkish customs union was considered a step above the bilateral association treaties the EU had signed with the CEEC (Wilkens 1998: 19). Turkey would be the only country in the world with a customs union with the EU. In Çiller's view this could only lead to full membership. Financial assistance was expected to ease the economic shock of opening the Turkish market to further European competition. In Turkey, public opinion was very much divided over the issue. Small- and medium-sized entrepreneurs joined forces with anti-Western elements in opposing the customs union (Wilkens 1998: 19). Moreover, right from the start of the negotiations the EU made it clear there was no link whatsoever between the customs union and possible future EU membership of Turkey.

Negotiations moved slowly because the EU wanted Turkey to abide by its rules on intellectual property, cartels and free trade. For this, Turkey asked financial compensation. There were also political problems. Kurdish parliamentarians had been arrested in the national assembly building (March 1994). For the European Parliament – which had always been much more critical of Turkey's human-rights record than national governments – it was impossible to sign a customs union agreement with a country that violated human rights as flagrantly as Turkey did (Zürcher 1997: 331). Therefore the EU first wanted certain political conditions to be fulfilled. On 23 July 1995 the Turkish Parliament complied with this by adopting a package containing amendments to fourteen articles of the 1983 Constitution. Associations and trade unions would be able to engage in political activities; civil servants were allowed to join trade unions. Political parties were given the right to establish women and youth branches (Zürcher 1997: 312). For the time being these amendments seemed to satisfy EU governments. Greek opposition to the customs union in the EU was overcome by offering membership to Cyprus: on 6 March 1995 the EU–Turkey customs union was linked to the start of negotiations on Cyprus's accession. In the end – because of considerable pressure from governments and from the USA – the European Parliament also gave in. It approved the customs union agreement less than two weeks before the December 1995 national elections. The customs union took force on 1 January 1996. In contrast to the Association Agreement and the Additional Protocol, it did not mention anything about free movement of workers, services or capital. This should have set a warning bell ringing in Turkey.

The EU in the 1990s: *Agenda 2000*

After the partial failure of the Amsterdam Intergovernmental Conference, the Commission could no longer wait to publish its views on enlargement. Therefore, in July 1997 *Agenda 2000* was put forward. This very important document put enlargement in the framework of the necessary restructuring of the EU, as asked for by the European Council (Faucompret *et al.* 1999: 124–5). Further, *Agenda 2000* announced a reform of certain EU policies (the CAP, regional policy and budget) and of the financial framework for the period 2000– 6. It addressed all the political, economic and social issues relating to enlargement and comprised – in the third part of the report – the Commission's opinion on the accession applications submitted by the CEEC. No separate opinion was issued on Turkey. Nevertheless, in the first part of *Agenda 2000* the Commission made a very critical outline assessment of economic, political, and social conditions in all candidate countries, including Turkey, and of their relations with the EU. The Commission observed that 'Turkey had a government and a parliament resulting from multi-party democratic elections and an administration capable of framing and applying legislation compatible with the *Acquis communautaire*' (CEC 1997: 72).

However, in view of the economic and the political situation in Turkey and because of its regional problems, the Commission concluded that Turkey did not qualify for EU membership. More particularly, the following socio-economic problems were mentioned: macroeconomic instability, poor taxation system, necessary restructuring of social security, necessary privatization of state-owned enterprises and the need to restructure farming. The main political problems were: the lack of freedom of expression, the Kurdish problem, the National Security Council and the conflicts with Greece and Cyprus. Notwithstanding all these problems, the EU should continue to support Turkey's efforts to solve them (CEC 1997: 72).

Though expected, the conclusions of the Luxembourg European Council (December 1997) were very disappointing for Turkey. The Council decided to launch an accession process with the ten CEEC. Moreover, to please Greece – which otherwise would probably have vetoed the accession of any other new member state to the EU – Cyprus was also put on the list of first-wave candidates. Though Turkey's eligibility was reaffirmed, its application was put in a separate category from the other applicants. It was not accepted as a candidate country. Instead, and in contrast to previous final communiqués of European Councils, this time a lot of attention was spent on Turkey, for which a pre-accession strategy was set out designed to help it to enhance its candidacy for membership (Andrews 1998: 27; Larrabee and Lesser 2003: 51):

> The Council confirms Turkey's eligibility for accession to the European Union. Turkey will be judged on the basis of the same criteria as the other applicant States. While the political and economic conditions allowing accession negotiations to be envisaged are not satisfied, the European Council considers that it is nevertheless important for a strategy to be drawn up to prepare Turkey for accession by bringing it closer to the European Union in every field. This strategy should consist in: development of the possibilities afforded by the Ankara Agreement; intensification of the Customs Union; implementation of financial cooperation; approximation of laws and adoption of the *Acquis communautaire*; participation in certain programmes and in certain agencies. (Conclusions of the Presidency 1997: 7)

Yet the European Council added the following:

> The European Council recalls that strengthening Turkey's links with the European Union also depends on that country's pursuit of the political and economic reforms on which it has embarked, including the alignment of human rights standards and practices on those in force in the EU; respect for and protection of minorities; the establishment of satisfactory and stable relations between Greece and Turkey; the settlement of disputes, in particular by legal process, including the International Court of Justice; and support for negotiations under the aegis of the UN on a political settlement in Cyprus on the basis of the relevant UN Security Council Resolutions. (Conclusions of the Presidency 1997: 7)

The EU invited Turkey to a European conference together with the candidate countries. However, the Turks – incensed by what they called the discriminatory attitude of the EU – rejected the EU's invitation to participate in the conference. Instead, Prime Minister Yilmaz announced that political dialogue with the EU would be suspended indefinitely. Wherever possible, Turkey would choose non-EU contracts over EU ones (Wilkens 1998: 23). To add insult to injury, the special fund for Turkey, proposed by the Commission in its grand action plan, was vetoed by Greece. Relations between Turkey and the EU were soured and political dialogue was temporarily cut off. Public opinion in Turkey was convinced that the real reasons for not letting their country in had nothing to do with the Copenhagen criteria but lay elsewhere: Turkey was poor, large and, most important of all, Muslim. According to Prime Minister Yilmaz: 'Opposition to membership did not stem from humanistic, democratic concerns, but only from cultural and religious biases. Apparently the EU only wanted to bring in the poor, unstable, former hostile but Christian countries of Eastern Europe' (Andrews 1998: 28; Waxman 1998: 5).

Turkey threatened to annex the northern part of Cyprus if the island were to join the EU before a political settlement between the two communities had been reached. Two years later the EU changed track. Helmut Kohl, vocal opponent to Turkish membership, had left the political scene, while his successor, Gerhard Schroeder, became Turkey's ally. Relationships between Turkey and Greece had improved after Greek Prime Minister Simitis took office, and devastating earthquakes in 1999 initiated humanitarian aid efforts. The parallel enlargement of NATO into Eastern Europe might have faced a Turkish veto if the EU door had remained closed (Dahlman 2004: 556; Kafyeke 2006: 43). At the European Council of Helsinki (1999), Germany, Austria and Greece gave up their resistance to Turkey. The EU accepted Turkey's candidacy, provided it complied with the Copenhagen criteria. Turkey had rather suddenly become a candidate country with a vocation to join the Union:

> The European Council welcomes recent positive developments in Turkey as noted in the Commission's progress report, as well as its intention to continue its reforms towards complying with the Copenhagen criteria. Turkey is a candidate state destined to join the Union based on the same criteria as applied to the other candidate states. Building on the existing European strategy, Turkey, like other candidate states, will benefit from a pre-accession strategy to stimulate and support its reforms. This will include enhanced political dialogue, with emphasis on progressing towards fulfilling the political criteria for accession with particular reference to the issue of human rights, as well as on the issues referred to in paragraphs 4 and 9(a).[12] Turkey will also have the opportunity to participate in Community programmes and agencies and in meetings between candidate states and the Union in the context of the accession process. An accession partnership will be drawn up based on previous European Council conclusions while containing priorities on which accession preparations must concentrate in the light of the political and economic criteria and the obligations of a member state, combined with a national programme for the adoption of the *Acquis*. Appropriate monitoring mechanisms will be established. With a view to intensifying the harmonisation of Turkey's legislation and practice with the *Acquis*, the Commission is invited to prepare a process of analytical examination of the *Acquis*. The European Council asks the Commission to present a single framework for coordinating all sources of European Union financial assistance for pre-accession. (Conclusions of the Presidency 1999b)

The EU proposed the following instruments for Turkey (Conclusions of the Presidency 1999b):

- a so-called 'Pre-Accession Strategy' – a road map for the accession – in order to prepare Turkey for EU membership;
- a single framework for coordinating all sources of EU assistance;
- an enhanced political dialogue;
- the Turkish participation in EU programmes and agencies.

According to Harun (2003: 72), the EU post-Helsinki policy has effectively delayed the eventual Turkish membership for the near future by making it conditional on the settling of a number of political issues.

The EU in the new millennium: Nice

The Nice European Council (December 2000) concluded the new Intergovernmental Conference. Again, it proved impossible to adapt the EU decision-making process to the forthcoming enlargement with the CEEC, Malta and Cyprus, as becomes clear from the vague wording in the final communiqué:

> The meeting of the European Conference at the level of heads of state or government on 7 December 2000 provided an opportunity for discussion in depth of institutional reform and the operation of the European Union in the longer term. The European Council regards the European Conference as a useful framework for dialogue between the Union's member states and the countries in line for membership. It proposes that the countries covered by the stabilization and association process and the EFTA countries be invited to attend as prospective members. (Conclusions of the Presidency 2000)

The Nice treaty – signed on 26 February 2001 and entering into effect on 1 February 2003 – created a complicated institutional framework, as becomes evident from the following:

- Composition of the European Commission: with effect from 2005, the Commission will comprise one representative for each member state (instead of two for the large member states, as was the case earlier). Once the Union reaches twenty-seven member states, there will be fewer commissioners than there are member states. The commissioners will be selected by a system of rotation. The president and the members of the Commission will be appointed by the Council acting by qualified majority after approval of the body of commissioners by the European Parliament.
- The scope of decision making by qualified majority in the Council of Ministers is enlarged. There are twenty-seven items, which change over completely or partly from unanimity to qualified-majority voting (e.g. judicial cooperation in civil matters; the conclusion of international agreements in the area

of trade in services and the commercial aspects of intellectual property (with exceptions); industrial policy; economic, financial and technical cooperation with third countries). Taxation and social policy are excluded from qualified majority decision making. Regional policy is deferred until 2007.

- Most of the legislative measures, which require a decision from the Council acting by qualified majority, will be decided with the European Parliament via the co-decision procedure. (The treaty has not extended the co-decision procedure to legislative measures that already come under the qualified majority rule – e.g. CAP or trade policy.)
- The possibility for 'enhanced cooperation' is expanded, with a minimum of eight member states required, for instance, in the area of the common foreign and security policy. However, enhanced cooperation of this kind cannot be used for issues that have military implications or that affect defence matters. The Council gives the authorization for enhanced cooperation after receiving the opinion of the Commission. The Council will decide by qualified majority, but each member state may ask that the matter be referred to the European Council for the purposes of a unanimous decision.
- Upon a proposal of one-third of the member states, the Parliament or the Commission, the Council, acting by a four-fifths majority of its members and with the assent of the European Parliament, can declare that a clear danger exists of a member state committing a serious breach of fundamental rights and address to that member state appropriate recommendation.

The last two items are not very relevant. As to enhanced cooperation, none of the larger member states is interested in this, and, without them, it does not make sense to go ahead with only a limited number of states. Take, for instance, defence. Notwithstanding the 1998 Saint-Malo Agreement on a European Rapid Reaction Force, France and the UK have fundamentally different views on organizing a common European defence, while neither of them wants to engage EU institutions in it. This is in contrast with countries like Belgium that want to set up a common European army with the involvement of the Commission and the European Parliament. The same holds for the last item: this so-called democracy clause was a late reaction to the coming-to-power of the FPÖ in Austria and the mostly symbolic EU sanctions issued thereon. The real problem tabled at the European Council of Nice – how to create a more efficient decision-making system to prepare the EU for a growing number of member states – was not solved. In the Council, member states defend their national interests. Therefore, voting procedures are very important. There are three dominant axes in the EU with contradictory interests: big versus small member states; member states favouring a federal union versus member states favouring cooperation between sovereign governments; member states that are net contributors to the budget versus member states that are net receivers (Müftüler-Bac 2005: 152). In most cases, member states decide by qualified majority. This qualified majority system is biased in favour of small states. The Amsterdam Treaty Protocol on the institutions provided that, in the case of further EU enlargement, the Commission should comprise one national of each of the member states, on condition that, by that date, the votes in the Council were reweighed in a manner acceptable to all (read: large) member states. The Nice treaty still gives small countries more voting power per capita than larger countries. For a decision to be adopted, a number of qualified votes has to be reached, a majority of member states and – if a member state insists – a majority of 62 per cent of EU population. According to Baldwin and Widgrén (2004: 4), the Nice solution is bad, because the 'passage probability' of a Commission proposal and thus efficient decision making is lower than it would have been without any reform. The power of a large nation depends mostly on its population share, since its weight in the EU population is much larger than its weight in the number of members. The Nice population threshold – if invoked by a member state – will shift power to large nations whose population shares exceed their membership rates. Thus, large new member states like Turkey could be significant allies for the big countries as well as for the small ones (Aleskerov *et al.* 2002: 388; Kafyeke 2006: 31). There is no denial that, with 15 per cent of the total EU population, Turkey will have an important voice in the decision-making process (Littoz-Monnet and Villanueva Penas 2005: 13). Yet, under the Nice rules, the power differences among Turkey and the three other big member states would be small (Baldwin and Widgrén 2005: 9). Turkey's membership would have only moderate implications for the passage probabilities.

The Nice European Council made abundantly clear that the EU was not yet ready for enlargement but that at the same time the link between deepening the EU and enlargement was being given up:

> There has to be a deeper and wider debate about the future of the European Union ... The subjects to be considered include the demarcation of respon-sibilities between the Union and the member states, the status of the charter of fundamental rights of the European Union, simplification of the treaties, and the role of the national parliaments in the institutional architecture of the European Union. The Intergovernmental Conference agrees that once this preparatory work has been completed another Intergovernmental Conference will be convened in 2004 to deal with these matters, but the conference will in no way impede or be a pre-condition to the enlargement process. (Conclu-sions of the Presidency 2000)

For Turkey, the Nice European Council seemed to be positive. The 'Accession Partnership Document' put forward by the Commission on 8 November 2000 was approved by all member states:

> The European Council welcomes the progress made in implementing the pre-accession strategy for Turkey and is very pleased at the agreement reached on the framework Regulation and on the Accession Partnership at the Council meeting on 4 December 2000. It highlights the importance of that docu-ment for making relations between the Union and Turkey closer along the lines mapped out by the Helsinki European Council conclusions. Turkey

is requested swiftly to submit its national programme for adoption of the
Acquis, basing it on the Accession Partnership. (Conclusions of the Presidency 2000)

On the other hand, Turkey was annoyed by the fact that, when calculating the
future votes in the Council and the seats in EU institutions, the Nice treaty took
into account the CEEC, Cyprus and Malta but left Turkey out of the equation. In
contrast with other candidate countries, it took a long time for Turkey to prepare
its National Programme for the Adoption of the *Acquis communautaire*. Opponents and proponents of more liberalization of the Turkish economy were at odds.
The first National Programme of Action, presented in March 2001, was vague and
evasive on the most critical issues, such as Cyprus, treatment of minorities and the
role of the military. In October 2001 the Turkish National Assembly passed a first
series of reforms that significantly eased restrictions on human rights. In February
2002 the Parliament passed a new package containing reforms in the Turkish
Penal Code and antiterrorism law (Larrabee and Lesser 2003: 53). In August 2002
the fourth reform package was passed, containing, *inter alia*, the abolishment of
the death penalty in times of peace and the legalization of broadcasting and private
tutoring in Kurdish. Thus, the new National Programme was finally ready, and it
went well beyond the restrictive proposals in the first National Programme. Yet in
the 2002 Progress Report, the Commission made clear that Turkey still had a long
way to go to fulfil the Copenhagen criteria.

The Copenhagen European Council

The Copenhagen European Council (December 2002) officially closed negotiations with the CEEC, Cyprus and Malta. Even if EU structures had not been yet
adapted to an increasing number of member states, the countries were welcomed
as prospective new member states, as becomes clear from the final communiqué
of the meeting:

> The European Council in Copenhagen in 1993 launched an ambitious process
> to overcome the legacy of conflict and division in Europe. Today marks an
> unprecedented and historic milestone in completing this process with the
> conclusion of accession negotiations with Cyprus, the Czech Republic,
> Estonia, Hungary, Latvia, Lithuania, Malta, Poland, the Slovak Republic
> and Slovenia. The Union now looks forward to welcoming these States
> as members from 1 May 2004. This achievement testifies to the common
> determination of the peoples of Europe to come together in a Union that has
> become the driving force for peace, democracy, stability and prosperity on
> our continent. As fully-fledged members of a Union based on solidarity, these
> States will play a full role in shaping the further development of the European
> project. (Conclusions of the Presidency 2002)

The Council also had warm words for Bulgaria and Romania:

The successful conclusion of accession negotiations with ten candidates lends new dynamism to the accession of Bulgaria and Romania as part of the same inclusive and irreversible enlargement process. The Union welcomes the important progress achieved by these countries, which is duly reflected in the advanced state of their accession negotiations. The Union looks forward to consolidating the results achieved so far. Following the conclusions of the European Council in Brussels and depending on further progress in complying with the membership criteria, the objective is to welcome Bulgaria and Romania as members of the European Union in 2007. The Union confirms that accession negotiations with these countries will continue on the basis of the same principles that have guided the accession negotiations so far, and that each candidate country will be judged on its own merits. (Conclusions of the Presidency Copenhagen 2002)

For Turkey, the European Council had some encouraging words but the conclusions seemed evasive:

The European Council recalls its decision in 1999 in Helsinki that Turkey is a candidate state destined to join the Union based on the same criteria as applied to the other candidate states. It strongly welcomes the important steps taken by Turkey towards meeting the Copenhagen criteria, in particular through the recent legislative packages and the subsequent implementation measures, which cover a large number of key priorities specified in the Accession Partnership. The Union acknowledges the determination of the new Turkish government to take further steps on the path of reform and urges in particular the government to address swiftly all remaining shortcomings in the field of the political criteria, not only with regard to legislation but also in particular with regard to implementation. The Union recalls that, according to the political criteria decided in Copenhagen in 1993, membership requires that a candidate country has achieved stability of institutions guaranteeing democracy, the rule of law, human rights and respect for and protection of minorities. The Union encourages Turkey to pursue energetically its reform process. If the European Council in December 2004, on the basis of a report and a recommendation from the Commission, decides that Turkey fulfils the Copenhagen political criteria, the European Union will open accession negotiations with Turkey without delay. (Conclusions of the Presidency Copenhagen 2002)

To the great disillusionment of the Turks, the European Council gave ten states the green light for membership in 2004, while Bulgaria and Romania received the prospect of membership three years later. At the same time, the European Council once again put off the decision to start accession negotiations with Turkey. However, Turkey was determined to reach the deadline set in the Copenhagen final communiqué. It set in motion a new reform movement. Parliament passed in total seven reform packages, including two sets of amendments to the Constitution.

The ill-fated constitutional treaty

Realizing that enlargement with twelve new member states had come too soon, the EU tried to deepen the European integration process by calling first a Convention (December 2001) and, following this, a new Intergovernmental Conference (June 2003). Out of these came the European Constitutional Treaty, which was signed on 29 October 2004, six months after the accession of ten new member states.

The Treaty Establishing a Constitution for Europe (EU 2004) was to replace all existing treaties and simplify European law. It contained the following:

- The treaty would extend EU rights into some new areas, most importantly into justice policy, especially asylum and immigration. It did away with the old structure of pillars under which some policies came under the EU and some under intergovernmental arrangements.
- The principle of voting by qualified majority would become general. There would be a veto only with respect to foreign policy, defence and taxation. A country outvoted on an issue could always take its case to the European Council, though it could still be outvoted there. The European Parliament would have an equal say on decisions requiring majority voting.
- A qualified majority was now defined as at least 55 per cent of the members of the Council, comprising at least fifteen of them and representing member states comprising at least 65 per cent of EU population.
- The European Council would elect its president by qualified majority, for a term of two and a half years, renewable once. The European Parliament would then have to approve the candidate. The rotating presidency with each member state holding the chair for six months would disappear.
- The European Council, deciding by qualified majority, with the agreement of the president of the Commission, would appoint the Union Minister of Foreign Affairs, who would conduct the EU common foreign and security policy.
- The Commission would be slimmed down to a number of members corresponding to two-thirds of the number of member states (unless the European Council, acting unanimously, decided to alter this figure).
- The Charter of Fundamental Rights would be incorporated in the Constitution. It sets out rights, freedoms and principles. These include a whole list from the right to life and the right to liberty down to the right to strike.
- The EU would have legal personality.
- Member states would be allowed to leave the EU.

Unfortunately, the treaty was rejected by popular referendum in both France and the Netherlands (May/June 2005), two founding members of the EU. Opponents focused on the Euro, which had made life expensive, the increasing loss of national sovereignty to the anonymous Brussels bureaucracy and the enlargement with the CEEC and possibly with Turkey, which was to cost numerous jobs and would lead to an uncontrolled flood of immigrants. The campaigns also degenerated into attacks on sitting governments, emphasizing the distance existing between government and nation. Proponents were unable to explain the legal phraseology of the text and to focus on the benefits of European integration. As the treaty was an intricate compromise between twenty-five member states, it was very difficult to explain the improvements it would bring compared with previous treaties.

Negotiations at last

In its October 2004 report the Commission reached a positive conclusion with respect to Turkey. Realizing that the EU had opened negotiations with Romania and Bulgaria too soon and ignoring last-minute opposition from Austria,[13] the European Council (December 2004) finally gave the green light for accession negotiations with Turkey. Yet the final communiqué (Conclusions of the Presidency 2004) showed that the consensus on the matter had been very weak and that the enthusiasm that had accompanied previous enlargements was lacking:

- The European Council welcomed the adoption of the six pieces of legislation[14] identified by the Commission. It decided that, in the light of the Commission report and recommendation, Turkey sufficiently fulfilled the Copenhagen political criteria to open accession negotiations if it brings into force these specific pieces of legislation.
- The European Council welcomed Turkey's decision to sign the Protocol regarding the adaptation of the Ankara Agreement, taking account of the accession of the ten new member states (thus including Cyprus).
- Negotiations, which will be conducted in an intergovernmental conference with the participation of all member states on the one hand and Turkey on the other, where decisions require unanimity, will be broken down into a number of chapters, each covering a specific policy area. The Council, acting by unanimity on a proposal by the Commission, will lay down benchmarks for the provisional closure and, where appropriate, for the opening of each chapter.
- Long transition periods, derogations, specific arrangements or permanent safeguard clauses, may be considered. The Commission will include these, as appropriate, in its proposals for each framework, for areas such as freedom of movement of persons, structural policies or agriculture. Furthermore, the decision-taking process regarding the eventual establishment of freedom of movement of persons should allow for a maximum role of individual member states. Transitional arrangements or safeguards should be reviewed regarding their impact on competition or the functioning of the internal market.
- The financial aspects of accession of a candidate state must be allowed for in the applicable financial framework. Hence, accession negotiations yet to be opened with candidates whose accession could have substantial financial consequences can be concluded only after the establishment of the financial framework for the period from 2014 together with possible consequential financial reforms.

- The shared objective of the negotiations is accession. These negotiations are an open-ended process, the outcome of which cannot be guaranteed beforehand.
- In the case of a serious and persistent breach in a candidate state of the principles of liberty, democracy, respect for human rights and fundamental freedoms and the rule of law on which the EU is founded, the Commission will, on its own initiative or on the request of one third of the member states, recommend the suspension of negotiations and propose the conditions for eventual resumption. The Council will decide by qualified majority on such a recommendation, after having heard the candidate state, whether to suspend the negotiations and on the conditions for their resumption.

The Council set two political conditions before negotiations could be started. First, Turkey was required to bring into force the six pieces of legislation. Turkey did this on 1 June 2005. Secondly – and this was politically much more difficult for the government – Turkey was expected to sign the Additional Protocol to the Ankara Agreement, which extended the association to the new member states (among them Cyprus).[15] Many elements in the Brussels final communiqué were hardly reassuring for the Turks: permanent safeguard clauses in areas such as the freedom of movement of persons, structural policies or agriculture; the preliminary agreement of member states on the financial framework for 2014–20; the right to veto opening and closing of negotiations on each of the items held by each single member state; possible suspension of negotiation in case of a breach of domestic law; and so on. The following remark in the final communiqué was the most upsetting: 'If Turkey was not in a position to assume in full all the obligations of membership it had to be insured that Turkey was fully anchored in the European structures through the strongest possible bond' (Conclusions of the Presidency 2004).

On many occasions, Turkey has made it explicitly clear that it rejected the notion of privileged partnership with the EU. On the day negotiations were to start (3 October 2005) Minister of Foreign Affairs Abdullah Gül even refused to board the plane until it was quite clear that in the Negotiation Framework there was no wording alluding to 'privileged partnership' (Kirişçi 2006: 57). Negotiations did not start under a lucky star: right from the beginning, the Cyprus issue was going to impinge on them. Moreover, negotiations with Turkey could not have come at a worse moment. The negative 2005 referenda outcomes plunged the EU into a deep crisis. It took almost two years before agreement was reached on a mandate to negotiate a new 'Reform Treaty' to replace the rejected Constitutional Treaty (June 2007). The draft Reform Treaty was a compromise between the eighteen member states that had ratified the Constitutional Treaty and those that had not. Although the new treaty is shorter, it leaves the substance of the Constitutional Treaty largely untouched if one takes into account annexes and separate declarations. It retains EU legal personality, the EU presidency and the position of foreign minister (but under a different name: high representative for foreign affairs and security policy). It also increases the number of decisions that will be taken by qualified majority voting and maintains the co-decision power of the European Parliament. Yet the new voting system in the Council will be phased in, beginning only in 2014 and fully implemented only three years later. The Charter of Fundamental Rights has been given legal force but will apply only to laws or actions by the EU institutions within the EU treaties. There is a specific exemption to say that it does not apply to the domestic law of the UK. Member states can opt in or out of policies concerning frontiers, asylum and police and judicial cooperation. National control over foreign policy is not given up in favour of the EU. The role of national parliaments is to be strengthened: national parliaments would receive all EU proposals eight weeks before they go to the Council to mandate their ministers before Council meetings and would also gain the right to object directly to draft legislation if they feel it goes beyond EU competence. The Copenhagen enlargement criteria are included in the treaty. On 6 December 2007 the Reform Treaty was signed in Lisbon. The treaty will enter into effect after ratification by the twenty-seven member states.

Conclusion

From the preceding, we can draw the following conclusions:

- The EU is a product of the cold war. It is an international organization with far-reaching delegation of powers by member states to the institutions of the organization. Its economic achievements are exceptional: it evolved from a customs union into a fully-fledged internal market and eventually into a strong monetary union. The EU political integration has been less successful. Since Maastricht, there has been cooperation in the field of foreign and security policy and in the area of home affairs and justice. Yet the results are often the lowest common denominator of member states' policies.
- With respect to non-member states, there were two strategies that the EU could have pursued. It could have waited for other European countries to make the necessary adjustments, or it could continue with the economic integration process, thus enabling other states to join later on. The EU opted for the second strategy. All previous enlargements had been successful. Unfortunately, the EU has neglected to adapt its institutional rulings and decision-making process to the growing number of its members. Structures designed for six member states are inappropriate for twenty-seven or more member states.
- Turkey's pro-Western orientation was the corollary of its domestic political system. At the same time, it was a geopolitical necessity brought about by its geographical location and the policy of the USSR. The EC tried to fend off the Turkish request for membership as long as possible. The Association Agreement and the customs union were offered as alternatives. However, Turkey kept on insisting that it wanted to become a full member of the EC. Turkey's economic problems in the 1970s and political problems in the 1980s were a welcome excuse for the EC to freeze relations.

- Because of the end of the cold war, ten former hostile Warsaw Pact countries joined the EU. It then became even more difficult for the EU to reject the application of Turkey, which had always been a staunch NATO ally. By formulating the rigid Copenhagen criteria as separate preconditions for membership, the EU upped the ante and put off the definitive decision on the Turkish application yet again. But Turkey embarked on an ambitious reform path, thereby forcing the EU to face the challenge.
- In December 2004 the EU had to give in. Yet the outcome of the negotiations looks very dark. Turkey refuses to recognize the Republic of Cyprus. Leaders of some member states have declared themselves openly against Turkish EU membership. Public opinion in the EU is very much against it. Since the start of negotiations (October 2005) the pace of reforms in Turkey has slackened. In Turkey, more and more people are asking themselves whether it still makes sense to go on with negotiations.

3　The Copenhagen economic criteria

In order to reach the Copenhagen economic objectives, the Commission has laid down four subsets of criteria by which Turkey has to abide. The first relates to the existence of a functioning market economy. The second deals with the capacity to compete in EU markets. The third refers to the EMU, while the fourth deals with the so-called *Acquis communautaire*. In the following four sections, we will deal with each of these criteria in detail. Based on an analysis of the successive Progress Reports, we shall categorize each of the different criteria into three groups: those where, according to the Commission, progress has been made, those with no progress and those with limited progress. While there is some degree of latitude in this classification, we consider this approach as a first attempt to analyse the underlying problems.

A functioning market economy

In Table 3.1 we show the six chapters being dealt with by the Commission under the heading 'A functioning market economy'. In the following section we will further analyse each of these chapters:

- economic policy essentials;
- macroeconomic stability;
- free interplay of market forces;
- free market entry and exit;
- adequate legal system;
- sufficiently developed financial sector.

Table 3.1 The existence of a functioning market economy, Turkey, 1998–2006

Criterion 1	Progress	No progress	Limited progress
Economic policy essentials	X		
Macroeconomic stability			X
Free interplay of market forces	X		
Free market entry and exit	X		
Adequate legal system	X		
Sufficiently developed financial sector	X		

Source: Based on CEC (1998, 1999, 2000, 2001, 2002, 2003b, 2004c, 2005, 2006a).

Economic policy essentials

It is not always easy to find a trend with respect to the criterion 'Economic Policy Essentials' from the different Commission Progress Reports. We will discuss the item 'macroeconomic stability' in the next section, but first it is important to measure the results of the 'steady reform course' of the Turkish government. We have, therefore, looked for key indicators that could be compared with the rest of the EU. We decided to use the following indicators to typify the Turkish economic and social situation: GDP per capita, human development, income inequality and global competitiveness.

GDP per capita

Table 3.2 shows GDP, population and GDP per capita for the EU-15, the new member states and Turkey. Turkish GDP in 2005 is about 2.8 per cent of EU-15 GDP and about 52 per cent of GDP in the twelve new member states. Turkish population in 2003 was about 18 per cent of EU-15 population. Turkey's long-term growth of real GDP per capita is lower than the growth of its total real GDP because of its high population growth. Turkey's average GDP in purchasing power standards in 2005 is lower than the average GDP of the new member states, but similar to that of Bulgaria and Romania.

Because of the customs union, one could have expected free trade with the EU to determine a certain convergence of the Turkish GDP per capita towards the average EU-15 GPD per capita. Economic theory in fact predicts that opening up to trade is ultimately welfare enhancing for a country.[1] This has not happened

Table 3.2 GDP, population and GDP per capita, EU-27 and Turkey, 2003–5

Country	GDP 2005 (market current prices; billion Euro)	Population (2003)	GDP per capita in PPS (EU-25=100) 2005
EU-15	10,286.3	383,706,397	108.3
Bulgaria	21.4	7,823,557	32.1
Czech Republic	99.7	10,207,362	73.8
Estonia	11.1	1,353,557	60.1
Cyprus	13.4	722,752	83.3
Latvia	12.8	2,325,342	47.2
Lithuania	20.6	3,454,205	52.1
Hungary	88.8	10,129,552	61.4
Malta	4.5	398,582	69.5
Poland	243.4	38,204,570	49.8
Slovenia	27.6	1,995,733	80.6
Slovakia	38.1	5,379,607	55.0
Romania	79.3	21,742,013	34.7
Turkey	290.5	70,430,489	30.7

Source: Eurostat (2006a).

Table 3.3 GDP per capita in PPS, EU-27 and Turkey, 1995–2005 (EU-25=100)

Country	1995	1996	1997	1998	1999	2000	2001	2002	2003	2004	2005
EU-25	100.0	100.0	100.0	100.0	100.0	100.0	100.0	100.0	100.0	100.0	100.0
EU-15	110.7	110.4	110.1	110.0	109.9	109.7	109.6	109.3	108.9	108.6	108.2
Bulgaria	30.8	27.6	25.6	26.0	26.0	26.5	28.0	28.3	31.0	31.8	32.9
Czech Republic	68.8	71.5	69.2	66.8	65.9	64.7	65.8	67.7	70.7	72.1	73.7
Estonia	33.6	35.0	38.4	39.3	38.7	42.1	43.7	46.8	51.2	53.4	59.8
Cyprus	82.1	81.3	79.6	80.7	81.4	82.2	84.4	82.6	85.3	87.7	88.9
Latvia	29.9	30.9	33.0	33.9	34.0	35.3	37.1	38.7	41.2	43.6	48.0
Lithuania	34.2	35.4	37.2	38.8	37.4	37.9	40.1	41.9	47.1	49.0	52.1
Hungary	48.9	48.8	49.8	50.9	51.7	53.9	56.9	59.1	60.8	61.3	62.5
Malta	n/a	n/a	n/a	77.8	77.1	78.0	73.8	74.9	74.3	71.3	70.4
Poland	40.7	42.4	44.2	45.1	45.8	46.7	46.1	46.3	46.9	48.7	49.7
Romania	n/a	n/a	n/a	n/a	25.3	24.9	26.2	28.1	29.9	32.6	34.1
Slovenia	68.2	69.5	71.0	71.9	73.6	72.7	73.9	74.5	77.4	79.9	81.9
Slovakia	44.7	47.0	47.4	47.6	46.9	47.4	48.7	51.0	52.8	54.4	57.1
Turkey	29.8	30.8	32.3	31.9	29.2	29.8	25.6	26.1	26.2	26.8	27.6

Source: Eurostat (2006a).

in the EU–Turkey case. Table 3.3 and Figure 3.1 show that new member states have generally converged with EU-15. All EU-10 member states have reduced the distance separating them from EU-15, and Bulgaria and Romania started to do this recently. However, for Turkey the distance from EU-15 has increased rather than decreased.

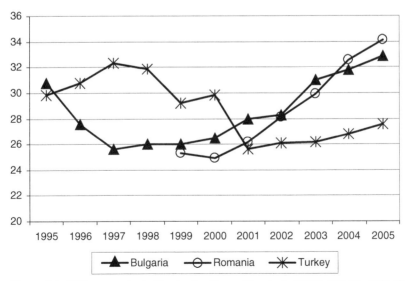

Figure 3.1 GDP per capita in Purchasing Power Standards (PPS) (EU-25=100) (Source: Eurostat (2006a)).

Human development

Table 3.4 shows the UN Human Development Index (HDI). The HDI ranks nations according to their citizens' quality of life rather than strictly by a nation's traditional economic figures. The criteria for calculating rankings include life expectancy, educational attainment and adjusted real income. The 2005 index is based on 2003 figures. Table 3.4 makes it clear that all EU member states other than Romania fall into the category of highly developed countries. The EU-15 member states even rank among the first 27 out of 177 countries with an EU average of 0.922. Turkey and Romania fall into the category of medium-developed countries. Compared to the EU-27, Turkey performs poorly.

Income inequality

In Table 3.5 EU member states and Turkey are ranked by income inequality figures, sorted in ascending order, according to their Gini coefficient (survey years vary between 1997 and 2002). A lower Gini coefficient tends to indicate a higher level of

Table 3.4 Human Development Index, EU-27 and Turkey, 2005

Country	Rank	HDI
Luxembourg	4	0.949
Sweden	6	0.949
Ireland	8	0.946
Belgium	9	0.945
Netherlands	12	0.943
Finland	13	0.941
Denmark	14	0.941
United Kingdom	15	0.939
France	16	0.938
Austria	17	0.936
Italy	18	0.934
Germany	20	0.930
Spain	21	0.928
Greece	24	0.912
Slovenia	26	0.904
Portugal	27	0.904
Cyprus	29	0.891
Czech Republic	31	0.874
Malta	32	0.867
Hungary	35	0.862
Poland	36	0.858
Estonia	38	0.853
Lithuania	39	0.852
Slovakia	42	0.849
Latvia	48	0.836
Bulgaria	55	0.808
Romania	64	0.792
Turkey	94	0.750

Source: UN (2005).

Table 3.5 Gini coefficients, selected countries, 2005

Country	Rank	Gini coefficient
Denmark	1	24.7
Sweden	3	25.0
Belgium	4	25.0
Czech Republic	5	25.4
Slovakia	7	25.8
Finland	10	26.9
Hungary	11	26.9
Germany	14	28.3
Slovenia	15	28.4
Austria	19	30.0
Romania	21	30.3
Netherlands	24	30.9
Lithuania	28	31.9
Bulgaria	29	31.9
Spain	31	32.5
France	34	32.7
Latvia	41	33.6
Poland	42	34.1
Greece	48	35.4
Ireland	50	35.9
United Kingdom	51	36.0
Italy	52	36.0
Estonia	61	37.9
Portugal	65	38.5
Turkey	70	40.0
Cyprus	n/a	n/a
Luxembourg	n/a	n/a
Malta	n/a	n/a

Source: World Bank (2005a).

social and economic equality. As far as Turkey is concerned, it has the highest Gini coefficient of the countries mentioned. The share of the highest 10 per cent of households is 13.3 higher than that of the lowest 10 per cent. Turkey belongs to a group of countries with extreme inequality of income distribution. There are several reasons for this. First, the successive economic crises. Secondly, migration flows from rural to urban areas: income distribution and inequality in rural areas remained nearly constant, whereas income inequality significantly increased in urban areas (Oskam *et al.* 2005b: 20). Thirdly, Turkey lacked effective tax and transfer policies to alter market distribution (Gültekin and Yilmaz 2005: 72). High- and middle-income groups remain largely exempt from income taxation; wealth taxes are insufficient and wage-earners bear 80 per cent of the income tax burden (Tocci 2001: 23).

Global competitiveness

Table 3.6 shows the World Economic Forum Global Competitiveness Index (GCI) rankings. The GCI provides an overview of factors that are critical to driving productivity and competitiveness of countries and groups these factors into nine

Table 3.6 Global Competitiveness Index, EU-27 and Turkey, 2005–6

Country	Rank 2006 (2005 in parentheses)
Finland	2 (2)
Sweden	3 (7)
Denmark	4 (3)
Germany	8 (6)
Netherlands	9 (11)
United Kingdom	10 (9)
Austria	17 (15)
France	18 (12)
Belgium	20 (20)
Ireland	21 (21)
Luxembourg	22 (24)
Estonia	25 (26)
Spain	28 (28)
Czech Republic	29 (29)
Slovenia	33 (30)
Portugal	34 (31)
Latvia	36 (39)
Slovakia	37 (36)
Malta	39 (44)
Lithuania	40 (34)
Hungary	41 (35)
Italy	42 (38)
Cyprus	46 (41)
Greece	47 (47)
Poland	48 (43)
Turkey	59 (71)
Romania	68 (67)
Bulgaria	72 (61)

Source: World Economic Forum (2006).

categories: institutions, infrastructure, macroeconomy, health and primary education, higher education and training, market efficiency, technological readiness, business sophistication and innovation. All EU member states rank in the top 50 out of 125 countries. Turkey ranks 59.

Conclusion

When comparing key economic indicators of Turkey with the EU we can draw the following conclusions:

- Compared to EU-15, Turkey lags significantly behind when four economic key indicators are chosen: GDP per capita, human development, income inequality and global competitiveness.
- There is less divergence between the EU-12 and Turkey.
- There is no minimum norm being fixed in the Progress Reports as to economic and social development.

- EU membership will contribute to the economic development of Turkey: GDP per capita, human development and global competitiveness are bound to increase while income inequality will probably decrease.

Macroeconomic stability

We will deal with the following main indicators:

- economic growth;
- rate of employment;
- rate of inflation;
- balance of payments.

Economic growth

In its 2006 Progress Report the Commission mentions the following (CEC 2006a):

- Real annual GDP growth slowed down slightly compared to 2005.
- Private consumption and investment bolstered GDP.
- Gross fixed capital formation slowed down.
- The external sector contributed negatively to GDP.
- There are growing external imbalances.
- The authorities reacted promptly by fiscal and monetary tightening.
- Economic growth has remained quite strong and has become more balanced.

According to the Commission, the economic growth prospects do not look bad for Turkey. It was different in the past. The economic history of Turkey since 1971 has been a story of chronic macroeconomic imbalances (see Figure 3.2). While

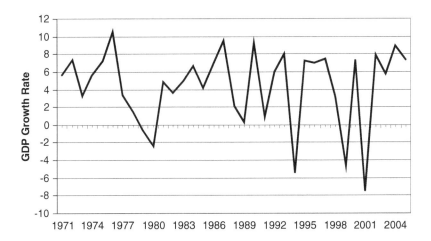

Figure 3.2 Real GDP growth rate, Turkey, 1971–2004 (Source: Eurostat (2006a)).

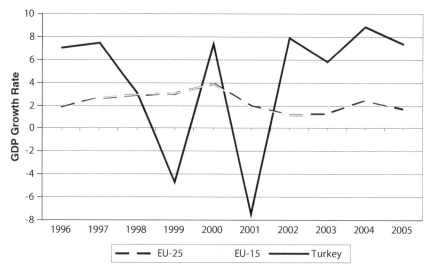

Figure 3.3 Real GDP growth rate, Turkey and EU, 1996–2005 (Source: Eurostat (2006a)).

in the period 1996–2005 the EU-15 and EU-25 rates of economic growth were modest but stable, Turkish growth rates were erratic (see Figure 3.3). Years of high growth were followed by years of crisis. There were four major economic crises: in 1978, 1994, 2000 and 2001. We shall briefly describe their causes.

By the late 1970s Turkey ran into its first crisis, which was characterized by recession, galloping inflation and a severe shortage of foreign exchange. To get out of the crisis, the government adopted a package of devaluation and liberalization in line with IMF prescriptions. Turkey had to become a more export-oriented economy; it had to make a serious effort to combat inflation and it had to reduce the deficit on its balance of payments. Liberalization did away with the ceiling on interest rates and the prices of public goods (Uğur 2004: 77). Wages were frozen (thanks to the 1980 coup, trade unions were suppressed). The drop in real purchasing power was about 40–60 per cent (Zürcher 1997: 316).

Turkey started the 1980s with a stabilization and liberalization programme. The Central Bank adopted a managed exchange-rate policy to control inflation. High interest rates and the wage freeze succeeded in curbing inflation in the first half of the 1980s. The programme achieved strong macroeconomic adjustment. However, macroeconomic imbalances reappeared after 1987. Inflation and fiscal imbalances rose again. The cause was not high consumer demand but the government deficit. Inefficient taxation, the huge losses of state enterprises, the large civil service and policies to compensate popular demands were to blame for this (Zürcher 1997: 320; Akyüz and Boratav 2003: 3). Before fiscal discipline had been secured and inflation brought under control the capital account was first partially and then in 1989 fully liberalized. This liberalization was premature: there was no corresponding adjustment of fiscal balances. Budget deficits were monetized. There was liberalization without stabilization. Lax monetary policy went hand in hand with fiscal indiscipline.

Turkey followed a policy mix characterized by an activist fiscal and an accommodating monetary policy (Uğur 1999: 68; Akyüz and Boratav 2003: 3; Önis 2006:
244). The Turkish government used export subsidies, surcharges on imports and an
undervalued exchange rate among other instruments, to stimulate economic growth
and to accommodate the demands of rent-seeking industries (Uğur 2004: 81). For
instance, the Özal government put state income into separate funds. Surcharges
were imposed on several items and activities (for example, on imports of luxury
products or on Turkish labourers abroad), and they were put in funds that remained
outside the budget and parliamentary control (Zürcher 1997: 321).

The outcome was a rapid build-up of public debt and the emergence of a finan-
cial system, which came to depend on high rates on government debt, compared to
international borrowing with large currency risks. The eventual appreciation of the
Turkish lira in 1989 increased the vulnerability of the economy to external shocks.
At the end of 1993 two prestigious American firms lowered their credit ratings for
Turkey twice in a row, and the Turkish government tried to impose lower interest
rates on banks participating in American treasure bill[2] auctions (Zürcher 1997: 322;
Akyüz and Boratav 2003: 4). These two events seemed to trigger a reversal of capital
flows. Portfolio investors expected a devaluation of the Turkish lira and began to
withdraw their funds. This led to a second crisis. At the end of 1994 inflation stood
at 150 per cent and short-term measures (increasing interest rates, rising prices of
government services and state products) plunged the Turkish economy into a deep
crisis (Zürcher 1997: 323; Akyüz and Boratav 2003: 8). The IMF wanted Turkey to
privatize its economy further, but this process moved very slowly.

The following years were a repetition of the preceding cycle. Capital inflows
generated booms (1995–7 and later in 2000), which increased fiscal and financial
fragility (1998 and the end of 2000), and reversal of capital flows accompanied
economic contraction and financial crisis (1999 and 2001) (Boratav and Özugurlu
2006: 181). Capital flows returned during 1995–7, when the economy enjoyed
three successive years of growth in excess of 7 per cent. In 1999 Turkey ran into
serious problems again with its public finances. This was partly due to external
shocks such as a major earthquake, higher oil prices, the rise in the value of the
American Dollar and the Asian and Russian financial crisis. Eight insolvent banks
had to be taken over by the public Saving Deposit Insurance Fund (Uğur 2004: 89;
Akyüz and Boratav 2003: 9; Önis 2006: 245). Moreover, the overvalued exchange
rate, used to achieve a rapid reduction in inflation, helped to undermine export
competitiveness. In December 1999 the government – in close cooperation with
the IMF – launched a stabilization programme. A gradual shift towards a more
flexible exchange-rate regime would start in July 2001 (Akyüz and Boratav 2003:
11). Private capital inflows and large-scale foreign borrowing by the government
resulted in a large increase in international reserves. Under the policy rule of non-
sterilization, this meant a considerable expansion of domestic liquidity, which
helped to lower interest rates, thereby supporting private and public consumption.[3] From the Turkish exchange-rate-based stabilization programme followed an
increase in capital inflows, a positive evolution in economic activity, an appreciation of the currency and increasing trade deficits (Akyüz and Boratav 2003: 15).

It is difficult to identify a single event behind the collapse of confidence and flight from domestic assets that occurred in November 2000 – the third crisis that brought the country to the verge of financial collapse. The events included disappointing economic forecasts, problems with the EU, the economic situation in Argentina, disclosure of irregularities in banks and competitive manoeuvring between private banks. Again, the IMF rode to the rescue of the Turkish economy with a $10.5 billion financial rescue package. The government agreed to further spending cuts and tax increases, abolishment of agricultural support policies, liberalization of markets, financial restructuring and privatization (Akyüz and Boratav 2003: 17). Stability proved short lived, and it soon became clear that the programme was unviable. Rising public debt, high inflation and the continued appreciation of the Turkish lira were initially behind the new crisis. The precipitating cause was a row between Prime Minister Ecevit and President Sezer.[4] In February 2001 Turkey experienced the worst economic crisis in its history. Investors pulled $5 billion out of the country on one day alone. At that rate, foreign reserves would soon have run out. Overnight interest rates soared to 6,200 per cent. The Central Bank sold dollars to stop the speculative assault on the lira. One quarter of its foreign currency reserves were spent to no avail. Queues formed outside banks, as panic ensued over the falling lira. In the end the government allowed the Turkish lira to float freely – in other words to devalue.[5] It lost 45 per cent of its value. Many people lost their jobs, not only in the banking sector, but also in small and medium-sized enterprises. Bankruptcies were expected to increase, as companies continued to struggle with high interest rates for their debts. Ordinary Turks, already struggling with unemployment and a drop in consumer spending, were likely to suffer heavily from the latest crisis (*The Economist* 2001; Buğra 2004: 53; Lejour *et al.* 2004: 17; Akyüz and Boratav 2003: 18; Önis 2006: 252). In May 2001 a new IMF programme was set in place – with an additional stand-by credit of $8 billion – to address the two bottlenecks of the economy: the government budget deficit and the government debt, and the banking system. Fiscal transparency and privatization were central in the plan. The IMF set high targets on primary surpluses on the public budget. Rising rates of indirect taxation and cutting back of public expenditures signified reduction of social transfers (Boratav and Özugurlu 2006: 181).

We can conclude that nearly every decade ended in Turkey with a major stand-by agreement with the IMF (Gültekin and Yilmaz 2005: 64). Over time Turkey has had sixteen IMF stand-by agreements receiving approximately $30 billion, which makes it the second highest borrower from the IMF after Brazil (Tocci 2001: 27; Eder 2003: 230). The latest three-year stand-by agreement was signed in May 2005, a $39.5 billion rescue package. It included the following:

- further liberalization of the economy, with significant restructuring of the agricultural and banking sector;
- institutional reforms: independence of the central bank and creation of regulatory boards in banking, telecommunication, energy, and tobacco and sugar that operated independently of the government;

- a tight fiscal policy (with a 6.5 per cent surplus in the primary budget for purposes of interest payments).

Some economists remain very sceptical about Turkey's commitment to stabilization: 'Each stabilization programme had to be abandoned within one to two years after its adoption' (Uğur 2004: 89). The public budget is overburdened by debts accumulated during the 1990s – to such an extent that over half of the government spending has to be allocated to interest payments on the debt (Buğra and Keyder 2006: 212). The reason for the volatile macroeconomic environment has been the inability of successive governments to deal with the underlying causes of poor public finances (see Table 3.7). According to Tocci (2001: 21–2), 'it is widely recognized that weak and unstable governments in Turkey have traditionally relied more on creating money in a cheap way than on effective tax reform to finance public deficits'. Other economists (among them the European Commission) think that – after eighteen previous failures – Turkey has learned from its past mistakes. The government knows that heavy domestic borrowing to finance large fiscal deficits is a recipe for a crisis. Export competitiveness, increasing domestic savings capacity and current account balance are being taken care of. Neglect of these elements, based on the assumption that large capital inflows and significant international reserves provide the necessary protection, represents a clear invitation to a crisis (Önis 2006: 247). According to Larrabee and Lesser, the economic reform package will have significant implications for Turkish politics, because the old system of patronage using state-controlled banks has been the basis for influence of Turkey's leading political parties. Turkey has two options. If it sticks to the IMF programme, economic reforms, greater democratization, EU

Table 3.7 Public deficit as percentage of GDP, Turkey, 1989–2005

Year	Deficit
1989	5.3
1990	7.4
1991	10.2
1992	10.6
1993	12.0
1994	7.9
1995	5.2
1996	8.3
1997	7.6
1998	7.2
1999	11.5
2000	7.8
2001	33.0
2002	12.9
2003	11.3
2004	5.7
2005	1.2

Source: Tocci (2001: 19); Eurostat (2006a).

membership and the continued modernization of Turkish society will be necessary. If it rejects the programme, there will be no economic and political reform, and a deepening crisis could strengthen nationalist forces in society (Larrabee and Lesser 2003: 16–17).

The AKP government – in power after 2002 – clearly opted for the first approach. It realized all too well that Turkey's ability to go along with the IMF was part of the programme leading to EU membership. This one-party government has displayed a stronger commitment to fiscal discipline and reform than its multi-party predecessors, who had to satisfy the clients who had brought them to power in the first place. This has helped to increase investor confidence as well as to create the basis of an economic recovery process. Resisting populist opposition to fiscal discipline, the government has combated inflation, depreciated the lira and paid off past-due loans. It shrank the pension system, downsized the public sector and reformed bankruptcy law (Phillips 2004: 94; Önis 2006: 254). Yet it is realized that Turkey is still very much reliant on investor confidence. While debt has gone down from 90 to 70 per cent of GDP, the government has had to refinance it almost every month. As 75 per cent of the debt is held domestically, the government has to keep the trust of its people; moreover, it should not worry foreign bankers and it should bring EU accession to a successful conclusion (Friends of Europe 2004: 33). This is a giant task that is not easy to accomplish in a democracy, where governments have to face the electorate at regular intervals and where the opposition uses all means to come to power by obstructing the government.

Rate of unemployment

In its 2006 Progress Report the Commission states the following with respect to unemployment (CEC 2006a):

- The unemployment rate ranges between 8 and 10 per cent.
- The skill mismatch between labour demand and supply hampers job creation.
- Unemployment is much higher among the young and is of a long-term nature for more than half of job-seekers.
- There are large pockets of underemployment in the economy.
- Female employment remains low.
- Participation in the labour market is low and falling.

We think the Commission is relatively moderate when assessing the employment problem in Turkey. First, participation rates and rates of total employment are extremely low (see Table 3.8). Secondly, the informal sector, which absorbs many workers, will be unable to compete with the rest of the economy, while EU regulations require that it is abolished. Table 3.9 shows that both the Turkish participation rate and the rate of total employment are substantially below those in the EU-25. This is mainly due to the low participation and employment rates of women in Turkey. Unpaid family workers mainly consist of women in the

Table 3.8 Labour market indicators, 2003–4

Labour market	EU-15	EU-25	Turkey
Active population (15–64 years), 2004 (000)	180,277	214,155	24,188
Participation rate (15–64 years), 2004 (%)	770.6	69.7	51.5
Unemployment rate, 2004 (%)	8.1	9.1	10.3
Employment rate, 2003 (%)	n/a	62.9	45.5
Employment rate for women, 2003 (%)	n/a	55.1	25.2

Source: Eurostat (2006a).

agricultural sector and they are the largest category among different groups of informal workers (Buğra and Keyder 2006: 217). In Turkey employment rates and labour-force participation even seem to decline over time, not only for women but also for men (see Table 3.10). This decline is partly due to a problem of categories, where men in agriculture are considered fully employed, while they are allowed to go out of the labour force once they are in cities.

Turkey's official unemployment level in 2004 was not very different from that of EU-15 or EU-25. Yet, comparisons are difficult, because the Turkish figures are official unemployment figures; while 50 per cent of Turkey's economic activity is in the informal sector (farming and certain services). Some put the estimate of the informal urban workforce at as high as 30–40 per cent of the total (Hughes 2004: 15). On the other hand, it is thought that unemployment in the informal sector is at more or less the same level as it is in the official sector (Oskam *et al.* 2005b: 14). Unlike the EU, Turkey counts unpaid family work as employment. Economists think that only 20–25 per cent of the working-age population has a normal full-time salaried job and that only 44 per cent of the potential labour force is in fact employed at all, a figure that compares rather unfavourably with the EU average of 63 per cent (Barysch 2005: 6; Buğra and Keyder 2006: 218). If the workforce in agriculture were cut to match the sector's contribution to the economy, 4.4 million jobs would have to be found elsewhere. Because of the increase in the population in working age (one million persons a year), the growing participating rate of female workers and the decline of farming, Turkey will have to create at least a million jobs every year (Derviş *et al.* 2004b: 9).

Table 3.9 Labour-force participation and employment rates according to gender, Turkey, 1988–2005 (%)

Year	Male employment rate	Female employment rate	Male labour-force participation	Female labour-force participation
1988	77.1	33.0	81.4	36.0
1993	71.9	24.3	75.9	32.7
1998	69.6	25.6	74.9	29.3
2003	62.9	23.9	70.4	26.6
2005	64.8	22.3	72.2	24.8

Source: ILO (2006).

Table 3.10 Inflation rates, selected countries, 1997–2005 (harmonized indices of consumer prices)

Country	1997	1998	1999	2000	2001	2002	2003	2004	2005
EU-15	1.7	1.3	1.2	1.9	2.2	2.1	2.0	2.0	2.1
EU-25	2.6	2.1	1.6	2.4	2.5	2.1	1.9	2.1	2.2
Turkey	85.6	82.1	61.4	53.2	56.8	47.0	25.3	10.1	8.1

Source: Eurostat (2006a).

Rate of inflation

In its 2006 Progress Report the Commission states the following with respect to inflation (CEC 2006a):

- Disinflation policies succeeded in decreasing the inflation rate.
- This process was driven by a tight fiscal policy, major improvements in productivity and the strength of the lira.
- However, after strong disinflation, inflation rose again. This was due to energy prices and more recently a weaker lira.

As stated by the Commission, the government did succeed in bringing down inflation. It had been quite different in the past. Table 3.10 and Figure 3.4 show that inflation rates in Turkey have been decreasing since the mid-1990s, but until 2004 they were still at very high levels. Table 3.11 shows there was a certain link between the growth of money supply and inflation. The correlation between both of these variables was 0.42. According to Gültekin and Yilmaz (2005: 72), the

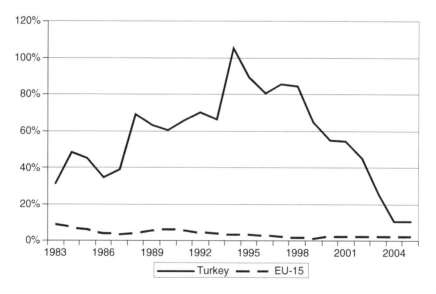

Figure 3.4 Inflation rates, Turkey and EU-15, 1983–2005 (Source: OECD (2006b)).

Table 3.11 Money supply growth and inflation, Turkey, 1969–2004 (annual %)

Year	Money and quasi money growth	Inflation, GDP deflator
1969	17.0	7.4
1970	21.9	9.0
1971	28.1	17.5
1972	26.0	11.3
1973	28.4	21.8
1974	25.7	28.4
1975	28.0	21.0
1976	23.4	15.1
1977	33.8	23.7
1978	36.5	46.7
1979	61.7	75.7
1980	39.9	88.1
1981	35.1	44.1
1982	38.0	28.2
1983	47.9	26.3
1984	19.0	48.2
1985	39.4	53.1
1986	320.1	36.0
1987	50.5	33.6
1988	65.3	69.4
1989	68.9	75.5
1990	53.2	58.2
1991	82.7	58.9
1992	78.7	63.7
1993	64.4	67.8
1994	145.3	106.5
1995	103.6	87.2
1996	117.3	77.8
1997	97.5	81.5
1998	89.7	75.7
1999	100.3	55.6
2000	40.5	49.9
2001	86.2	54.8
2002	29.1	44.1
2003	14.6	22.5
2004	22.1	9.9
Correlation Coefficient		0.42

Source: World Bank (2005b).

rapid decline in inflation was mainly accomplished by an overvalued Turkish lira and significant erosion in real wages. Table 3.12 deals with comparative price levels between EU-15, EU-25 and Turkey. Figures for 2005 are provisional only; figures for Turkey are estimates. Between 1994 and 2004 comparative price levels have in all probability risen faster than those in the EU-15. The gap in average living standards between Turkey and the EU-15 has increased. Ahmet Insel (2004: 120) is very pessimistic: 'Turkish inflation was produced by socio-political insta-bility and has in turn produced instability. Inflation has performed a regulatory

Table 3.12 Comparative price levels, EU and Turkey, 1995–2005 (EU-25 = 100)

Country	1995	2000	2005
EU-25	100.0	100.0	100.0
EU-15	104.4	104.0	103.7
Turkey	49.9	60.5	65.6

Source: Eurostat (2006a).

role in the short run but it has undermined the confidence of economic actors. Social conflicts were avoided but the instability remains.'

Balance of payments

In its 2006 Progress Report the Commission states the following with respect to the balance of payments (CEC 2006a):

- The current account deficit increased during recent years.
- It was driven by strong domestic demand, higher oil prices and lower tourism earnings.
- Turkey can still easily finance the deficit thanks to its foreign currency reserves earned through privatization.
- The current account deficit was also driven by higher investment; this should enhance export capacity.

We are a little less positive about the balance of payments compared to the Commission. Table 3.13 provides an overview of the balance of payments. To stem recurrent current-account deficits Turkey adopted a floating exchange rate in 2001. Yet the current-account deficit grew continuously between 2001 and 2003 because of the increasing deficit on the balance of trade (see Table 3.14). Tourism is the main service that earns foreign exchange. Worker remittances provide more

Table 3.13 Balance of payments, Turkey, 2003–5 ($m.)

Balance of payments	2003	2004	2005
Current account	−8,036	−15,604	−23,155
Goods	−14,010	−23,878	−32,926
Services	10,504	12,784	13,966
Income	−5,557	−5,637	−5,663
Direct investment	−405	−796	−734
Portfolio investment	−1,207	−1,195	−964
Other investment	−3,945	−3,646	−4,005
Financial account			
Direct investment	1,253	2,024	8,726
Portfolio investment	2,465	8,023	13,437
Other investment	3,424	4,187	16,611

Source: IMF (2006).

Table 3.14 Trade between Turkey and EU/rest of world, 2000–3 (billion Euros)

Turkey	2000	2001	2002	2003
Exports to EU	15.745	18.027	19.505	21.614
Imports from EU	29.024	20.422	24.601	27.383
Trade balance	–13.278	–2.395	–5.096	–5.769
Exports to non-EU	14.436	17.028	18.627	17.784
Imports from non-EU	30.420	25.834	29.877	31.690
Trade balance	–15.984	–8.805	–11.250	–13.905

Source: Eurostat (2006a).

than half of current transfers. There is a deficit on income from foreign investments. To finance the deficit on the current account Turkey had recourse to portfolio and other investments (especially trade credits and loans). Unlike direct investments, these are debt-creating capital inflows, which explain the growing debt service on the current account, the government debt of almost 50 per cent of GDP and dwindling foreign-currency reserves.

Conclusion

The following conclusions can be drawn from the preceding:

- Since the 1970s the Turkish economy has been in bad shape: erratic economic growth, high unemployment, sky-rocketing inflation, significant current-account deficits.
- Because of strong American support, the IMF bailed Turkey out time and again. Thanks to this aid, it was able to survive four major economic crises.
- The main reason for the bad economic situation is related to the huge government deficit and the lobbying of special interest groups.
- Since 2002 the economic policy of the new government, in close cooperation with the IMF and the EU, seems to have taken a turn for the better.
- Servicing the debt and creating jobs for the unemployed are the most important tasks for the government. Because of country flight and the growth of active population, more than a million jobs need to be created every year.

Free interplay of market forces

It is clear from the Progress Reports that the Commission considers that the following are necessary conditions for the free interplay of market forces: privatization, liberalization of entry and exit, imposition of hard budget constraints on both public and private enterprises and a liberal trade regime.

In its 2006 Progress Report the Commission mentions the following under this heading (CEC 2006a):

- Progress has been made with the free interplay of market forces.

- Special privileges of state-owned banks are being phased out.
- State-owned enterprises now account for about 5 per cent of GDP and about 15 per cent of value added in the manufacturing sector; state banks make up nearly one third of the value added in the banking sector.
- Staff in state enterprises and banks comprises only 2.5 per cent of total employment.
- The share of administered prices in the consumer price index amounts to 10.2 per cent of the total weight of the consumer price index basket.
- Price liberalization is fairly advanced but there are exceptions – for example, electricity prices are far below production costs.

We will elaborate on this further. Since the 1980s, Turkish foreign trade has been significantly liberalized. To promote competition Turkey eliminated quantitative restrictions and substantially reduced the level of custom's duties (see Table 3.15). Unfortunately, processing industries tried to secure inputs at preferential rates (Hartler and Laird 1999: 7). According to Hartler and Laird, these 'made-to-measure' tariffs were the historical result of political pressures from various Turkish industries.

The trade liberalization policy generated significant results. The 1984 Import Programme provided an excellent 'natural' experiment with which to test the 'imports-as-market-discipline' theory. International competition led to the decrease of mark-ups in imperfectly competitive industries (mark-ups rose in industries where protection was increased) (Levinsohn 1993: 20).

It is the opinion of the Commission that the economy should be privatized to generate free interplay of market forces. Before 1995 the Turkish state-owned sector accounted for over 50 per cent of fixed capital formation, about 40 per cent of employment in firms employing 10 employees or more, 50–60 per cent of total value added in the manufacturing sector and 40–60 per cent of imports (Uğur 1999: 16). Since its membership of the WTO (1995), Turkey has withdrawn most of its investment and export incentives (Togan 2001: 32). The share of the Turkish public sector has decreased significantly. According to the European Bank for Reconstruction and Development, the share of the public sector in value added and in employment in the EU-12 varies between 35 and 20 (EBRD 2005). In Turkey its share is nowadays no higher than that. However, Table 3.16 shows that the public sector is still important in Turkey. It dominates industries like petroleum and coal, tobacco and beverages. State-owned enterprises are overstaffed. In general they have performed poorly because of the soft-budget constraints

Table 3.15 Tariff by stage of processing, Turkey, 1998 (*ad valorem* duties)

Goods	Third countries	EU
Raw materials	21.6	19.7
Intermediate	7.3	1.1
Processed goods	14.1	9.0

Source: Hartler and Laird (1999: 17).

Table 3.16 Characteristics of Turkish manufacturing industries, 2000 (%)

Sector	Share of sector in total value added	Share of sector in total employment	Share of public sector of total value added in sector
Food processing	11.45	15.41	13.01
Beverages	2.22	0.68	50.58
Tobacco	2.60	1.14	78.25
Textiles	12.29	18.56	1.11
Wearing apparel and footwear	3.75	9.62	1.25
Fur and leather products	0.27	0.62	0.00
Wood and cork products	1.29	4.08	0.01
Furniture and fixtures	1.10	4.35	0.01
Paper and products	3.21	3.41	8.48
Chemicals	9.71	3.59	7.24
Petroleum and coal	12.49	0.60	89.83
Rubber and plastic products	3.85	3.65	0.27
Non-metallic minerals	6.62	5.56	0.85
Basic metals	5.41	3.96	20.52
Metal products	4.75	7.98	2.58
Machinery	4.45	6.07	5.29
Electrical machinery	5.42	4.14	2.00
Transport equipment	7.86	5.09	2.55
Professional and scientific measuring equipment	0.61	0.68	4.80
Other manufacturing industries	0.66	0.82	2.16
Total manufacturing	100.00	100.00	18.91

Source: Hoekman and Togan (2005: 115).

they face (Martin *et al.* 2002: 121; Hoekman and Togan 2005: 328). They are not subject to commercial code and therefore they escape bankruptcy laws (Hoekman and Togan 2005: 328).

Turkey is also under pressure from the World Bank and the IMF to privatize more of its industrial and financial holdings. Privatization was promised a long time ago. However, actual implementation of the programme has been very slow because of union and popular opposition to lay-offs, and because of corruption (Martin *et al.* 2002: 121). Previous plans have also fallen through because of the state's inability to make the businesses sufficiently attractive to buyers. Since 2005 privatization seems to have taken off. Tupras, an oil refinery, was sold to a consortium of Turkey's Koc Holding and Royal Dutch/Shell. Turk Telecom was sold to Saudi Oger and Telecom Italia. However, in both cases workers' unions have launched legal proceedings against the deals. Many state-owned enterprises remain in need of restructuring (Hughes 2004: 12; *The Economist*, 2005a, b).

In order to encourage further free interplay of market forces the Commission wants the Turkish industry to deconcentrate. According to UNIDO, in spite of Turkey's liberalization programme, domestic industrial structure is still fairly concentrated by international standards. The average three-firm concentration ratio across all selected products is abnormally high – even compared to the CEEC: it is over 86 per cent. In addition to high levels of concentration, ownership of productive assets across product groups is concentrated through the predominance of a few large industrial holdings and associated banks. There are large family-run conglomerates, such as Koc Holding (108 companies), Sabanci Holding (50 companies) and Cukorova Holding (commercial vehicles, paper, telecommunications and banks) (Martin *et al.* 2002: 127). The fifteen largest private companies in Turkey controlled over 500 separate industrial enterprises in 1988. Many of these large private holdings also control Turkey's largest financial institutions. However, over time one can observe a reduction in concentration (UNIDO 1995: 145). High domestic producer concentration ratios do not mean per se that there is no or insufficient competition. Removal of import barriers and efficient competition laws can offset possible negative effects caused by high concentration ratios in the domestic economy.

Free market entry and exit

In the previous section we discussed the positive liberalization and privatization trend of Turkey. In its Progress Reports the Commission points out that a significant effort to create favourable free market entry/exit conditions in Turkey continues. For instance, in the 2006 Progress Report the Commission reports 'that in 2005 almost 100,000 enterprises were established and more than 26,000 went bankrupt. The latter figures are about 5 per cent higher than in 2004' (CEC 2006a: 28).

This development reflects the removal of entry and exit barriers, and constitutes a positive change for the Turkish economy. Indeed, economic theory suggests that the establishment of new and the liquidation of old firms is a crucial element of the resources reallocation process in an economy. When distortions are removed, market forces can freely select the most efficient enterprises, and this enhances efficiency and welfare growth. Free market entry and exit are thus also essential in order to realize fully the potential gains associated with trade liberalization and privatization.

The presence of a significant number of small and medium-size enterprises (SMEs) is also an important factor enhancing market dynamism. SMEs in Turkey already account for 75 per cent of employment and 27 per cent of value added. Twenty five per cent of firms employ fewer than ten persons and 49 per cent employ fewer than twenty-five persons (Buğra 2004: 56). However, according to the Commission, many of these firms still operate in the informal economy, which restrains their ability to improve productivity. Access to finance is also a major problem for SMEs in Turkey. Bank loans cover only about 10 per cent of SMEs' financing needs, and owners' assets remain the major source of capital, because of high interest rates and collateral requirements. As suggested by UNIDO, Turkey would gain by creating more favourable conditions for SMEs, bringing them under the umbrella of the formal economy and stimulating their export activities (UNIDO 1995: 242).

Adequate legal system

In the Negotiating Framework, the Council wants 'Turkey to provide for a well-functioning and stable public administration built on an efficient and impartial civil service, and an independent and efficient legal system' (Council of the European Communities 2006a).

In the 2006 Progress Report the following is mentioned (CEC 2006a):

- The legal system, including the regulation of property rights, is in place.
- However, the time lag between the adoption of legislation and its implementation is often long.
- The enforceability of the decisions of authorities and courts continues to prove difficult.
- The implementation of the legislation on property rights, including intellectual property rights, is not appropriate.
- Training of judicial personnel is not always adequate.

According to the Commission, the legal institutions have been established but they do not work properly. As in many other developing countries, it takes more time for mores and minds to evolve than for institutions. Courts are not familiar with the Western conceptions of human rights and economic freedom. We think that Turkey's major problem in this respect is the lack of economic freedom. The Heritage Foundation 2006 *Index of Economic Freedom* measures 161 countries against a list of 50 independent variables divided into 10 broad factors of economic freedom. Low scores are more desirable. The higher the score that is reached on a factor, the more there is government interference in the economy. These 50 variables are grouped into the following categories:

- trade policy;
- fiscal burden of government;
- government intervention in the economy;
- monetary policy;
- capital flows and foreign investment;
- banking and finance;
- wages and prices;
- property rights;
- regulation;
- informal market activity.

On the one hand, from Table 3.17 we learn that Turkey still has a long way to go before it can be called economic free. Apart from Romania, all other EU member states do better. On the other hand, compared to the previous year, Turkey has improved 0.3 point based on improved scores in trade policy, fiscal burden of government, monetary policy and banking and finance. Overall, Turkey is classified in the category 'mostly unfree'. In that group it is kept company by some

Table 3.17 Index of Economic Freedom, Europe, 2006

Country	2006 Index of Economic Freedom	Rank on 161 countries
Austria	1.95	18
Belgium	2.11	22
Bulgaria	2.88	64
Czech Republic	2.10	21
Cyprus	1.90	16
Denmark	1.78	8
Estonia	1.75	7
Finland	1.85	12
France	2.51	44
Germany	1.96	19
Greece	2.80	57
Hungary	2.44	40
Ireland	1.58	3
Italy	2.50	42
Latvia	2.43	39
Lithuania	2.14	23
Luxembourg	1.60	4
Malta	2.16	24
Netherlands	1.90	16
Poland	2.49	41
Portugal	2.29	30
Romania	3.19	92
Slovenia	2.41	38
Slovakia	2.35	34
Spain	2.33	33
Sweden	1.96	19
Turkey	3.11	85

Source: Heritage Foundation (2006).

African countries. A small consolation is that countries including Ukraine (99), Russia (122), India (121) and China (111) do worse. According to the Heritage Foundation, there are still a lot of formal and informal barriers in Turkey that create legal uncertainty: excessive bureaucracy, weaknesses in the judicial system, high and inconsistently collected taxes, weaknesses in corporate governance, unpredictable decisions taken at the municipal level and unclear changes in the legal and regulatory environment.

Sufficiently developed financial sector

In the 2006 Progress Report the Commission mentions the following (CEC 2006a):

- Efficiency of the financial intermediation has been increasing, as shown by the gradual decline in spreads between average lending and deposit rates.
- Increased foreign participation in banks has enhanced competition. Majority-owned foreign banks account for about 15 per cent of Turkish banking assets.

- The return on assets and on equity declined. This indicates declining profit margins for banks.
- Supervision of the financial sector has benefited from a new banking law. Most of the secondary regulations have been put in place. The regulatory and supervisory power on financial holding, leasing, factoring and consumer finance companies is to be transferred to the Banking Regulation and Supervisory Agency.

In the Commission's view, the situation of the Turkish financial sector does not look bad. In view of past mistakes, much has been done to make the financial sector healthy. Until 1980 the Turkish financial sector was heavily regulated. It had to help the state to implement its development strategy. Then, at the beginning of the 1980s trade and capital flows were liberalized in Turkey. These measures were aimed at developing an efficient and competitive banking system, which was expected to support the functioning of a more liberal economy (UNIDO 1995: 52). Reforms led to major changes in the banking sector. Reduction of legal barriers attracted new banks, both domestic and foreign. Product variety increased, and the quality of financial services improved. Unfortunately, financial reforms did not go far enough. The government did not privatize the state banks and did not stop subsidizing banks and industries (Eder 2003: 223).

In November 2000 and again in February 2001 Turkey found itself engulfed in serious economic and financial crises. What appeared to be one of the fundamental causes of the crises was the weakness of the under-regulated banking system, which helped to undermine confidence and resulted in massive capital flight. The November 2000 crisis reflected the weakness of the private banking system, whereas the February 2001 crisis was associated with the public banks (Önis 2006: 250). State-owned enterprises had borrowed heavily from the Central Bank, domestic commercial banks and foreign creditors (Uğur 1999: 60). Both public and private banks were engaged in speculative and even fraudulent operations. Turkish government bonds and treasury bills had higher returns than bank deposits or private securities. Banks bought government bonds and borrowed from foreign investors (Buğra 2003: 463). When foreign capital flew out, many banks made large losses. The Central Bank attempted to rescue the banking system at the expense of the stability of the Turkish lira, exacerbating problems for many small and medium-sized banks (Tocci 2001: 28). The Turkish lira was devalued by 120 per cent. Interest rates reached astronomic heights, and some banks could not pay off their debts (Gültekin and Yilmaz 2005: 67). The government bailed out bankrupt companies and banks. Hence, a total sum roughly equal to one-third of Turkey's predicted GNP for 2002 was used for financial rescue operations (Buğra 2003: 465).

At the insistence of the EU and the USA, the Turkish government signed agreements with the IMF and the World Bank. Bank reform was the cornerstone of the IMF aid programme. The Turkish Central Bank became independent. State and private banks were put under the supervision of an independent institution, the Banking Regulation and Supervisory Agency (BSRA), which had to deal with the privatization of the large public banks. The Saving and Developing Insurance Fund (SDIF) had to take care of the administration, liquidation and the possible merger of banks coping with financial difficulties. The fund has taken over nineteen banks since 1997. Finally yet importantly, the public banks were to be restructured and recapitalized, and undercapitalized private banks would be sold or closed while their deposits would be insured.

However, as reported by the World Bank, several issues remain. State ownership in the sector is still very large, with three big deposit-taking state banks accounting for 34 per cent of assets in the total banking system. Foreign ownership remains small, and almost all the major private banks are affiliated with large financial and industrial conglomerates. This creates transparency problems and distortions in terms of access to credit (World Bank 2006a: 161–3). Banks are still tempted to buy high-interest government bonds and to avoid lending to domestic firms, risking new financial fiascos in the future. Buyers of troubled banks have picked out a few of their loans, leaving the rest with the SDIF. Major mergers in the banking system have yet to take place. A pro-competitive policy would need to encourage rivalry among the leading banks, which continue to dominate the system. This, in turn, requires the entry of new banks with a reasonable number of branches (UNIDO 1995: 69). The Turkish financial system is too dependent on the American dollar and banking services are still primitive compared to EU standards. The capital market is underdeveloped. Loans to the private sector represent less than 14 per cent of GDP, a low share even compared to Russia (Faivre 2004: 106).

Conclusion

The following conclusions could be drawn from the preceding:

- Since the years 2000 Turkey has concentrated its efforts on privatization, while not enough attention has been paid on creating fair competition in domestic markets.
- Turkey's domestic industrial structure is too concentrated, with large family-run companies dominating the scene.
- Turkey should stimulate private entrepreneurs to set up new companies. With help from the Commission, it is possible to do this without infringing European laws on competition and state aid.
- In order to attract new investors, both foreign and domestic, more legal transparency is required.
- Turkey's financial sector is on the road of deregulation, yet requires sufficient attention from the government.

The capacity to compete in EU markets

In its Progress Reports the Commission put six topics under this heading (see Table 3.18) (CEC 2006a):

- sufficient investment in human capital (and care for the socially underprivileged);
- sufficient investment in physical capital (and sufficient foreign direct investment);
- positive physical-infrastructure-related factors;
- structural transformation of the economy;
- state influence on competitiveness and enterprise restructuring;
- growing trade integration of goods and services with the EU.

To measure whether Turkey meets these criteria we assume that EU member states fully comply with each of them. Turkey's objective must be to reach the average EU-25 level as soon as possible. Therefore, it should devise a strategy to catch up with the EU.

Sufficient investment in human capital

In the 2006 Progress Report the Commission states the following (CEC 2006a):

- The government wants to spend more on education. The increase not only reflects the rising costs of the growing young population, but also aims to enhance the coverage and quality of education.
- However, considerable income-, gender- and regional differences in educational attainment and in the quality of education persist.
- The average level of knowledge for pupils in secondary education is low. Weaknesses in quality, transparency and accessibility of higher education are significant.
- Labour force participation rates are low, particularly for women and older people.
- The fast-growing working-age population and the move out of the agricultural sector create a strong need for job creation.
- There has been little effort to reduce the substantial employment in the informal economy.

Table 3.18 The capacity to cope with competitive pressure and market forces within the EU, Turkey, 1998–2006

Criterion 2	Progress	No progress	Limited
Sufficient human capital			X
Sufficient physical capital	X		
Sufficient infrastructure	X		
Structural transformation of the economy	X		
State influence on competitiveness			X
Trade integration with the EU	X		

Source: CEC (1998, 1999, 2000, 2001, 2002, 2003b, 2004c, 2005, 2006a).

- The legal focus remains on protecting jobs, and less than 4 per cent of unemployed workers get unemployment benefits.
- The non-wage costs of hiring labour remain large.

We shall elaborate on this further. We shall deal first with education. Human capital formation is an engine of growth in developing economies. In Turkey government-provided education through to age 14 or the eighth grade is compulsory. However, according to a World Bank Study, only 40 per cent of Turkish youth have a secondary school diploma (*The Economist* 2006d). A UNICEF report shows that in Turkey in 2003 over 50 per cent of girls between 7 and 13 and over 60 per cent of girls between 11 and 15 did not attend school (US Department of State 2004: 21). Table 3.19 shows the number of students in the EU-15, the new member states and Turkey, by gender aged 15–24 years as a percentage of the corresponding age population. With respect to literacy, not only does Turkey lag behind the level in the EU, but there also seems to be significant gender inequality. Table 3.20 shows that, compared to the EU-15 and the new member states, Turkey does not invest enough in education. Consequently, the share of adult population with tertiary education is lower than the corresponding shares in EU-15, the new EU member states, Bulgaria and Romania. The share of Turkish population aged 20–24 having completed at least upper secondary education was 42 per cent (2004); in the EU-25 it was 77.1. The total of Turkish tertiary graduates in science and technology per 1000 of population aged 20–29 was 5.6 (2004). In the EU-25, the corresponding figure was 12.7.

In order to reach a growth rate that would put Turkey on a path of convergence with the EU, the Commission wants Turkey to invest more in human capital. Inadequate spending on public education has led to the commercialization of the education system and caused a severe gap in educational opportunities. Policy-makers have been wasting time with debates on whether girls should wear headscarves at school and on whether graduates of religious schools should attend universities (Gültekin and Yilmaz 2005: 73). On the positive side, Turkey has been brave enough to take part in the International Assessment Programme (PISA), allowing its education system to be compared with those of other OECD countries. The main finding was that provision within the country differs wildly. Some schools and some students perform very well by any standard. On average, Turkish education is of poor quality. However, prospects are improving. In 1997 the government increased the period of mandatory education from five years to eight, and in 2005 – for the

Table 3.19 Students aged 15–24 as share of corresponding age population, EU and Turkey, 2004 (%)

Country	Males	Females
EU-15	57.3	61.8
EU-10	62.4	66.7
Turkey	30.6	23.1

Source: Eurostat (2006a).

Table 3.20 Education, Turkey, 2003–4

Country	Total expenditure on education as % of GDP	% of adult population with tertiary education
EU-15	5.20	3.1
New member states	5.37	4.6
Bulgaria	4.24	2.9
Romania	3.44	3.1
Turkey	3.74	2.7

Source: OECD (2006b).

first time in the history of Turkey – education received a larger share of the (official) national budget than the armed forces. The number of universities has grown rapidly and now totals seventy-eight (*The Economist* 2005a).

In chapter 19 of the 2006 Progress Report the Commission refers to social well-being (CEC 2006a: 53). According to the results of a poverty study conducted by TURKSTAT, 1.29 per cent of the population lives below the hunger line, while 25.6 per cent live below the poverty line. The share of the latter increases to 40 per cent in the rural areas. According to the same study, the child poverty rate (below 6 years of age) is 34 per cent, while this rate reaches 40 per cent in rural areas.

The Commission states that well-functioning market economies need to protect the underprivileged strata of society. Table 3.21 shows the at-risk-of-poverty rate after social transfers. It is measured by the share of persons with a disposable income below the risk-of-poverty threshold, which is set at 60 per cent of the national median disposable income, after social transfers. From these figures, it is not clear whether for Turkey the informal sector has been taken into account. Still, in both cases the Turkish government needs to act. Apart from Slovakia, in no EU member state does more than one-fifth of the population live below the minimum subsistence level. Gaps in social security and health insurance programmes leave approximately 20 per cent of families and their children without coverage. Redistribution could be helped by a change in the tax system. At present Turkey relies

Table 3.21 At-risk-of-poverty rate after social transfers, EU and Turkey, 2000–3 (% of population)

Country	2000	2003
EU-15	15	15
Bulgaria	14	14
Czech Republic	n/a	8
Estonia	18	18
Cyprus	n/a	15
Latvia	16	16
Lithuania	17	15
Hungary	11	12
Malta	15	n/a
Turkey	n/a	26

Source: OECD (2006b).

heavily on indirect taxes – which are easily collected but hurt the poor – and more lightly on direct taxes, which are harder to collect (US Department of State 2004: 21; *The Economist* 2005a). According to Sozen and Shaw (2003: 111–12), the provision of public services has not been given high priority by the government. The state machinery relating to national security policies has been overdeveloped, while that relating to the provision of welfare services has remained weak. Emphasis has been put on the duties of citizens towards the state – such as paying taxes and military conscription – rather than on the rights of citizens as individuals

While the traditional political parties dealt with their clients and public services were lacking, the Islamic parties built their own social networks in the cities, offering financial and other aid to the destitute and poor, thereby filling a void. Local governments controlled by the Islamists and NGOs of an Islamic character have been especially successful in mobilizing charitable donations and channelling them to destitute people (Buğra and Keyder 2006: 224). That is why the traditional and religious countryside values have entered the Turkish cities (Rochtus 2002: 179) and support for Islamic parties has grown.

Sufficient investment in physical capital

As far as investment in physical capital is concerned, the Commission stipulates the following (CEC 2006a):

- Gross fixed capital formation amounted to around 20 per cent of GDP.
- Foreign direct investment had increased to 2.8 per cent of GDP.
- The privatization process had proceeded and supported capital inflows.
- Foreign ownership was most prominent in the wholesale and retail sectors, where 36 per cent of the companies with foreign ownership operated.

We would like to elaborate a little bit further on foreign direct investment (FDI). In a labour-abundant economy like Turkey's with its rapidly expanding workforce, gross capital formation should increase labour productivity and real wages. Table 3.22 shows the gross fixed capital formation of Turkey compared to EU-15 and some of the new member states (data were not available for the other new member states and for Bulgaria and Romania). Whereas in the past the growth

Table 3.22 Gross capital formation as percentage of GDP, EU and Turkey, 2004

Country	Gross capital formation
EU-15	20.4
Poland	18.2
Czech Republic	27.3
Slovakia	24.7
Hungary	22.6
Turkey	17.8

Source: OECD (2006b).

in Turkey was capital intensive, this trend seems to have halted at the beginning of the twenty-first century. In Table 3.23 we give an overview of the number of foreign affiliates for Belgian, French and UK domestic manufacturing firms by countries, grouped together in geographical categories (affiliates are included if 10 per cent or more of the capital is directly controlled). We find for all three countries a preference for Western Europe, while Mediterranean Europe ranks second. Geographical neighbourhood and traditional links seem to explain much of the FDI streams. In view of its large market and its central geographical position, Turkey could do much better.

Table 3.23 Number of foreign affiliates for domestic manufacturing firms, EU and Turkey, 2007

Country	Belgium	France	UK
Austria	30	57	4
Luxembourg	76	56	1
Germany	312	728	171
Netherlands	311	205	78
Belgium	—	343	8
France	632	—	171
UK	225	593	—
Ireland	20	37	79
Subtotal	*1,606*	*2,019*	*512*
Sweden	52	78	5
Denmark	27	51	17
Finland	8	22	1
Subtotal	*87*	*151*	*23*
Cyprus	1	6	0
Spain	103	563	39
Greece	18	40	3
Malta	1	2	0
Italy	133	445	10
Portugal	29	106	1
Subtotal	*285*	*1,162*	*53*
Estonia	3	1	5
Hungary	38	63	2
Czech R.	72	83	1
Latvia	0	2	0
Lithuania	4	1	1
Poland	102	175	18
Slovenia	10	15	0
Slovakia	32	34	0
Subtotal	*261*	*374*	*27*
Romania	39	114	16
Bulgaria	15	14	0
Turkey	27	53	1

Source: AMADEUS (n.d).

In January 2004 the independent organization COFACE[6] turned Turkey's @ rating regarding investing conditions from C into B. The B stands for 'an unsteady political and economic environment that is likely to affect further an already poor payment record'. Compared to EU member states, both old and new, Turkey scores the poorest (see Table 3.24).

Table 3.25 shows the FDI intensity: the average value of inward and outward FDI flows divided by GDP, multiplied by 100. Compared to all other countries, Turkey scores poorly. Table 3.26 compares the FDI of Turkey with the FDI in three of the new member states. The conclusion is similar: the annual average share of investments in GDP is extremely low. In recent years the situation has improved. Where in 2002 FDI was only $1.14 billion, in 2006 the total was $20.2 billion (*De Standaard* 2007b).

Turkey's FDI policies contain many of the standard practices of developed countries, such as equal rights and obligations for both domestic and foreign firms, agreements to solve double taxation problems, adherence to various international conventions on the free flow of capital and invisible transactions and reductions

Table 3.24 @ratings, EU and Turkey, 2006

Country	@rating
Austria	A1
Belgium	A1
Bulgaria	A4
Czech Republic	A2
Cyprus	A3
Denmark	A1
Estonia	A2
Finland	A1
France	A1
Germany	A1
Greece	A2
Hungary	A3
Ireland	A1
Italy	A2
Latvia	A3
Lithuania	A3
Luxembourg	A1
Malta	A3
Netherlands	A1
Poland	A3
Portugal	A2
Romania	A4
Slovenia	A2
Slovakia	A3
Spain	A1
Sweden	A1
Turkey	B
United Kingdom	A1

Source: COFACE Belgium (2006).

Table 3.25 FDI intensity, EU and Turkey, 1997–2004 (investment/GDP)

Country	1997	2000	2004
EU-15	1.1	3.5	1.0
Bulgaria	n/a	4.0	5.4
Czech Republic	1.2	4.6	2.3
Estonia	4.1	4.1	5.8
Cyprus	3.3	5.6	5.5
Latvia	4.3	2.7	2.9
Lithuania	1.9	1.7	2.3
Hungary	2.9	2.3	NA
Malta	n/a	8.6	5.5
Poland	1.6	2.7	2.6
Slovenia	n/a	n/a	1.7
Slovakia	0.6	5.3	1.0
Romania	n/a	1.4	n/a
Turkey	0.4	0.5	0.6

Source: Eurostat (2006a).

in bureaucracy. Taxation policies provide for exemptions from corporate tax, and there are free port zones with duty-free production (Balasubramanyam and Corless 2001: 54). However, even after establishing the customs union with the EU, Turkey failed to attract FDI.

In a joint study by Tüsiad and Yased (2004: 1–14), the attractiveness of Turkey for FDI is compared to fifteen other countries. Their report constructs an FDI attractiveness score by taking into account thirty-one factors that foreign investors consider during their evaluations, when deciding where to invest (see Table 3.27). The thirty-one factors can be grouped together in seven categories: general macroeconomic environment, political environment, labour, energy, taxes/incentives, infrastructure for transport and telecom and expenditures for R&D. The FDI attractiveness score is between 0.001 and 100. Notwithstanding favourable conditions – a generous law to attract FDI, a skilled workforce, a convertible currency for almost fifteen years, a large domestic market and the closeness to large markets – Turkey ranks second to last on the list. Turkey falls severely behind the other countries in criteria like political stability, legal framework, share of labour force, energy cost, taxation, bureaucratic procedures and R&D. According to Balasubramanyam and Corless (2001: 59), statistical evidence on

Table 3.26 FDI, Turkey, Poland, Czech Republic and Hungary, 1991–2000

GD/FDI	Turkey	Poland	Czech Republic	Hungary
GDP 2000 ($m.)	199,267	157,598	51,433	46,604
FDI inflows 1991–2000 (annual average, $m.)	814.5	4,545	4,498	2,198
Share annual average FDI inflows in GDP (%)	0.4	2.8	8.7	4.7

Source: Hoekman and Togan (2005: 265).

Table 3.27 FDI attractiveness score, selected countries, 2004

Rank	Country	FDI attractiveness score
1	Ireland	67.53
2	Malaysia	63.46
3	Czech Republic	62.07
4	Germany	60.50
5	Estonia	56.56
6	Hungary	56.56
7	Slovenia	54.18
8	Slovakia	52.46
9	Portugal	51.33
10	China	48.90
11	Brazil	48.46
12	Russia	42.45
13	Poland	42.34
14	India	41.16
15	Turkey	37.23
16	Argentina	34.14

Source: Tüsiad and Yased (2004).

the determinants of FDI shows that the most important factors influencing FDI are per capita income, the trade policy of the host country, price stability and the efficiency wage rate. It is even possible that the customs union with the EU has diverted FDI away from Turkey to more stable countries in the neighbourhood like Greece.

Positive physical-infrastructure-related factors

On physical infrastructure, the Commission mentions the following (see Table 3.28) (CEC 2006a):

- Infrastructure investments have been suppressed to support the primary surplus target.
- No significant changes have occurred concerning road and rail network.
- The Baku–Tblisi–Ceyhan pipeline is an important addition to energy infrastructure.

Table 3.28 Physical infrastructure-related factors, EU and Turkey, 2001–4

Physical infrastructure	EU-15	EU-25	Turkey
% households with Internet access (2004)	45.00	42.00	7.00
Mobile phone subscriptions per 100 inhabitants (2003)	85.00	81.00	40.00
Consumption of energy/GDP per 1,000 Euros (2004)	187.48	204.89	452.45
Number of hospital beds (per 100,000 inhabitants) (2002)	611.3	639.1	262.1
Environmental expenditures by public sector in % of GDP (2001)	0.58	0.58	0.22

Source: Eurostat (2006a).

- Spending on R&D remains low. However, public spending on this item is budgeted to increase.
- So far improvements in infrastructure have been modest.

We think it is useful to compare Turkey with EU member states. Table 3.27 shows a number of physical-infrastructure-related factors. (Items have been chosen where Eurostat figures were available). Compared to EU-15 and EU-25, Turkey demonstrates a number of weaknesses. Internet access is relatively limited. Energy efficiency is low. Health care is insufficient, and in the environmental sector, a lot remains to be done.

Structural transformation of the economy

With respect to structural transformation of the Turkish economy, the 2006 Progress Report stipulates the following (CEC 2006a):

- There is progress with respect to the structural transformation of the economy.
- The share of agriculture in employment decreased markedly.
- Jobs were created in the industrial sector, and its share in the total labour force rose.
- However, job creation in industry and services was not strong enough fully to compensate for the reduction in agricultural employment.
- Industry gained in importance while services remained stable.

Basically we share the Commission's view. We would like to elaborate a bit further on the structure of the Turkish economy and especially the place still occupied by agriculture. Economic theories have a number of roles for agriculture in the process of economic growth (Stern 1996: 75):

- a supplier of labour;
- a producer of food for non-agricultural workers;
- a source of savings;
- a supplier of foreign exchange.

Important as farming may be, as incomes rise across countries we see that both the fraction of output coming from agriculture and the share of agricultural employment in the total fall. For lower-middle-income countries the share in 1990 in value added was 17 per cent and for upper-middle-income countries it was 9 per cent. For most OECD countries, it was 4 per cent or less. The figures for employment drop correspondingly rapidly with income, although for lower-middle-income countries we still find around half of the employment in agriculture, and for upper-middle-income countries around a quarter. The shares of output and employment from agriculture drop sharply with income. The change can happen fairly rapidly: even for richer countries the drop over time can be

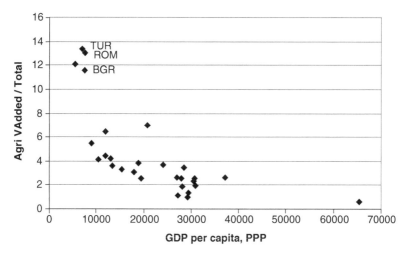

Figure 3.5 Share agricultural sector in GDP versus GDP per capita, 29 European countries, 2003 (Source: World Bank (2006b)).

large (Stern 1996: 8). Figures 3.5 and 3.6 make this inverse relationship between the share of the agricultural sector in the GDP of a country and its GDP per capita abundantly clear.

Compared to the EU-15 and the EU-10, Turkey – as well as Romania and Bulgaria – has a high share of agricultural value added in total value added (see Table 3.29). Therefore, Turkey has more in common with countries like Russia

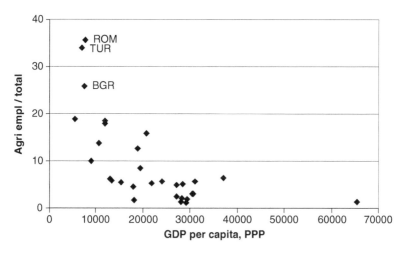

Figure 3.6 Share of agricultural employment in total versus GDP per capita, 29 European countries, 2003 (Source: World Bank (2006b)).

Note: Figures for Bulgaria from 2001.

Table 3.29 Sectoral distribution of value added, EU and Turkey, 2004 (%)

Country	Agriculture	Industry	Services
EMU	2	27	71
Bulgaria	11	31	58
Czech Republic	3	38	59
Estonia	4	29	67
Hungary (2003)	3	31	66
Lithuania	6	34	60
Latvia	4	22	73
Poland	3	33	64
Romania	14	37	49
Slovak Republic	4	30	67
Slovenia (2003)	3	37	61
Turkey	13	22	65

Source: World Bank (2006b).

and Ukraine than with the EU-25. However, Tables 3.30 and 3.31 show that between 1985 and 2005 both the share of agriculture in GDP and the share of agricultural employment in total employment in Turkey went down and that the share of services went up. In addition to that, Table 3.32 shows that in industry and services Turkish productivity is higher than productivity in certain new member states. In construction, it ranked fourth and in agriculture it ranked third compared to these selected member states. Because of agricultural reforms, the share of farming will further go downward. By how much and for how long is by no means certain. Swinnen and Rozelle state that agricultural output fell steeply in the first years of transition in almost all CEEC. Yet the length of time between the beginning of reform and the bottom of the trend line varied among nations (Swinnen and Rozelle 2006: 15–16). Development does generally involve a movement out of agriculture into both services and industry. In turn, it is development in the industry and in services that provides the fuel for agricultural development through the expansion of demand for its products and of supply of the necessary inputs. Product markets and factor markets for capital and non-agricultural labour also appear to be key ingredients to ensure not only greater productivity, but also greater profitability of agriculture (Scandizzo 1998: 37).

Table 3.30 Sectoral gross value added, Turkey, 1985–2005 (% of GDP)

Sectors	1985	1995	2005
Agriculture	20.4	16.4	11.9
Industry and construction	27.1	30.0	23.7
Services	52.5	53.5	64.5

Source: World Bank (2006b).

Table 3.31 Sectoral employment, Turkey, 1985–2005 (% of GDP)

Sector	1985	1995	2005
Agriculture	44.1	36	29.5
Industry and construction	22.0	24	24.7
Services	33.9	40	45.8

Source: World Bank (2006b).

State influence on competitiveness and enterprise restructuring

In the 2006 Progress Report the following is mentioned (CEC 2006a):

- The work of the Competition Authority is satisfactory, and the privatization process supports its role in the market.
- Transparency in the corporate sector has improved and accounting standards have been upgraded although not yet fully implemented.
- No improvements have been made concerning monitoring of state aids. This has had a negative effect on the competitive climate.
- Public procurement policies continue to be undermined by exceptions made to the regulatory framework.

This information being very concise, it is important to say something more about the state influence on the competitiveness and enterprise restructuring in Turkey. This is related to the quality of government. As far as the quality of government is concerned a large gap exists between the EU and Turkey. Table 3.33 shows the governance indicators for Turkey in 2005 as calculated by the World Bank. The following elements are taken into account: voice and accountability; political stability/no violence; government effectiveness; regulatory quality; rule of law; control of corruption. Each of these indicators is put on a scale ranging between –2.5 and +2.5 – the higher the value the better the government rating. Turkey scores poorly, and does so again when compared to the EU-10 (see Table 3.34). It is tempting to conclude that the situation in Turkey has improved slightly compared to 1996. Yet, according to the World Bank, one has to be very cautious when comparing figures over time. According to UNIDO (1995: 132), the Turkish

Table 3.32 Sectoral gross value added per person employed, selected countries, 2000 (Euros)

Country	Agriculture	Industry	Construction	Services	Total
Bulgaria	4,289	3,696	3,176	4,292	4,073
Czech R.	9,707	12,391	8,867	12,060	11,739
Hungary	7,629	11,962	8,566	12,090	11,531
Poland	2,093	11,841	12,049	13,511	10,874
Romania	1,149	5,779	6,224	7,466	4,188
Turkey	4,577	13,523	8,508	15,657	10,890

Sources: Derviş *et al.* (2004: 6); Eurostat (2006a).

Table 3.33 Governance indicators, Turkey, 1996–2005

Governance indicator	1996	2005
Voice and accountability	−0.47	−0.04
Political stability/no violence	−1.40	−0.54
Government effectiveness	−0.16	+0.27
Regulatory quality	+0.44	+0.18
Rule of law	−0.02	+0.07
Control of corruption	+0.10	+0.08

Source: World Bank (2006b).

Note
Scale between −2.5 and +2.5.

government's approach to restructuring and rehabilitation of companies has serious shortcomings. A major one is that it does not clearly distinguish between economic efficiency and socio-political objectives. As a result, restructuring decisions often appear arbitrary and lacking objective criteria (UNIDO 1995:132).

Growing trade integration of goods and services with the EU

In the 2006 Progress Report we read the following (CEC 2006a):

- Exports and imports of goods equalled around 54 per cent of GDP in 2005.
- Imports from and exports to the EU declined as imports from and exports to other markets rose more rapidly.
- The EU remained Turkey's largest trading partner, but other markets are gaining in importance. Overall trade openness continued to increase, and the trade partners were diversified.

Table 3.34 Governance indicators, EU-10, 2005

Country	Voice and accountability	Political stability/ no violence	Government effectiveness	Regulatory quality	Rule of law	Control of corruption
Bulgaria	0.59	0.16	0.23	0.63	−0.19	−0.05
Czech Republic	1.01	0.69	0.94	1.04	0.70	0.42
Estonia	1.05	0.68	1.03	1.43	0.82	0.88
Hungary	1.10	0.79	0.79	1.11	0.70	0.63
Latvia	0.89	0.83	0.68	1.03	0.43	0.33
Lithuania	0.90	0.88	0.85	1.13	0.46	0.26
Poland	1.04	0.23	0.58	0.82	0.32	0.19
Romania	0.36	0.03	−0.03	0.17	−0.29	−0.23
Slovak Republic	1.04	0.69	0.95	1.16	0.41	0.43
Slovenia	1.08	0.94	0.99	0.86	0.79	0.88

Source: World Bank (2006b).

Note
Scale between −2.5 and 2.5.

- Labour productivity improved and rose in both the private and the public sectors.
- The real effective exchange rate based on unit labour cost rose considerably at the beginning of 2006. Owing to a sharp exchange-rate depreciation, this trend was strongly reversed.

We would like to spend a lot of attention on the trade integration of goods and services of Turkey with the EU. We will first offer a general picture of trade relations between the EU and Turkey as far as goods are concerned. Next, we will pay attention to the intra-industry specialization and the revealed comparative advantages. Finally we will deal will trade relations in the field of services.

General picture of EU–Turkey trade relations with respect to goods

Table 3.34 compares Turkish trade integration of goods with EU-15, the ten new member states and Bulgaria and Romania. If the index (imports plus exports divided by GDP) increases over time, it means that the country is becoming better integrated in the international economy. Table 3.35 shows that Turkey performs relatively well in the field of goods. It has one of the highest increases in the EU, more than the EU-15 and several new member states. Only Poland and Hungary do better.

Table 3.36 shows that the EU share in Turkey's imports and exports is significant, though smaller than the EU share in EU-10 imports and exports. Turkish exports to the EU did not increase significantly in the years after the customs union took effect. This does not seem difficult to explain. Turkey had already been exempted from paying nominal tariffs on industrial exports to the EU and

Table 3.35 Trade integration of goods, EU and Turkey, 1995–2004 (%)

Country	1995 (M+X/GDP)	2004 (M+X/GDP)	% variation
EU-15	7.9	10.5	33
Bulgaria	40.3	48.3	20
Czech Republic	42.2	63.3	50
Estonia	54.0	66.8	24
Cyprus	24.8	20.5	–17
Latvia	64.1	40.8	–36
Lithuania	47.7	51.7	8
Hungary	31.5	57.0	81
Malta	n/a	57.6	n/a
Poland	18.6	33.5	80
Slovenia	43.4	51.4	18
Slovakia	44.8	67.8	51
Romania	n/a	35.5	n/a
Turkey	16.9	26.2	55

Source: Eurostat (2006a).

Table 3.36 EU share in total imports and exports of ten new member states/Turkey, 2003–5 (%)

Country	2003	2004	2005
EU share in total imports			
Czech Republic	71.0	79.9	81.1
Estonia	64.8	73.6	75.9
Cyprus	59.4	68.0	68.3
Latvia	75.3	75.5	75.2
Lithuania	55.8	63.3	59.0
Hungary	63.1	66.9	67.4
Malta	68.0	72.6	74.9
Poland	69.1	74.8	74.7
Slovenia	75.6	81.3	78.2
Slovakia	74.0	79.0	78.9
Turkey	46.4	46.6	42.2
EU share in total exports			
Czech Republic	86.3	86.0	84.2
Estonia	82.4	80.3	77.9
Cyprus	59.6	65.3	71.7
Latvia	79.3	77.3	76.4
Lithuania	62.5	66.9	65.3
Hungary	81.2	79.4	76.3
Malta	48.7	50.3	51.6
Poland	80.8	79.1	77.2
Slovenia	66.9	66.0	66.4
Slovakia	84.7	85.1	85.4
Turkey	54.8	54.5	52.4

Source: Eurostat (2006a).

quotas had been abolished, apart from some sensitive products. Moreover, Turkey faced tough competition from similar economies with preferential access to the EU market. Yet, Turkish imports from the EU did increase after the customs union agreement took effect. This too is easy to explain. Before 1 January 1996 Turkey imposed tariffs and quantitative restrictions on EC imports of industrial goods. After 1 January 1996 they were abolished.

Table 3.37 shows the share of individual sectors in total exports of Turkey both before and after the customs union agreement with the EU. There is some change in the share held by individual sectors. In 1995 the three top sectors (food products and beverages; textiles; wearing apparel) accounted for 63.4 per cent of total exports. In 2005 the share of food products and beverages had gone down from 9.3 per cent to 5.5 per cent. The share of motor vehicles had increased from 4 to 19 per cent and that of machinery and equipment from 2.7 to 6.6 per cent. The new three top sectors (wearing apparel; textiles; motor vehicles) accounted for 54.6 per cent of total exports. As far as specialization is concerned, we can see a tendency to upgrade, although the bulk of Turkey's trade with the EU consisted of traditional and low-technology product groups and was still disadvantaged in terms of quality.

Table 3.37 Share of Nace 2 sector in total exports of Turkey to the EU, 1995–2005

Ranking 1995			Ranking 2005		
Description	Nace 2	Share	Description	Nace 2	Share
Tobacco	16	0.000	Tobacco	16	0.000
Office machinery and computers	30	0.001	Publishing and printing	22	0.001
Publishing and printing	22	0.001	Office machinery and computers	30	0.001
Wood products	20	0.002	Wood products	20	0.001
Pulp and paper products	21	0.003	Pulp and paper products	21	0.003
Medical, precision, and optical instruments, watches and clocks	33	0.003	Medical, precision, and optical instruments, watches and clocks	33	0.003
Leather	19	0.005	Leather	19	0.004
Furniture, manufacturing not elsewhere classified	36	0.010	Energy products	23	0.013
Energy products	23	0.015	Other transport	35	0.013
Fabricated metals	28	0.019	Furniture, manufacturing not elsewhere classified	36	0.021
Radio, television and communication equipment and apparatus	32	0.020	Electrical machinery	31	0.022
Rubber and plastic	25	0.023	Chemicals	24	0.024
Machinery	29	0.027	Fabricated metals	28	0.029
Electrical machinery	31	0.028	Mineral products	26	0.032
Other transport	35	0.035	Rubber and plastic	25	0.032
Mineral products	26	0.037	Food and beverages	15	0.055
Motor vehicles	34	0.040	Basic metals	27	0.056
Chemicals	24	0.043	Machinery	29	0.066
Basic metals	27	0.053	Radio, television and communication equipment and apparatus	32	0.077
Food and beverages	15	0.093	Textiles	17	0.129
Textiles	17	0.193	Motor vehicles	34	0.192
Wearing apparel	18	0.348	Wearing apparel	18	0.225

Source: Eurostat (2006a)

Intra-industry specialization and revealed comparative advantages

Many studies have found that, the more advanced and developed an economy, the more specialized its trade structure will be. Thus, industrialized countries tend to have greater levels of intra-industry trade than developing countries (Gönel 2001: 61). The smooth adjustment hypothesis predicts that adjustment costs due to trade liberalization are lower when the trade pattern of a country is intra-industry style. We did some further research on this.

Table 3.38 shows the intra-industry specialization index between Turkey and the EU at the two digit-level.[7] In the case of perfect intra-industry specialization (exports is equal to imports) the index is 1. If there is no intra-industry trade at all, the index is 0. Thus, higher values of the latter index point to deeper complementarities in the trade structure within each sector.

The average specialization index increased from 0.48 (1995) to 0.51 (2005). New top sectors emerged in 2005 compared to 1995: rubber and plastic products; luxury products; fabricated metal products; communication equipment; basic metals and motor vehicles are doing well. The figures show that in a number of sectors there is intra-industry specialization for Turkey vis-à-vis the EU, which

Table 3.38 Intra-industry specialization index, between Turkey and the EU, 1995–2005 (%)

Ranking 1995			*Ranking 2005*		
Description	*Nace 2*	*Index value*	*Description*	*Nace 2*	*Index value*
Office machinery and computers	30	0.04	Office machinery and computers	30	0.04
Wearing apparel	18	0.06	Tobacco	16	0.06
Tobacco	16	0.06	Wearing apparel	18	0.09
Pulp and paper products	21	0.13	Medical, precision, and optical instruments, watches and clocks	33	0.14
Medical, precision, and optical instruments, watches and clocks	33	0.14	Pulp and paper products	21	0.17
Machinery	29	0.16	Chemicals	24	0.19
Chemicals	24	0.31	Wood products	20	0.33
Motor vehicles	34	0.42	Textiles	17	0.47
Publishing and printing	22	0.42	Machinery	29	0.48
Radio, television and communication equipment and apparatus	32	0.50	Publishing and printing	22	0.50
Basic metals	27	0.52	Mineral products	26	0.51
Leather	19	0.54	Energy products	23	0.53
Textiles	17	0.54	Food and beverages	15	0.55
Fabricated metals	28	0.63	Other transport	35	0.57
Furniture, manufacturing not elsewhere classified	36	0.63	Electrical machinery	31	0.61
Electrical machinery	31	0.64	Leather	19	0.72
Other transport	35	0.73	Basic metals	27	0.80
Mineral products	26	0.75	Furniture, manufacturing not elsewhere classified	36	0.85
Wood products	20	0.78	Radio, television and communication equipment and apparatus	32	0.86
Rubber and plastic	25	0.79	Motor vehicles	34	0.87
Food and beverages	15	0.83	Fabricated metals	28	0.95
Energy products	23	0.97	Rubber and plastic	25	0.99

Source: Eurostat (2006a).

could lead to the conclusion that adjustment costs of trade liberalization might be tolerable. Nevertheless, the measurement of the indicators in other sectors shows that a significant part of Turkey's trade with the EU is still vertical, which has to be seen as inter-industry trade – that is, involving goods of a different quality produced within the same industry. So higher than expected adjustment problems may occur in those sectors.

Table 3.39 shows the revealed comparative advantages (RCA) index for Turkey in its trade with the EU.[8] In case of an index of more than 1, Turkey has a comparative advantage in a certain sector. The higher the RCA index is, the more successful the trade performance of Turkey is in a particular area of industry.

Table 3.39 Revealed comparative advantages index, Turkey versus the EU, 1995–2005

Ranking 1995			Ranking 2005		
Description	*Nace 2*	*Index value*	*Description*	*Nace 2*	*Index value*
Office machinery and computers	30	0.03	Office machinery and computers	30	0.03
Tobacco	16	0.05	Tobacco	16	0.04
Pulp and paper products	21	0.10	Medical, precision, and optical instruments, watches and clocks	33	0.09
Medical, precision, and optical instruments, watches and clocks	33	0.11	Pulp and paper products	21	0.12
Machinery	29	0.12	Chemicals	24	0.13
Chemicals	24	0.27	Wood products	20	0.25
Motor vehicles	34	0.39	Machinery	29	0.40
Publishing and printing	22	0.39	Publishing and printing	22	0.42
Radio, television and communication equipment and apparatus	32	0.49	Energy products	23	0.44
Basic metals	27	0.51	Other transport	35	0.50
Leather	19	0.54	Electrical machinery	31	0.55
Fabricated metals	28	0.67	Leather	19	0.71
Furniture, manufacturing not elsewhere classified	36	0.67	Basic metals	27	0.83
Electrical machinery	31	0.69	Motor vehicles	34	0.97
Other transport	35	0.83	Fabricated metals	28	1.12
Wood products	20	0.93	Rubber and plastic	25	1.27
Rubber and plastic	25	0.96	Radio, television and communication equipment and apparatus	32	1.64
Energy products	23	1.56	Furniture, manufacturing not elsewhere classified	36	1.68
Food and beverages	15	2.04	Food and beverages	15	3.25
Mineral products	26	2.41	Mineral products	26	3.67
Textiles	17	3.92	Textiles	17	4.06
Wearing apparel	18	47.97	Wearing apparel	18	26.50

Source: Eurostat (2006a).

Since 1995 Turkey has maintained its comparative advantage in food products and beverages, other non-metallic mineral products, textiles and wearing apparel. Moreover, it has developed a comparative advantage in new sectors: fabricated metal products, rubber and plastic products, communication equipment and furniture, jewels and other products. Competitiveness has also improved a lot for basic metals and motor vehicles. The six sectors in which Turkey improved its performance in 2005 are the ones with the highest increase in intra-industry trade (see Table 3.38). Trade integration has developed in new sectors with higher value-added productions. Turkey is moving in the right direction from trading textiles, apparel, food and beverages to trading goods with higher value added.

Trade relations in the field of services

Table 3.40 shows the part played by the exports and imports of services in GDP. Over time – compared to the EU-15 and some of the new member states – Turkey seems to have become less integrated in the international economy. The highly state-controlled and monopolized service sectors are probably to blame for this. In Table 3.41 and Figure 3.7 we deal with outsourcing and insourcing of services in Turkey.[9] Until 2001 Turkey was a net exporter of these services. From 2002 on – possibly because of the economic crisis – the situation changed significantly.

Conclusion

The following conclusions can be drawn:

• Turkey should invest more in human capital and it should devote part of its government budget to social benefits on behalf of those who need it.

Table 3.40 Trade integration of services, EU and Turkey, 1995–2004 (M+X/GDP)

Country	1995	2000	2004
EU-15	2.5	3.6	3.6
Bulgaria	10.3	15.3	14.5
Czech Republic	10.5	11.1	8.5
Estonia	18.3	22.3	20.3
Cyprus	22.3	23.9	27.6
Latvia	18.8	11.8	10.8
Lithuania	7.7	7.6	9.1
Hungary	9.8	11.4	10.6
Malta	n/a	23.5	21.3
Poland	6.4	5.7	5.1
Slovenia	8.5	8.6	9.3
Slovakia	10.8	10.2	8.6
Romania	n/a	5.1	4.9
Turkey	5.8	7.4	5.5

Source: Eurostat (2006a).

Table 3.41 Outsourcing and insourcing services, Turkey, 1993–2005

	1993	*1995*	*2000*	*2005*
Credit	1,580	2,630	6,022	267
Debit	512	426	1,602	371
Net	1,068	2,204	4,420	–104

Source: Eurostat (2006a).

- Compared to other developing countries, Turkey has attracted only a very limited number of foreign investors. Its complicated legal system, the endemic corruption, the weak physical infrastructure and the political instability are the main reasons for this. Yet the new government seems to be doing better: since it took power, FDI has risen.
- Turkey is on the right track as regards the structural transformation of its economy. Industry and services are becoming more important to the detriment of agriculture.
- Trade integration of goods between Turkey and the EU is strong. Both the intra-industry specialization and the revealed comparative advantages indexes prove that Turkish firms will be able to compete with European firms in the large internal market.
- Trade integration of services is weaker. From a net outsourcer of services Turkey has turned into a net insourcer.

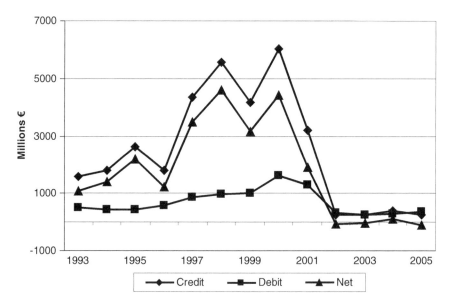

Figure 3.7 Outsourcing and insourcing services, Turkey, 1993–2005 (Source: Eurostat (2006a)).

The EMU

Unlike all other policies of the EU, the EMU is designed in the expectation that not all member states will join at the same time. However, the Accession Partnership stipulates that 'Turkey will participate in the EMU, from accession as a member state with derogation. It shall adopt the Euro as its national currency following a Council decision to this effect based on an evaluation of its fulfilment of the necessary conditions' (Council of the European Communities 2006a).

This means that candidate countries that have achieved economic and budgetary results in line with the Maastricht criteria have to join the single currency. Unlike the UK and Denmark, they cannot opt out of the EMU.[10] EMU members lose the power to pursue an independent monetary as well as an independent exchange-rate policy.

In the 2006 Progress Report the Commission thinks Turkey has created favourable conditions for the EMU but significant steps have yet to be taken (CEC 2006a):

- Turkey has adopted new legislation that prohibits privileged access of public-sector authorities to financial institutions.
- There is some progress regarding the Central Bank's independence.
- The Central Bank of Turkey has yet to adopt a secondary objective that allows for general economic objectives of the EC to take precedence over domestic objectives.
- Turkey has not yet adopted the necessary rules and structures with a view to integrating its Central Bank into the European System of Central Banks by the time of EU accession.
- Banks are no longer required to keep a certain amount of compulsory reserves in the form of Turkish treasury bonds.
- However, the Investor Protector Fund is obliged to invest its assets in government bonds and deposits to be kept with state banks.
- All public institutions except the central government must either deposit their funds in state banks or buy government bonds.
- Overall in the area of monetary policy Turkey is advanced.

Even if all institutional requirements are not fulfilled, we think that cautious optimism is justified here. Table 3.42 shows that – because of IMF pressure –Turkey is slowly converging towards the Maastricht criteria with the exception of the interest-rate criterion. The Turkish economy recovered in 2002 and output growth has since remained strong, while inflation came down quickly. The Central Bank has cut interest rates, thus encouraging companies to borrow and to invest cheaply. Turkey's economy, however, remains fragile, highly indebted and very much dependent on the inflow of short-term capital. Most of Turkey's government debt is in short-term foreign currency bonds that expire on average every two years. Therefore, the government constantly has to go back to the markets to refinance its debt. Half of the government's budget is still spent on interest payments (Barysch 2005: 6).

Table 3.42 The Maastricht criteria, Turkey, Bulgaria and Romania, 2000–5

	Inflation rate (%)					
	2000	2001	2002	2003	2004	2005
Turkey	54.9	54.4	45.0	25.3	9.9	n/a
Bulgaria	10.1	7.9	5.8	2.3	n/a	n/a
Romania	45.7	34.5	22.5	15.3	n/a	n/a
Norm	2.8	3.3	3.0	2.7	2.9	n/a

Sources: Hoekman and Togan (2005: 20); OECD (2006b).

	Budget deficit (% of GDP)				
	2001	2002	2003	2004	2005
Turkey	−33.0	−12.9	−11.3	−5.7	−1.2
Bulgaria	1.9	0.1	0.3	1.9	3.1
Romania	−3.3	−2.0	−1.7	−1.3	−0.4
Norm	−3.0	−3.0	−3.0	−3.0	−3.0

Source: Eurostat (2006a).

	Government debt (% of GDP)				
	2001	2002	2003	2004	2005
Turkey	104.4	93.0	85.1	76.9	69.6
Bulgaria	66.2	54.0	46.1	38.6	29.9
Romania	n/a	23.8	20.7	18.0	15.2
Norm	60.0	60.0	60.0	60.0	60.0

Source: Eurostat (2006a).

Interest rates, 10-year bonds, 2004 (%)	
Turkey	28.5
Bulgaria	5.4
Romania	17.3
Norm	6.2

Source: Eurostat (2006a).

Exchange rate against parity, 2001–3 (%)	
Turkey	16.3
Bulgaria	−0.8
Romania	−19.2
Norm	±15.0

Source: Eurostat (2006a).

Economic theory suggests that the main benefit of joining an optimum currency area is enhanced price stability, while the main cost is higher business cycle volatility if the country's output is not sufficiently positively correlated with that of the currency area as a whole. The more synchronized the business cycles among the member countries, the lower the probability of asymmetric shocks. Furceri and Karras (2006: 37) find that Turkey should expect both high cyclical costs and high price-stability benefits. Sayek and Selover (2002: 236) find that the divergence between Turkish and EU business cycles may be due to many domestic and regional shocks specific to Turkey and unfelt elsewhere in Europe. As Turkey's business cycle is negatively or not correlated with that of the EMU as a whole, it seems highly improbable that Turkey will benefit from EMU membership. However, one could also argue the opposite: if Turkey entered the EMU, its business cycles would tend to be more synchronized with the European business cycles. Membership in the EMU might impose valuable monetary stability and discipline on the Turkish economy. The EU would replace the IMF and the stability it engendered would be longer lasting (Sayek and Selover 2002: 236). Some economists even argue that Turkey should adopt the Euro and transfer the control over monetary policy to the European Central Bank. By renouncing control over monetary policy, the government could engage seriously in a reform of the banking system (Tocci 2001: 28–9).

The *Acquis communautaire*

The ability to implement the *Acquis communautaire* is the main obligation imposed by the EU on candidate states. However, in the past no country that joined the EU had complied fully with the *Acquis* at the time of entry. Countries such as Greece, Spain and Portugal were allowed to adopt the *Acquis* – which at that time was less extensive than in 2007 – in transitional stages. For example, Spain and Portugal achieved the abolition of import tariffs within seven years and they were granted six extra years to complete their customs union. In the meantime they had voting power and benefited from substantial financial assistance (Harun 2003: 35). Nowadays applicant countries need to complete the *Acquis communautaire* in full before their accession.

Thus, negotiations between member states and Turkey focus almost exclusively on the necessary adoption by Turkey of EC law. In this sense the word 'negotiations' is misleading. The discussions focus on 'how' Turkey will adopt European standards and not on 'whether' Turkey will adopt them (Rehn 2005b). This is not always easy to accept by the Turkish government. The conviction that the EU should bend its rules to accommodate Turkey rather than the other way round seems firmly rooted in the state psyche (*The Economist* 2000a). Table 3.43 gives a short overview of the situation as described in the Commission's Progress Reports. Upon reading the Progress Reports we find – not surprisingly – that progress has been made in the fields more or less related to the customs union, but that much remains to be done in these and in other fields. Even fulfilment of short-term priorities under the Accession Partnership is lagging behind in a number of

Table 3.43 Turkey's adoption of the *Acquis communautaire*, 1998–2006

Chapter	Progress	No progress	Limited progress
Free movement of goods	X		
Freedom of movement for workers			X
Right of establishment and freedom to provide services			X
Free movement of capital		X	
Public procurement		X	
Company law		X	
Intellectual property law	X		
Competition policy and state aid			X
Financial services			X
Information society and media	X		
Agriculture			X
Food safety, veterinary and phytosanitary products		X	
Fisheries		X	
Transport policy			X
Energy			X
Taxation			X
Economic and monetary union	X		
Statistics			X
Employment and social policy			X
Enterprise and industrial policy	X		
Trans-European networks			X
Regional policy and coordination of structural instruments			X
Judiciary and fundamental rights	X		
Justice, freedom and security	X		
Science and research	X		
Education and culture	X		
Environment		X	
Consumer and health protection			X
Customs Union	X		
External relations	X		
Foreign, security and defence policy	X		
Financial control			X
Financial and budgetary provisions			X
Institutions			
Other			

Source: CEC (1998, 1999, 2000, 2001, 2002, 2003b, 2004c, 2005, 2006a).

areas. Much improvement is needed in Turkey's institutional and administrative capacity. This means that reforms that are more horizontal are necessary, such as strengthening corporate governance and regulatory frameworks. According to the Commission, full adoption by Turkey of the 90,000-page *Acquis communautaire* will be a costly process (CEC 2004a: 29).

In this section we will deal with some difficult issues:

• the free movement of goods;

- the right of establishment and the freedom to provide services;
- competition policy and state aid;
- employment and social policy;
- freedom of movement for workers;
- agriculture;
- regional policy and coordination of structural instruments;
- financial and budgetary provisions;
- foreign, security and defence policy;
- justice, freedom and security;
- education and culture.[11]

The free movement of goods

According to the Commission, the overall level of Turkish alignment in the customs union is high. Turkish trade integration with the EU has remained stable, and Turkey has significantly improved the function of its market economy. Problems still remain with respect to the Turkish Free Trade Zones and the protection of intellectual property rights.[12] The Commission does not go into further detail with respect to the customs union. That is why we will elaborate on it further. First, we will deal with the customs union in general. After that, we will pay attention to a topic that is unnoticed in the 2006 Progress Report: anti-dumping measures. We will conclude with the topic discussed at length by the Commission in the report: technical and administrative barriers to trade.

The customs union

Economists have tended to be rather sceptical of the benefits of customs unions. Apart from the trade-creating effect between customs union partners, there is trade diversion vis-à-vis third countries. Welfare could be reduced by diverting imports from the least-cost source outside the EU to a higher-cost source inside the EU. However, Turkey seems to satisfy many of the criteria for the customs union to be welfare enhancing (Hartler and Laird 1999: 3). Trade ties between the EU and Turkey were already very close before the customs union. The Turkish economy is quite diverse. Turkey's trade barriers were substantial before the customs union (see Table 3.44). The simple average tariff declined from 26.7 per cent in 1993 to 12.7 per cent in 1998 (Hartler and Laird 1999: 4). In general Turkey's tariffs were

Table 3.44 Overall tariff profile, Turkey, 1993 (in % *ad valorem*)

Tariffs	Third countries	EU
Whole economy	26.7	22.2
Standard deviation	13.1	12.9
Duty-free lines (%)	1.4	7.2
Maximum tariff	132.5	130.0

Source: Hartler and Laird (1999: 15).

set on an *ad valorem* basis (98 per cent of the items), but specific, formula and alternate duties applied to 337 items at the HS twelve-digit level.[13]

As a result of the customs union Turkey has become an open economy in the non-agricultural sectors. Based on Turkey's import shares it is estimated that the average nominal tariff on non-agricultural imports is less than 2 per cent (zero for imports from the EU and 3–4 per cent on average for third countries) (Harrison *et al.* 1996: 2). If one takes into account agricultural products, nominal protection rates with the EU are 1.34 per cent; with third countries: 6.92 per cent; for General System of Preferences beneficiaries: 2.71 per cent (Togan 2000: 23).

By establishing a customs union instead of a free trade zone, the risk of trade diversion and the resulting welfare loss were minimized. The adoption of the EU common external tariff by Turkey resulted in more secure access to the Turkish market for most industrial products by third countries. Turkey had bindings on some 31 per cent of tariff lines, equivalent to 34 per cent of non-oil imports. The EU's tariff schedule is 100 per cent bound, at generally lower rates than Turkey's. Because of the customs union Turkey's tariff schedule is de facto subject to the same binding commitment as that of the EU (Hartler and Laird 1999: 4). This clearly favours trade with third countries. Apart from this static effect, there is the dynamic effect of the customs union. According to Kursat Tuzmen, Turkish Minister for Foreign Trade and Customs:

> the customs union was designed to be a transitional process that would ulti-mately carry Turkey to full EU membership. It encouraged Turkey to become more competitive and its industry to adapt to new conditions. The legal order that governed production and trade had been upgraded and aligned to the EU, so that Turkey now has a greater degree of industrial and commercial integra-tion with the EU than most countries. (Friends of Europe 2004: 25)

In the 2006 Progress Report the Commission praises Turkey: its level of align-ment with the EC's common commercial policy is advanced and in line with Turkey's customs union obligations (CEC 2006a).

However, we think that for Turkey there are some disadvantages attached to this common commercial policy. Because the EU sets rules (customs cooperation, rules of origin, competition law, standards, government procurement, intellectual and industrial property rights, taxation, and investment codes[14]), third countries have to change their legal regulations unilaterally. Countries like Turkey had to give up their independence in trade policy, even when they could not take part themselves in the framing of EU trade policy (the so-called Commission 113 meetings). Secondly, in the WTO Turkey qualified for developing-country status, but because of the customs union it cannot (fully) benefit from this. It also means that in multilateral trade negotiations Turkey has to align its point of view to those of the EU. In the 2003 Progress Report (CEC 2003b) it was (mildly) chided for not doing so in the Doha Round.[15] In the 2006 Progress Report the Commission mentions the following: 'The level of coordination of Turkey with the EU within the WTO, in particular as regards GATS, the Doha Development Agenda, and the

OECD, needs attention. Frequently Turkey does not align its position with the EU' (CEC 2006a: 71).

Thirdly, WTO member states might introduce cases against Turkey for not complying with commitments under the multilateral trading system. If Turkey raises tariffs or imposes quotas on products, third countries might ask for compensation if they exported these products to Turkey. This was done by India (1998) with respect to EU quotas imposed by Turkey on imports of textiles.[16] Fourthly, in accordance with article 16 of the customs union agreement, Turkey had to sign by 2001 free trade agreements with EU privileged trading partners. By 2007 only seven of these agreements had entered into force (EFTA, Israel, Tunisia, Palestine, Bosnia-Herzegovina, FYR Macedonia and Croatia). Negotiations continued with other countries. This situation disfavours Turkish exporters: third-country exporters could export duty-free to an EU member state and then re-export to Turkey, while Turkish exports do not enjoy the same benefit. Turkey has also signed other trade agreements with non-EU countries – for example, in 2003 the 'Economic Cooperation Organization Trade Agreement' (ECOTA) with Afghanistan, Iran and Tajikistan.[17] This probably violates the Negotiating Framework: 'The resulting rights and obligations … imply the termination of … all other international agreements concluded by Turkey that are incompatible with the obligations of membership' (Council of the European Communities 2006a).

Anti-dumping measures

In spite of the customs union between Turkey and the EU and in marked contrast with the agreement with the EFTA countries ('European Economic Area'), it is possible for both partners to invoke 'trade defence instruments', such as anti-dumping and countervailing measures and safeguards (Yasar 2006: 32). Anti-dumping policy is an industrial policy tool that nullifies advantages attached to a customs union. Instead of keeping 'unfair imports' out, it is often aimed at fostering the interests of domestic producers (Konings and Vandenbussche 2005 151). Konings and Vandenbussche show that mark-ups of EU firms increase significantly during anti-dumping protection against dumped imports. In the case of anti-dumping procedures, the EU has not treated Turkey differently from any other third country. Between 1987 and 2003 the Commission started anti-dumping proceedings in twenty-seven cases, mostly in low-skilled sectors (textiles, iron ore and steel). In nine cases, final *ad valorem* duties were imposed; in one case Turkey had to sign a minimum price agreement (see Table 3.45). As for Turkey itself, Vandenbussche and Zanardi (2006:17) qualify it as 'a tough new user' of anti-dumping measures. It ranks among Brazil, Mexico, India, Taiwan, China, Egypt, Indonesia, Lithuania and Poland, having initiated at least four anti-dumping cases on average per year. Turkey initiated proceedings against the EU in eleven cases where final duties were imposed in eight of them (see Table 3.46). Because there have been cases where the allegedly dumping Turkish firm has a negligible share of the market (below 5 per cent) and for that matter a *de minimis* rule could have been applied, some authors argue that European applicants were mainly protecting their

Table 3.45 Anti-dumping proceedings, EU versus Turkey, 1987–2003

Year	Product	*Final* ad valorem *duty (%)*
1987	Synthetic textile fibres	11.90
1987	Polyester yarn	13.20
1987	Iron or steel sections	39 ECU/ton
1989	Denim	
1989	Welded tubes of iron ore	18.50
1990	Bathrobes, toilet and kitchen linen	
1990	Asbestos cement pipes	
1990	Cotton yarn	12.10
1990	Polyester yarn	Agreement on minimum price
1990	Rods of alloy steel	
1990	Products of alloy steel	16.00
1990	Wire rod	
1991	Pig iron	
1992	Portland cement	
1992	Colour television receivers	
1993	Synthetic yarn	
1994	Cotton fabrics	
1994	Bed linen	
1996	Unbleached cotton fabrics	
1997	Cotton fabrics	
1999	Steel wire rod	
2000	Iron or steel ropes and cables	31.00
2000	Paracetamol	
2000	Colour television receivers	
2001	Tubes and pipes of iron and steel	6.00
2001	Flat-rolled products of iron and steel	11.50
2002	Hollow sections	

Source: Eurostat (2006a).

dominant position in the EU market (Ülgen and Zahariadis 2004: 12). According to UNIDO (1995: 215), anti-dumping policy has gained notoriety as an instrument of protection 'masquerading as a defender of honest commercial values'.

The case of television receivers is a particularly interesting one. Anti-dumping duties were imposed by the EU on Turkish imports because the television sets

Table 3.46 Anti-dumping proceedings, Turkey versus EU, 1987–2003

Investigated country	Products	Final duty
Finland	Paper	*Ad valorem*
Germany	Printing and writing Paper + polyvinyl chloride	Specific duty + none
Italy	Polyester fibres + polyvinyl chloride	*Ad valorem* + specific duty
Netherlands	Benzoic acid + polyvinyl chloride	Specific duty + specific duty
Belgium	Polyvinyl chloride	Specific duty
EU	Bearings	None
France	Printing and writing paper	None
Greece	Polyvinyl chloride	Specific duty

Source: Eurostat (2006a).

contained Chinese cathode tubes imported by Turkey at prices that were too low. Turkey argued that the television sets had become of Turkish origin, while the Commission retorted that the value added in Turkey was too small for them to qualify as 'Turkish products'. Turkey applied the same rules of origin as the EU regarding third-country trade. These rules differ between countries with and without preferential agreements. Through the customs union with the EU Turkey acceded to the Pan-European Cumulating System (PECS). The PECS provides for diagonal cumulating with respect to the origin of products. However, both EU member states and Turkey can invoke safeguard clauses if they feel their economy, certain industrial sectors or certain regions are threatened by imports.

Technical and administrative barriers

Apart from anti-dumping duties, non-tariff barriers have become the major instrument of protection in the EU (Togan 2001: 27). Technical and administrative barriers continue to hinder trade between Turkey and the EU. Non-tariff barriers result from different legislations on commercial, technical and marketing standards. On different occasions, the European Court of Justice blamed EU member states for hindering EU trade among themselves by a number of ubiquitous regulations. It was the view of the Court that products that are lawfully produced and marketed in one member state should in principle be admitted to other member states for sale, except in certain cases. We find a good illustration of the Court's view in the 'Dassonville' judgment: 'All trading rules engaged by member states which are capable of hindering, directly or indirectly, actually or potentially, intra-community trade are to be considered as measures having an effect equivalent to quantitative restrictions' (ECJ, 11 July 1974).

However in the landmark 'Cassis de Dijon' judgment the Court softened its stance:

> Obstacles to movement within the Community resulting from disparities between national laws relating to the marketing of products must be accepted in so far as those provisions may be recognized as being necessary in order to satisfy mandatory requirements relating in particular to the effectiveness of fiscal supervision, the protection of public health, the fairness of commercial transactions and the defence of the consumer. (ECJ, 20 February 1979 (case 120/78))

Since then the Court has applied the so-called rule of reason when judging whether national legislations obstruct free trade among member states, whereas member states refer to the 'Cassis de Dijon' judgment and to articles 28, 29 and especially 30 of the Treaty establishing the European Community (EU n.d.) to justify administrative and technical barriers:

> Article 28: 'Quantitative restrictions on imports and all measures having equivalent effect shall be prohibited between member states.'

Article 29: 'Quantitative restrictions on exports, and all measures having equivalent effect, shall be prohibited between member states.'

Article 30: 'The provisions of Articles 28 and 29 shall not preclude prohibitions or restrictions on imports, exports or goods in transit justified on grounds of public morality, public policy or public security; the protection of health and life of humans, animals or plants; the protection of national treasures possessing artistic, historic or archaeological value; or the protection of industrial and commercial property. Such prohibitions or restrictions shall not, however, constitute a means of arbitrary discrimination or a disguised restriction on trade between member states.'

The Commission complied with member states' requests, lest the internal market might not come into being. Thus, the mutual recognition of each other's technical standards by member states applies in only a limited number of product categories. For all other product categories, European rules had to be designed in order to liberalize trade. Here the Commission has opted for two different approaches. In the so-called 'old' approach (for example, motor vehicles) one single standard replaces the (now twenty-seven) existing ones before a product can be placed on the market of any other member state. Under the 'new' approach (for example, toys, pressure vessels, gas appliances) only minimum requirements are adopted for each product category. Three European standard institutions (CEN, CENELEC and ETSI) have to enquire into the conformity of member states' legislation with the minimum requirements. Importers need an inspection certificate from one of these institutions.

In trade relations with third countries, EU member states and the Commission are very strict in that they want trade partners not to jeopardize the high standards of production and marketing EU exporters themselves have to meet. The EU signed agreements with developed trade partners (for example, the USA, Australia, Israel) with respect to mutual acceptance of test certificates by conformity assessment institutions that correspond with EU legislation. With the twelve new member states, protocols on European conformity assessment have been signed. With Turkey, such an agreement has yet to be concluded. According to the 2006 Progress Report, 'provisions on the mutual recognition remain to be adopted'. However, it was the Commission's view that in the area of standardization, 'good progress was booked' (CEC 2006a: 33).

The number of mandatory standards invoked by Turkey declined significantly (from 300 in 2005 to 29 in 2006), especially with respect to 'new approach' fields. Turkey adopted 90 per cent of CEN and 88 per cent of CENELEC regulations. For a limited number of activities, progress was also achieved in the field of conformity assessment. However, problems remain. Turkey lacks the technical capacity and infrastructure to meet fully the needs of the testing and the certification process. Because of the lack of credible assessment institutions and the fact that the Turkish accreditation authority (TURKAK) is not internationally recognized, Turkish firms wishing to export to the EU usually contact European institutions that do the testing in their laboratories (Ülgen and Zahariadis 2004: 14; Hoekman and Togan 2005: 109). This procedure increases transport and administrative costs. There are also problems regarding market surveillance. Turkey and the Commission seriously disagree on verification fees and medicinal products.

The Commission thinks that the share of EU imports in the Turkish market could have been higher: 'There are still a number of barriers to trade, some of which are caused by Turkey's non-compliance with its obligations under the customs union' (CEC 2004a: 17).

In the 2006 Progress Report the Commission blames Turkey again (CEC 2006a):

- Progress has been uneven.
- There have been improvements both in areas such as accreditation, standardization and conformity assessment, and under the new approach directive.
- However, the removal of provisions contrary to the general principle of free circulation and mutual recognition has not been completed.
- Remaining import licensing requirements are contrary to articles 28–30 of the EC treaty.
- The conformity assessment structures have been developed in some areas for a limited number of activities.
- An effective market surveillance system in conformity with new approach principles is not yet in place.

Experts tend to agree with the Commission. According to Burrell (2005a: 155), Turkey's import is subject to 26,941 standards of which 1,264 are mandatory. The authorities stress that, although the procedure is obligatory only for mandatory standards, it is also 'highly recommended' for the marketing of products subject to non-mandatory standards. Trade between Turkey and the EU would possibly have been higher had technical barriers been removed. Mercenier and Yeldan (1997: 879) think that removing administrative and technical barriers will increase welfare. Domestic oligopolies will no longer be shielded from foreign competition at the expense of local customers. However, Lejour, de Mooij and Capel have simulated the gradual abolishment of administrative and technical barriers in EU–Turkey trade. Compared to the CEEC, the macroeconomic effects for Turkey are relatively small (average GDP increase of 0.8 per cent and average consumption increase of 1.4 per cent). Yet sectoral effects are more important for Turkey. As a result of their strong export orientation and relatively large non-tariff barriers, Turkish textiles and wearing apparel would benefit the most (Lejour *et al.* 2004: 41–4). Effects for the EU would be negligible.

The right of establishment and the freedom to provide services

This section is a very controversial one. Both Turkey and the EU focus on commitments to be taken by the other side. The freedom to establish and to supply services is the second main freedom provided for by the EU Internal Market Programme.

Articles 43 and 49 of the Treaty establishing the European Community (EU n.d.) state the following:

> Within the framework of the provisions set out below, restrictions on the freedom of establishment of nationals of a member state in the territory of another member state shall be prohibited. Such prohibition shall also apply to restrictions on the setting-up of agencies, branches or subsidiaries by nationals of any member state established in the territory of any member state. Freedom of establishment shall include the right to take up and pursue activities as self-employed persons and to set up and manage undertakings, in particular companies or firms within the meaning of the second paragraph of Article 48, under the conditions laid down for its own nationals by the law of the country where such establishment is effected, subject to the provisions of the chapter relating to capital.

> Within the framework of the provisions set out below, restrictions on the freedom to provide services within the Community shall be prohibited in respect of nationals of member states who are established in a State of the Community other than that of the person for whom the services are intended. The Council may, acting by a qualified majority on a proposal from the Commission, extend the provisions of the Chapter to nationals of a third country who provide services and who are established within the Community.

On the other hand, under strict conditions it is possible for member states to restrict both kinds of freedom. See Article 46:

> The provisions of this chapter and measures taken in pursuance thereof shall not prejudice the applicability of provisions laid down by law, regulation or administrative action providing for special treatment for foreign nationals on grounds of public policy, public security or public health.

and Article 54:

> As long as restrictions on the freedom to provide services have not been abolished, each member state shall apply such restrictions without distinction on grounds of nationality or residence to all persons providing services within the meaning of the first paragraph of Article 49.

As in the free movement of goods, the European Court had to intervene lest member states obstructed the freedom of establishment and the freedom to provide services. In the Gebhard case the Court stated the following:

> Where the taking-up or pursuit of a specific activity is subject to such conditions in the host member state, a national of another member state intending to pursue that activity must in principle comply with them. It is for this reason that article 44 provides that the Council is to issue directives, such as Directive

89/48, for the mutual recognition of diplomas, certificates and other evidence of formal qualifications or, as the case may be, for the coordination of national provisions concerning the taking-up and pursuit of activities as self-employed persons. It follows, however, from the Court's case-law that national measures liable to hinder or make less attractive the exercise of fundamental freedoms guaranteed by the Treaty must fulfil four conditions: they must be applied in a non-discriminatory manner; they must be justified by imperative requirements in the general interest; they must be suitable for securing the attainment of the objective which they pursue; and they must not go beyond what is necessary in order to attain it. (ECJ, 30 November 1995 (case C-55/94))

Since the 2004 EU enlargement the freedom to provide services in other member states has become a contentious issue among member states. In 2005 the Commission tried to introduce the country of origin principle with the so-called Bolkestein directive, but it had to backtrack because of fierce resistance in some member states. Apparently, member states did not want to inject new competition into their services markets, which account for two-thirds of EU-wide GDP (*The Economist* 2007a). Therefore, it is hardly surprising that the liberalization with respect to the establishment and the supply of services by third-country nationals has yet to be realized.

Although the principle of free trade in services is mentioned in the Ankara agreement and subsequently in the Additional Protocol, it was left out of the customs union on EU insistence (Ülgen and Zahariadis 2004: 24). Therefore, it is hardly likely that free trade of services will be dealt with outside the context of the enlargement negotiations, as Turkey had initially been hoping for. To the no small disappointment of Turkey, the EU does not want Turkish service providers to establish themselves on its territory, even if they fully comply with country-of-destination legislation. The official reason is that Turkey first has to adopt the entire *Acquis communautaire* in the services area. There is, of course, another reason behind this refusal: it could lead to the temporary employment of posted lower-skilled Turkish workers, who immigrate for this purpose. Moreover, Turkey itself has to eliminate barriers to services trade. So-called sensitive sectors are involved where the state still plays an important role as an economic agent: banking, insurance, transport, telecommunications, stock market, energy.

The 2006 Progress Report states the following in this respect (CEC 2006a):

- *Regarding the right of self-employed EU nationals to obtain a work permit*: Turkey requests immediate reciprocity.
- *Regarding company registration requirements*: in some sectors, foreign nationals cannot provide services even if their company is established in Turkey.
- *Regarding the professions*: certain professions are closed to foreigners.
- *Regarding the freedom to provide cross-border services*: service providers are required to register with relevant associations. Authorization procedures are cumbersome.

- *Regarding the regulated professions*: Turkey did not transpose regulations into its domestic legislation. Nationality requirements remain in vogue for many professions (lawyers, medical doctors, midwives, dentists, traffic controllers, private security services).

The conclusion of the Commission is obvious: overall alignment of Turkey with the *Acquis communautaire* is very limited in this area. In view of the preceding, this is an unexpected outcome: despite Turkey's relatively strong integration in the services area with the outside world, there is hardly any progress as far as relations with the EU are concerned.

Competition policy and state aid

As long as Turkey does not adopt the relevant clauses of the *Acquis communautaire* on competition and state aid, both Turkey and EU can take safeguard measures in foreign trade. Unfortunately, no deadline has been set in the customs union agreement. In 1994 the Turkish Parliament passed a competition law that is modelled on article 81 of the EEC treaty (Hoekman and Togan 2005: 114). Agreements between firms that restrict competition are prohibited. In 1997 a Competition Authority was set up, and a few years later it was authorized to impose fines. Yet Turkey does not have a law in line with article 82 of the EC Treaty. This article stipulates that any abuse by one or more firms of a dominant position is prohibited. Although the Commission has praised the Competition Authority for its efficiency (CEC 2004a: 21), evolution of European competition law does not facilitate things. In 1999, the EU changed its legal regime on so-called vertical agreements. Traditionally it was primarily legal-form based. Anti-competitive agreements were prohibited and automatically void. However, they could qualify for an exemption from the prohibition if their benefits outweighed the anti-competitive costs. This can be the case with respect to vertical agreements containing intellectual property rights (subcontracting; technology transfer) or when the market share does not exceed 30 per cent of the relevant market (Lorentzen and Møllgaard 2002: 2–3). Since 2003 the regime has become more flexible and calls for cooperation between European and national authorities and Turkey can hardly catch up (Ülgen and Zahariadis 2004: 18–19).

All in all, the Commission is relatively satisfied with respect to the way Turkey has implemented this part of the *Acquis communautaire*, as stated in the 2006 Progress Report (CEC 2006a):

- In the field of anti-trust, mergers included, progress can be reported. As regards enforcements, the Competition Authority continued to impose fines for the infringement of competition rules. However, legislative alignment is needed in some sectors.
- The Competition Authority continues to play an active role in merger control; especially important were privatization cases that made its presence more visible among market actors.

- The Competition Authority has administrative and operational independence. It has a sufficient administrative capacity to ensure anti-trust enforcement and merger control. It places high emphasis on continuous training of its staff.
- The administrative capacity of the Supreme Administrative Court is a matter of concern. Handling of appealed competition cases is slow.
- No development can be recorded with regard to the alignment of rules concerning public undertakings. Turkey needs to ensure transparency of financial relations between public authorities and public undertakings.

Whereas in the field of competition legislation in the view of the Commission, Turkey has made significant process, in the field of state aid Turkey has still a long way to go, as stated in the 2006 Progress Report 'No developments can be reported with regard to the adoption of state aid legislation or the establishment of an operationally independent state aid monitoring authority. Their absence results in serious distortions of competition' (CEC 2006a).

State aid can come in many forms and is not limited to direct subsidies. All measures that involve a public authority can contain elements of state aid – for example, investment grants, compensation for social security obligations, state guarantees created by a state-owned bank, tax allowances or tax credits. State aid can also be hidden in the sale of land or buildings by public authorities (Latham and Watkins 2003: 2). Turkey has an extensive state-aid system of tax exemptions and generous credit. The system is 'complex, non-transparent and generous' (Hartler and Laird 1999: 11). Textiles and clothing, followed by chemicals, are the main industry recipients. The manufacturing sector is the main beneficiary of duty concessions for exports as well as export credits and guarantees. Compared to Turkey, state aid in the EU-12 – though much criticized – pales into insignificance. Turkey has refrained from setting up an independent authority to monitor state aid. Moreover Turkey is blamed for requesting majority participation by Turkish citizens or companies in certain vital sectors (broadcasting, aviation, maritime transportation, value-added telecommunications services companies, and port facilities). There are also problems as to trade-related intellectual property rights (TRIPs). Turkey acceded to a number of international conventions, but the majority of them have yet to be transposed into domestic law.

In the view of the Commission, the level of state aid provided to Turkish firms explains partially why there are still high concentration rates in Turkish industry and why mark-ups are still higher in Turkish firms compared to EU firms. Indeed, Konings, Van Cayseele and Warzynski found that, in both Romania and Bulgaria, product market concentration and mark-ups were positively correlated. From estimates, it was inferred that, because of new-firm entry or enterprise break-ups, which resulted in lower product market concentration levels, mark-ups in Bulgarian and Romanian firms had declined during the transition process, suggesting that competitive pressure seems to discipline firms' pricing behaviour. Privatization as such did not solve the problem: privatized firms had even higher mark-ups than state firms. Turkey could learn from this: privatizing state-owned enterprises – as the government is now trying to do – without creating a competitive market environment may have little effect (Konings *et al.* 2005: 132).

Trade policy also plays a crucial role in enhancing competitiveness. Notwithstanding the customs union with the EU, Turkish firms are still relatively well protected against foreign competitors compared to those in the EU. This is likely to be another important reason for relatively higher mark-ups in Turkey. In Table 3.47 we compare average sectoral mark-ups[18] in Turkey and Belgium, the most open economy in the EU. As expected, mark-ups in Turkey are systematically higher than the Belgian ones. This confirms the view that Turkey should be further open to trade in order to foster competitiveness.

Employment and social policy

In the Commission's view, hardly any progress has been made in the field of employment and social policy (CEC 2006a):

- *Regarding the area of labour law*: there are shortcomings in the transposition of EU directives.
- *Regarding child labour*: Turkey does not comply with ILO conventions.
- *Regarding health and safety at work*: there is a good degree of alignment with the *Acquis communautaire*; however, the regulation transposing the Framework Directive into national legislation is still suspended.
- *Regarding social dialogue and trade-union rights*: Turkish laws are not in line with the *Acquis*.
- *Regarding employment policy*: there is no progress; the institutional capacity of the Turkish Employment Agency is weak.
- *Regarding the European Social Fund*: for the time being Turkey does not have the institutions to manage and monitor European Social Fund-type measures at national or regional level.
- *Regarding social inclusion*: there is no progress on a national integrated strategy.
- *Regarding social security*: Turkey's Parliament adopted a law in June 2006 on the complete reform of social security. However, the administrative and the inspection capacities require strengthening.
- *Regarding non-discrimination and equal opportunities*: there is no progress; the necessary institutions have yet to be set up.

Turkey seems to be reluctant about the full adoption of the *Acquis communautaire* in the field of employment and social policy. This is understandable. From Table 3.48 we learn that, for a developing country Turkey has a relative large share of income tax and social security contributions, comparable to wealthier EU member states. The average labour cost for employers is lower in Turkey than in developed EU member states, but it is relatively higher than in some of the new member states. If labour costs are important to some investors, then Turkey will not qualify as their first choice for investing.

Table 3.47 Average mark-ups, Turkey and Belgium, 1997–2000 (%)

Products	Turkey (1999–2000)	Belgium (1997–1999)
Food and beverages, tobacco	60.62	24.72
Textiles, apparel and leather	49.42	37.38
Wood products	62.55	41.47
Paper, paper products	56.00	54.27
Chemical products	73.72	44.39
Non-metallic minerals	109.65	56.55
Basic metals	32.81	29.16
Fabricated metal	60.16	46.90
Other manufacturing	49.40	37.72

Source: Hoekman and Togan (2005: 117).

Table 3.48 Labour costs, EU and Turkey, 2004

Country	Income tax + social security contribution (% of labour cost)	Labour cost ($)
Austria	45	34,030
Belgium	55	43,906
Bulgaria	n/a	n/a
Cyprus	n/a	n/a
Czech Republic	43	18,631
Denmark	43	36,690
Estonia	n/a	n/a
Finland	45	35,513
France	48	32,856
Germany	51	42,197
Greece	35	20,570
Hungary	46	11,934
Ireland	24	27,775
Italy	46	35,709
Latvia	n/a	n/a
Lithuania	n/a	n/a
Luxembourg	32	37,573
Malta	n/a	n/a
Netherlands	36	36,019
Poland	43	16,268
Portugal	32	15,376
Romania	n/a	n/a
Slovakia	42	13,249
Slovenia	n/a	n/a
Spain	38	27,156
Sweden	48	33,345
United Kingdom	30	32,557
Turkey	42	17,367

Source: OECD (2006b).

Table 3.49 illustrates Turkish labour market flexibility as compared to EU member states. The higher the figure, the less the labour market is flexible. The OECD puts Turkey among the countries with the strictest labour regulations. The figure for Turkey relates only to the formal sector (industry and some services). The inflexibility of the labour market is one of the reasons for the existence of the informal sector (the rest of the services and farming). Yet, the new labour law (No. 4857) introduces more flexibility by providing a legal basis for 'atypical' employment contracts like part-time and fixed-term contracts (Hoekman and Togan 2005: 240). If Turkey adopts the *Acquis communautaire* in the field of social policy, labour costs in the formal sector will increase. This is even more relevant for the informal sector, estimated at employing some 40 per cent of the urban workforce. It is thought that a great deal of the informal sector's firms will not survive such a move.

Freedom of movement for workers

Free movement of workers is one of the four most contentious issues in the negotiations. In the 2006 Progress Report the Commission concludes the following: 'Limited progress has been achieved. Progress was mainly realized in the area of co-ordination of social security systems. Alignment is at an early stage. The administrative capacity needs to be strengthened' (CEC 2006a).

We would like to elaborate on this topic, as it is one of the most delicate in the file. First, we will give a short historical overview of the free movement of Turkish workers to the EU. Next, we will evaluate the current EU point of view with respect to the free movement. Thirdly, we will try to evaluate the number of Turkish workers ready to emigrate in the eventuality of free movement of workers.

Historical overview

In the early 1960s north-western Europe had to look beyond European borders at a time when countries like Italy, Spain and Greece could not supply enough labour for the expanding needs of its labour markets and the Iron Curtain made immigration from Eastern Europe impossible. Thus, Turkey became involved in

Table 3.49 Labour market flexibility, selected EU countries and Turkey, 2004 (indicators of flexibility)

Countries	Version 1	Version 2
France	3.0	2.8
Germany	2.5	2.6
UK	0.5	0.9
Italy	3.3	3.4
Poland	1.6	2.0
Turkey	3.8	3.5

Sources: Derviş *et al.* (2004b: 10); OECD (2006b).

massive unskilled labour migration to European destination countries (Burrell 2005b: 282). The first recruitment agreement for labour was signed with Germany in 1961. Subsequently Turkey also concluded agreements with the Netherlands, Belgium and Austria in 1964, with France in 1965 and with Sweden in 1967 (Üçer 2006: 205). The annual exit of Turkish migrants to Germany rose to 66,000 in 1964; 130,000 in 1970 and peaked at 136,000 in 1973. It is estimated that between 1.5 and 2 million Turkish citizens went abroad for employment between 1961 and 1973, equivalent to 40 per cent of Turkish men aged 20–39. In 1973 labour migration to West European countries stopped abruptly because of the oil crisis and its economic aftermath. At that time there were one million Turks on the waiting lists of the Turkish Employment Service (Martin, *et al.* 2002: 122).

Yet, migration did not come to a complete end. Under certain circumstances, family reunification and marriages with spouses from the countries of origin were still possible.[19] Existing networks of migrants attracted new immigrants from the same countries of origin. This explains why Turkish nationals constitute by far the largest group of third-country nationals in the EU (about 25 per cent of all third-country nationals). There are currently 3.5 million legal Turkish immigrants living in EU countries, mainly in Germany, Austria, France and the Netherlands (see Table 3.50).

EU point of view

Article 36 of the Additional Protocol provided for freedom of movement in favour of Turkish workers, which had to be secured by progressive stages between the end of the twelfth and the twenty-second year after the agreement had come into force. However, apart from stating the principle of non-discrimination, the Protocol remained silent on the implementation of this stipulation. According to the Commission, it was up to the Association Council to deal with all questions arising in connection with geographical and occupational mobility of workers of Turkish nationality, such as social security measures, aggregation of periods of insurance or employment with respect to old-age pensions, death benefits, invalidity benefits, family allowances and health services, transfer to Turkey of old-age pensions, death benefits and invalidity pensions (CEC 2006a). By referring to the decisions of the Association Council, the European Court of Justice enabled

Table 3.50 Turkish population, selected EU member states, 2001

Country	In thousands	As % of total foreign population
Germany	1,998.5	27.4
France	208.0	6.4
Austria	134.5	17.7
Netherlands	100.8	15.1
UK	58.0	2.2
Belgium	56.2	6.5
Denmark	35.2	13.6

Source: Hughes (2004: 17).

legally resident Turkish workers to enjoy certain rights, as becomes obvious in the following judgment:

> As the Commission has correctly pointed out, there is no reason to give a different interpretation from that applied in relation to the Treaty – which, moreover, has already been applied by analogy in relation to the agreement concluded with Turkey of the prohibition … of all discrimination based on nationality as regards conditions of work. (ECJ, 4 December 2001 (case C-465/01))

The Court was also very much opposed to any discrimination of Turkish workers. This becomes evident from the following judgment:

> A Turkish worker who has been legally employed for more than four years in a member state, who decides voluntarily to leave his employment in order to seek new work in the same member state and is unable immediately to enter into a new employment relationship, enjoys in that state, for a reasonable period, a right of residence for the purpose of seeking new paid employment there, provided that he continues to be duly registered as belonging to the labour force of the member state concerned … (ECJ 23 January 1997 (case 171/95))

The Court also took Turkish residents into protection when member states tried to expel them without giving them the right to appeal (ECJ, 18 March 2003(case C-136/03)). Yet the Association Council did not make any progress on the free movement of Turkish workers (Uğur 1999: 153). Turkey realized that it was only as a member state that its workers would be able to gain free access to the German labour market. Turkey followed a two-pronged approach. First in its National Programme for the adoption of the *Acquis communautaire* Turkey called upon the EU to approve new Association Council decisions that would permit Turkish citizens working legally and residing in member states to exercise the right to free movement without having to wait for Turkey's full membership (Republic of Turkey, n.d.).

In 2003 a directive in this sense was approved, not only in favour of Turkish nationals but also in favour of all third-country nationals (Council of the European Communities 2003). Since then the European Union has been able to grant European resident status to third-country nationals who have resided legally and continuously within the territory of the member states for five years on condition that they can prove that they have stable resources and sickness insurance for themselves and their family. In principle, persons who have acquired long-term resident status will enjoy equal treatment with nationals as regards:

- access to paid and unpaid employment, conditions of employment and working conditions;
- education and vocational training, and recognition of qualifications;

- welfare benefits and sickness insurance;
- social assistance;
- social benefits, tax relief and access to goods and services;
- freedom of association and union membership, and freedom to represent a union or association;
- free access to the entire territory of the member state concerned.

However, member states may restrict equal treatment with nationals in respect of access to employment and to education (for example, by requiring proof of appropriate language proficiency). In the field of social assistance and social protection, member states may limit equal treatment to core benefits. Turkey has mixed feelings about this directive. First, because it does not accord a privileged position to Turkish nationals; and, secondly, because it remains to be seen how this directive will be transposed into national law. In any event, for Turkey it represents just a first step on the road to complete free movement for Turkish workers into the EU.

As far as free movement of workers from Turkey is concerned, member states remain extremely reluctant. On the one hand, because of the ageing of the EU population and the slow growth in employment, the EU will have to attract workers from outside the Union. At first sight, Turkey's dynamic and youthful immigrants could rejuvenate the EU demographical structure (see Table 3.51). On the other hand, EU member states do not welcome Turkish immigration for several reasons:

- Demographic trends will probably see the Islamic population grow faster than the indigenous one in certain member states.[20] Several reports indicate that some members of the existing Turkish (and Maghreb) communities do not integrate well into mainstream society (Oskam *et al.* 2004: 20). According to Tekin (2005: 293), the integration of Turkish workers in Germany was impeded by sharp differences between Turkish and European cultural views on the roles of men and women, and 'by the deep significance of Islam in the daily lives of Turks'. At the same time, it has to be acknowledged that EU

Table 3.51 Demographic distributions of age groups, Turkey, 1980–2020 (% share in total population)

Age	1980	2000	2020
Below 15	18.1	19.2	16.3
15–24	8.8	13.2	11.6
25–49	12.2	23.2	31.3
50–64	3.6	6.4	13.0
65–79	1.6	3.4	5.4
80+	0.3	0.5	1.4
Total (million)	44.6	65.8	78.7

Source: Laciner *et al.* (2005: 101).

governments do not take many initiatives to integrate immigrants into main-stream society. Unfortunately, with anti-immigrant platforms that play on citizens' aversion to Muslims, far right parties are winning elections every-where in Europe.

- Since the year 2000 EU employment rates have grown slowly while unemploy-ment rates have stood at 8 per cent (see Tables 3.52 and 3.53). Unemployment rates are generally higher for foreigners than for nationals or EU citizens.
- A significant number of blue-collar workers are of foreign origin (see Table 3.54 with data for Belgium). EU firms cannot fill vacancies, because skilled workers are needed. Instead of granting unlimited access to its labour markets and recruiting workers from abroad, EU governments give priority to retraining long-term structural unemployed.
- Member states favour Germany's 'new guest workers policy'. From 1989 onwards, Germany concluded specific agreements with former East Bloc countries about the limited temporary employment of a quota of sub-contract workers in project-tied employment. Only a small number of Turkish workers qualified for this approach.
- The existing mechanisms for importing labour to supply European business work well enough. EU member states follow a restrictive quota-based immi-gration policy. The inflow of foreign workers is carefully monitored. Vacan-cies are offered to non-EU nationals only if EU nationals cannot fill them.

However, the population dynamics of Turkey could contribute to offsetting the ageing of EU societies. In this context, the EU should encourage Turkey to reform and to invest in its education and training system. Total factor productivity is substantially lower in Turkey than in the EU. This suggests that a more efficient use of resources already available in Turkey has the potential to reduce the income gap vis-à-vis the EU (Boeri and Brücker 2001: 4).

How many Turkish citizens would emigrate?

The Eurobarometer Opinion Polls reveal that unemployed Turkish citizens are on average more mobile than EU-15 and EU-12 citizens (see Table 3.55). They have the highest inclination to move and work in the EU, but when it comes to firm inten-tions they are overtaken by other states (see Table 3.56). In contrast to potential

Table 3.52 Employment growth, EU and Turkey, 1994–2005 (%)

Country	1994	1995	1996	1997	1998	1999	2000	2001	2002	2003	2004	2005
EU-15	−0.1	0.8	0.6	1.0	1.7	1.9	2.2	1.4	0.7	0.5	0.7	0.8
EU-25	n/a	n/a	0.7	1.1	1.6	1.3	1.6	1.3	0.5	0.4	0.6	0.8
Turkey	n/a	3.7	2.1	−2.5	2.8	2.1	−0.4	−1.0	−1.8	−1.0	3.0	1.2

Source: Eurostat (2006a).

Note
Figures for Turkey 2000–5 are forecasts.

Table 3.53 Unemployment rates by nationality, EU-15, 2005 (%)

Country	Nationals	EU nationals	Non-EU nationals
Belgium	7.7	10.3	33.6
Denmark	4.6	n/a	13.7
Germany	10.2	13.2	24.4
Greece	10.0	NA	8.2
Spain	8.9	8.4	11.9
France	8.6	7.2	24.8
Ireland	n/a	n/a	n/a
Italy	n/a	n/a	n/a
Luxembourg	3.3	5.5	12.0
Netherlands	4.4	4.9	17.8
Austria	4.4	8.3	13.1
Portugal	7.5	n/a	12.4
Finland	8.2	14.8	25.0
Sweden	7.4	8.8	22.5
UK	4.5	5.6	9.3
EU-15	7.8	9.5	17.5

Source: Eurostat (2006a).

migrants from other states, the majority of would-be Turkish migrants have only primary education (see Table 3.57). It seems that the higher the level of education, the smaller the number of Turkish citizens who have the propensity to emigrate.

Several research studies have been undertaken on pull and push factors encouraging Turkish immigration into the EU following the lifting of legal barriers to immigration. They vary considerably, because they are based on different methodologies, such as opinion polls, extrapolations from earlier south-north migrations and analyses of past migration episodes. There are factors and circumstances that encourage Turkish citizens to emigrate. For instance: the low level of GDP compared to the EU; the wage differentials; the modernization of agriculture making workers redundant; the high unemployment rate; the growth of the working age population; the existing networks in Germany; the repression in Turkey; the generous EU welfare systems and the lack of a safety net at home.

Table 3.54 Workforce distribution in Belgium according to occupational status, by country of origin 2002–3 (%)

Category	Belgians	EU citizens	Moroccans/ Turks
Workers	26	35	74
Employees	33	35	12
Public sector	26	13	6
Self-employed	13	15	7
Menial worker	2	2	1
Total	100	100	100

Source: Okkerse and Termote (2004: 30).

Table 3.55 Potential mobility in case of unemployment, EU and Turkey, 2002 (%)

Intention	EU-15	13 candidates	Turkey
Would stay	34	36	37
Would move	38	45	57
Depends	16	12	2
Do not know	12	7	4

Source: Eurobarometer (2004).

One should also take into account the fact that there is in Turkey large internal rural–urban migration. An important pull factor is the possibility for migrants to live in *gecekondu* (squatter settlements on the outskirts of the cities), which allows them to migrate without incurring large costs. De Santis finds that around 750,000 migrant workers could move from rural areas to cities. The number of migrants may be too large to be absorbed by the Turkish cities (De Santis 2003: 350). Emigration to the EU could then become an alternative. According to Martin, Midgley and Teitelbaum (2002: 124), Turkey has one of the fastest population growth rates in Europe, about one million a year, and a labour force that is growing by almost 900,000 a year. Turkey hopes that EU aid and investment can create jobs for a number of displaced workers and new labour-force entrants. However, the Turkish government also takes the position that full EU membership cannot be divorced from freedom of movement for workers. Surplus-labour has to be exported to the EU.

The Commission has reported that forecasts of immigration from Turkey into the EU-15 (until 2025/2030) range between 0.5 and 4.4 million (CEC 2004a: 19). Erzan, Kuzubas and Yildiz (2004:11) reach lower estimations. Assuming free labour mobility starting in 2015 and using different scenarios, their simulation results for net migration from Turkey into EU-15 in the period 2004–30 are between 1 and 2.1 million. However, EU-10 immigration into the UK, one of the three member states to open its labour market immediately in favour of workers from new member states, was much higher than expected.[21] If the higher estimate of the European Commission becomes real and if Turkish citizens will preponderantly emigrate to Germany and Austria, this might cause problems for these two countries. In Germany, the share of non-nationals in 2004 was 8.9 per cent, while in Austria it was 9.4 per cent. In

Table 3.56 Intention to emigrate, EU and Turkey, 2002 (%)

Intention	EU-10	Turkey
General inclination	3.1	6.2
Basic intention	1.3	0.8
Firm intention	0.8	0.3

Source: Eurobarometer (2004).

Table 3.57 Breakdown of persons having general inclination for migration, EU-10 and Turkey, 2002

Category	EU-10	Turkey
Primary education	4.5	37.2
Secondary education	29.3	23.1
Tertiary education	18.5	18.9
Still studying	47.6	20.7
All	100.0	100.0

Source: Eurobarometer (2004).

Germany, the largest group of non-nationals is of Turkish origin. In Austria, they are of Serbian origin (Eurostat 2006b).

Agriculture

Agriculture is another delicate item in the negotiations file. In the 2006 Progress Report the Commission's conclusion is rather pessimistic (CEC 2006a):

*   The alignment with the *Acquis* remains limited.
*   Delays on the adoption of the necessary legislation and administrative structures put the timely implementation of the Instrument for Pre-Accession Assistance for Rural Development (IPARD) seriously at risk.
*   Most administrative structures related to the CAP have not yet been established.
*   The trend towards increasing support linked to production goes against the direction of the 2003 CAP reform.

We will deal first with the structure of farming in Turkey, and then with the CAP. Thirdly, we will confront both.

Turkish farming

Contrasts between Turkey and the EU are significant (see Table 3.58). Historically, Turkey has helped farmers. In Atatürk's view (Republic of Turkey 1923), farmers had the right to more prosperity than anyone else:

> Our people experienced many sufferings ... But we still live on this land and there is one main reason for that: because Turkish farmers, while fighting

Table 3.58 Agriculture, EU and Turkey, 2004

Share of agriculture	EU-25	Turkey
Per cent of GDP	2.1	11.5
Per cent of employment	4.9	33.8

Source: Eurostat (2006a).

with their swords in one hand, kept on ploughing their land which they never left with the other. If the majority of our nation wasn't farmers, we wouldn't exist in the world today.

For Atatürk the foundation of the national economy was agriculture: 'For that reason we consider it most important to progress in agriculture. Planned training and applied studies that spread down to the small villages will help us reach this goal.' Small farmers had to be protected: 'There shouldn't be any farmer left without land in the country.'

The amount of land owned and the size of farms had to be limited on the basis of the population density and the level of soil fertility in the area. Increasing the output of the farming sector to the limit was the cornerstone of Atatürk's economic policy: 'We must make every effort to use and produce machinery and scientific instruments that will increase the output and productivity of farmers and to take economic measures to assure maximum benefit from it.'

These were not only empty words but also the practical guidelines of Kemalist policy in the early years of the republic. The tithe (a medieval tax-in-kind collected by tax-farmers) was abolished. The loss in public revenue was compensated by rising rates of indirect taxes on necessities (Boratav and Özugurlu 2006: 161). Yet, despite Atatürk's concern for farmers, the government failed to implement an extensive agrarian reform in his lifetime or thereafter. The big landowners exercised an important influence in the RPP. Pretexts such as the lack of regular land surveys and the priority of settling first the immigrants led to the repeated postponement of land reform. Finally, even the Land Reform Bill – voted in 1945 – was effectively blocked and considerably diluted with later amendments (Karpat 1968: 333; Buğra 2003: 457).

Even today, about half of Turkey's area of some 79 million hectares is devoted to agriculture. In 2001 the average size of farm holding was 6.1 hectares, and 83.4 per cent of farms had less than 10 hectares of land. Land-tenure-based large-scale capitalist farming (for instance, in the west of the country and the Black Sea region), or semi-feudal relations (for instance, in Middle Anatolia) are rather exceptional (Hoekman and Togan 2005: 40; Boratav and Özugurlu 2006: 186) (Table 3.59). The family-owned farm is the basic unit of agricultural production, and family members provide most of the farm labour. Labour productivity is low,[22] and only a small fraction of the production is put on the market. Salaried workers in agriculture make up about 5 per cent of agricultural employment. Half of the labour force shares the household income as unpaid family labour (Cakmak 2004: 1–6). A large part of agriculture is informal: more than 90 per cent of workers in agriculture are unregistered (Temel 2005: 264). An employment rate of more than 30 per cent in farming is extraordinarily high, not only compared with EU member states but also with countries of the same level of development as Turkey. Although the majority of its population has become urban, Turkey could still be considered a 'pastoral country' (Buğra 2004: 56). Some of the farming families immigrated into the cities, where they found refuge in the *gecekondu*. These

Table 3.59 Agricultural holdings and land engaged in crop production, Turkey, 2005

Size of holdings (decares)	Number of holdings	Total area (decares)	Average size of farm holdings (decares)
Less than 5	177,893	481,605	3
5–9	290,327	1,951,672	7
10–19	539,507	7,374,515	14
20–49	950,539	29,523,341	31
50–99	559,999	38,123,216	68
100–199	327,330	43,881,626	134
200–499	153,688	42,076,313	274
500–999	17,431	11,218,554	644
1000–2,499	4,198	5,476,930	1,305
2,500–4,999	222	695,541	3,133
5,000+	56	3,526,174	62,967
Total	3,021,190	184,329,487	61

Source: Hoekman and Togan (2005: 41).

were set up on public grounds, but the government looked the other way. The occupants of the *gecekondu* got financial and material aid from their families left behind on the countryside. This made it unnecessary for the government to provide any kind of social security. In recent years *gecekondu* have been bought up by real-estate agents. The government will no longer be able to avoid responsibility for city immigrants (Buğra 2004: 57).

There is a wide range of different farming activities, and Turkey is a major world producer (CEC 2004a: 30). Major product groups are dried fruits, edible nuts, spices and herbs, as well as fresh and processed fruits and vegetables. Turkey is self-sufficient as far as animal products are concerned and is able to export a large amount of crop products (Burrell 2005a: 165). Turkey is the largest producer and exporter of agricultural products in the Near East and North African region. Despite the overall trade deficit of Turkey, the agricultural trade balance is significantly positive. Until 2001 the government opted for protective trade policies combined with government procurement, input subsidies and heavy investment in irrigation infrastructure (Oskam *et al.* 2004: 10). The benefits of the subsidies went to larger farmers and the support system strained the budget.

Under IMF pressure, Turkey had to make its agricultural policies more market friendly (Cakmak 2004: 9; Hoekman and Togan 2005: 48). The Agricultural Reform Implementation Project of 2001–5 saw a change of direction for agricultural policy. The aim was to shift from a production and input-oriented support system to an income support system. Domestic prices were to be cut while farmers were encouraged to switch to alternative crops. Fertilizer subsidies were eliminated and output price supports were reduced. In 2002 the cost of agricultural transfers (subsidies and direct income support) was reduced by over 2.3 per cent of GDP. According to Lundell *et al.* (2004: p. vii), by international standards the magnitude of the fiscal adjustment from Turkish agriculture and its quality were impressive.

However, the institutional reform of State Economic Enterprises and state-controlled Agricultural Sales Cooperatives is difficult. In contrast to the EU, Turkey does not have a structural policy (Oskam *et al.* 2004: 12). According to OECD estimates, total support given to farmers remains high. In 2002 it was $7.7 billion, or 4.1 per cent of GDP (Hoekman and Togan 2005: 49). The combined share in the Producer Support Estimate in Turkey in 2001–3 of market price support, input and output payments was 85 per cent, compared to 69 per cent in the EU-15, the difference being due to the greater emphasis in the EU-15 on direct payments. In the view of the Commission, reforms have slowed down lately.

The EU Common Agricultural Policy (CAP)

Whereas the EU generally believes in free trade, the CAP is the exception to the rule. The CAP consists of twenty-one different common market organizations, each with their panoply of rules of application, price supports and mechanisms to protect European farmers against foreign competitors and to subsidize EU exports. On 26 June 2003 EU farm ministers adopted a – long overdue – fundamental reform of the CAP. Since then most farm subsidies have been switched to direct payments, not linked to production and therefore not trade distorting. In the near future all subsidies will be paid independently from the volume of production (CEC 2003a). Member states may choose to maintain a limited link between subsidy and production under well-defined conditions and within clear limits. However, the Commission wants the Single Payment Scheme to draw in 90 per cent of direct payments to farmers (Boel 2006). These new single farm payments will be linked to the respect of environmental, food safety and animal welfare standards ('cross-compliance'). Direct payments to larger farms will be reduced and rural development will be strengthened. The CAP has to become increasingly market oriented with lower support prices and income transfers decoupled from production quantities, but linked to (maximum) farm size. Although it is recognized that these reforms are for the better, further reform is necessary because of budgetary constraints, EU enlargement and WTO pressure. The WTO wants export subsidies to be eliminated and tariffs to be further cut.

The agricultural sector is left out of the customs union with Turkey. The EU abolished *ad valorem* tariffs on agricultural imports from Turkey and it reduced rates for some specific tariffs. Yet there remain high specific tariffs for many of the core CAP products, and an entry price is charged for some fruit and vegetables (Burrell 2005a: 163). Overall, EU farming protection remains high. The same holds for Turkey. Turkish preferences mainly consist of tariff rate quotas with no tariff. Moreover, Turkey has introduced an import ban on red meat, and it requires control certificates from EU importers. At the WTO, Turkey has faced complaints about using sanitary and phytosanitary regulations for protectionist purposes and with insufficient scientific justification. In recent years, Turkey achieved a significant trade surplus in agricultural products with the EU-25.

Turkey and the CAP

Agricultural policy was an important issue in the 2004 EU enlargement. According to Swinnen (2004: 1), there were four reasons for this. First, agriculture fell outside the trade liberalization. Secondly, agriculture was regulated within a complex framework of EU-led instruments. Thirdly, agriculture made up a large share of employment. Fourthly, the share of agricultural production in the CEEC compared to the EU was much smaller than the relative share of labour, or that of land. These four reasons are even more relevant in the case of Turkey.

The agricultural sector encompasses the largest area in terms of adoption of the *Acquis communautaire*. Turkey would need considerable time to make a number of agricultural sectors more competitive in order to avoid substantial income losses for its farmers. In its 2006 Progress Report the Commission makes it very clear that it will not be possible to implement the EU agricultural policy without establishing an adequate infrastructure that is in conformity with the CAP (CEC 2006a):

- The new Turkish legal system puts emphasis on increasing productivity and ensuring food supply and gives lower priority to food safety and consumer-related matters.
- The administrative capacity of the Ministry of Agriculture and Rural Affairs has not improved.
- The new law (2006) moves Turkey further away from the principles of the reformed CAP by defining support linked to production as a key instrument of agriculture policy.
- The National Farmers Register System is not compliant with EU regulations.
- There is no progress on the setting-up of the Farm Accountancy Data Network.
- There is only limited progress as to the alignment with the common market organizations.
- The IPARD Agency does not have a legal basis yet and thus cannot start its financial aid programme.
- There is no progress in the field of quality control.

Complicating the adoption of the *Acquis* by Turkey is the fact that the CAP itself is in the process of reform. Moreover, the result of the WTO negotiations will also be of importance. In the end, several effects must be considered:

- For those products where Turkey is a net importer (animal products, cereals and oilseeds), Turkey would lose because of paying a higher price for EU products (EU prices are well above world market prices). For those products where Turkey is a net exporter (fruit, vegetables, industrial crops, pulses) it would gain.
- For products where the EU is a net exporter and Turkey a net importer, additional trade could be directed to Turkey and vice versa.

- The Turkish government will lose tariff revenue but will not have to pay export subsidies any more. However, its direct payments to farmers will be higher, because they could ask for income compensation in case prices are lowered (Temel 2005: 253).[23]
- Because the EU common external tariff is on average lower than that of Turkey, imports from third countries might increase.
- Because of lower EU support prices in many sectors (see Table 3.60), consumers will benefit, and small farmers might be squeezed out of the market. There will be income transfers from rural to urban groups (Cakmak 2004: 29).
- Today's CAP favours products of Northern and Eastern Europe (wheat, meat, milk and so on) over Mediterranean products (olive oil, wine, tobacco and so on) (Kafyeke 2006: 14). It is to be expected that Turkey will use its influence to change these rules.

The inclusion of Turkey into the CAP will have consequences for the EU budget. Table 3.61 summarizes the results of different studies. If the estimate of the European Commission proves to be accurate, about 5 per cent of the EU budget will be spent annually on Turkish farming. Taking into account the EU commitment to bringing down agricultural spending by means of a budgetary review in 2008, it is hard to see how countries like Poland and Turkey will receive what they think is their due.[24] However, one should not forget that these numbers depend to some extent on political negotiations on how much subsidy Turkey will get. In addition, one has to take into account that Turkey will contribute to the EU budget.

According to the Food and Agricultural Organization (FAO), with or without EU membership, Turkey should proceed further towards liberalization of agricultural trade. Turkey's first best solution is free trade instead of including agricul-

Table 3.60 Farm gate prices, Turkey and the EU, 2002–3

Product	Turkey (Euros per ton)	EU (Euros per ton)	Turkey/EU (%)
Wheat	158	119	132
Barley	143	105	136
Corn	144	133	108
Sunflower seed	360	270	133
Tobacco	3,254	2,102	84
Beef	2,868	2,410	119
Lamb	3,564	3,948	90
Poultry	1,198	948	120
Milk	257	315	82
Butter	6,280	3,282	191
Poor milk powder	4,300	2,055	209
Eggs	1,220	927	129
Sugar	599	712	84

Source: Grethe (2004: 158–9)

Table 3.61 Budgetary impact of Turkish membership as a result of the inclusion of Turkey into the CAP

Studies	Billion Euros
Hoekman and Togan (2005: 67)	1.196–2.999
Oskam *et al.* (2005a: 236)	3.392–4.218
CEC (2004a: 34)	5.960

ture in the customs union agreement with the EU (FAO 1999: 68; Grethe 2004: 173). Besides measures directly targeted at improving competitiveness of Turkish farmers, there need to be economic development and diversification in rural areas (CEC 2004a: 33; Oskam *et al.* 2004: 17).

Regional policy and coordination of structural instruments

Regional Policy is another difficult issue in the enlargement file. In the 2006 Progress Report the Commission concludes the following (CEC 2006a):

- Progress was made in adapting the legal framework and in the definition of regional structures for the implementation of regional policy.
- However, the role and functioning of these agencies require attention.
- There has to be a repartition of competences between ministries at both central and regional level.
- Preparation of programming documents for the implementation of the Instrument for Pre-Accession Assistance (IPA) should be accelerated.
- Overall, Turkey's alignment with the *Acquis* is modest.

In the view of the Commission, the main problem for Turkey in this field is of an institutional kind. The relevant law only came into force in February 2006. The agency to be set up in twenty-six regions will be staggered over a period of several years. The institutional framework and the administrative capacity remain weak. There are no structures, such as an interministerial coordination body in relation to regional development. However, some progress could be reported with respect to programming, monitoring and evaluation, which prove that the Turkish government attaches a growing importance to the regional perspective in the developmental context.

We will deal first with the EU Regional Policy. Next, we will briefly discuss regional inequalities in Turkey, which will enable us to evaluate the cost of including Turkey in the EU Regional Policy.

The EU regional policy

Like the CAP, EU Regional Policy is in evolution. Yet general principles remain the same. Council Regulation (EC) No. 1083/2006 (Council of the European Communities 2006b) lays down general provisions on the European Regional Development Fund (ERDF), the European Social Fund (ESF) and the Cohesion

Fund. The regions eligible for funding from the Structural Funds (ERDF plus ESF) are regions whose GDP per capita is less than 75 per cent of the average GDP of the EU. Member states eligible for funding from the Cohesion Fund are those whose GNI per capita is less than 90 per cent of the average GNI of the EU (the so-called EU-15 'poor four': Greece, Spain, Ireland and Portugal plus the EU-12). The funds provide assistance that complements national actions (co-financing), including actions at the regional and local levels, integrating them in EU priorities. Objectives are:

- convergence;
- regional ability to compete and employment;
- European territorial cooperation.

Total resources available for commitment from the funds for the period 2007–13 are 308.041 billion Euros, or on average 44 billion Euros annually. This amount will be broken down as follows (Council of the European Communities 2006b):

- 70.51 per cent for regions essentially located in the EU-12: the lion's share of the money;
- 23.22 per cent for the 'poor four' and the EU-12;
- 6.28 per cent for regions and member states that would have been eligible had the thresholds not changed because of the 2004 accession of new member states (in diplomatic terms this is called 'the statistical effect': essentially regions located in East Germany and the Mediterranean member states).

To control the absorption capacity of regions, the maximum level of transfer from the funds to each individual member state is limited to 4 per cent of GDP. Separate funds were allocated in favour of the EU-15 (239 billion Euros over the period 2000–6) and in favour of the EU-10 (40 billion Euros) (Hillyard and Barclay 1998: 29).

Regional inequalities in Turkey

The level of welfare in Turkey is not distributed equally across regions. Two regions, the Aegean and the Marmora region, are much richer than the rest of Turkey (see Table 3.62). There is a significant east–west division in Turkey, with the main centres of economic activity located in the western part of Turkey (see Table 3.63). Turkey demonstrates huge regional income inequality when compared to EU-25 countries. Table 3.64 shows the average GDP per capita level of Turkey, as well as the poorest and its richest regions compared to the EU-15 and the EU-25 per capita averages. Inequality of GDP per capita across regions is very high in Turkey. This has significant implications for structural policy in an enlarged EU. The inclusion of Turkey would seriously increase the socio-economic disparities across the EU. The changes that would be brought about by Turkey's accession to the EU are illustrated in Table 3.65.

Table 3.62 Regional disparities, Turkey, 2000

Region	Population (million)	Per capita GDP in % (Turkish average = 100)
Mediterranean	8.7	94
East Anatolia	8.1	28
Aegean	9.0	130
South-east Anatolia	6.6	54
Central Anatolia	11.6	97
Black Sea	8.4	76
Marmara	17.3	153

Source: Lejour *et al.* (2004: 23).

Budgetary impact

In case of accession to the EU, the entire territory of Turkey will fall under objective 1. Even the richest regions fall below the 75 per cent of EU GDP average, and the Turkish GNI is less than 90 per cent of the EU GNI per capita. Because the annual average EU per capita income will fall by about 2,520 Euros (at 2004 values and standardized purchasing power), some EU-27 regions will lose their eligibility because of the lowering of the EU average GDP level.

Oskam, Longworth and Vilchez (2005a: 238) have calculated that the total population of regions losing eligibility for the convergence regions under objective 1 is thirty-three million: twenty-seven million in the EU-15 and six million in the new member states. The potential 'statistical effect' of Turkish accession seems to be much larger than that experienced in the 2004 and 2007 enlargement. According to the Commission, per capita payments under objective 1 amounted in 2002 to 217 Euros per inhabitant. Under that assumption, Turkey would receive about 14.6 billion Euros. Yet transfers from the Structural Funds and Cohesion Fund cannot exceed 4 per cent of GDP. For Turkey, that requirement is binding. Therefore, payments could not exceed 8,664 billion Euros, and only when the Turkish government is ready to co-finance projects (Hoekman and Togan 2005: 69). Lejour, de Mooij and Capel (2004: 36) find almost the same figure: eight billion Euros a year. Oskam, Longworth and Vilchez (2005a: 238) find higher figures (in 2004 prices): 9.5 billion to 16.6 billion Euros in case of central growth projections, 8.3 billion to 14.5 billion Euros in case of lower economic growth for Turkey, 11.9 billion to 20.8 billion Euros in case of higher exchange rate for Turkey. In its Progress Reports the Commission hesitates to make predictions: 'The existing rules have never been applied to a country of similar size, similar

Table 3.63 East versus west, Turkey, 2003 (%)

Region	Share of population	Share of GDP	GDP/head (Turkey = 100)
East	37	22	60
West	63	78	123

Source: CEC (2004a: 40).

Table 3.64 GDP per capita levels in Turkey in relation to EU averages, 2003 (%)

Region	In relation to EU-15	In relation to EU-25
Poorest NUTS II Region's GDP per capita (Van)	9.5	11.5
Richest NUTS II Region's GDP per capita (Kocaeli)	42.5	52.0
Turkey average	28.5	35.0

Source: Republic of Turkey, Prime Ministry (2003).

level of economic development and similar intensity of regional disparities' (CEC 2006a).

Yet the 2025 transfers that the Commission computes are not very different from the ones found by Oskam, Longworth and Vilchez. Based on continued real annual GDP growth of 4–5 per cent, they would amount to just over 5.6 billion Euros (2004 prices) for each one percentage point of Turkey's GDP granted in regional aid. This means that about 6.5 per cent of the 2007 budget allowances would go to Turkey. Still the Commission adds that 'Structural Funds alone are not sufficient for catching-up if the economic policy framework is inadequate' (CEC 2004: 40).

Financial and budgetary provisions

In the 2006 Progress Report the Commission deals only with the necessity for Turkey to adopt the *Acquis communautaire* with respect to the EU common resources: 'Turkey will need to establish in due course the coordination structures and implementing rules to ensure the correct calculation, collection, payment and control of own resources as well as reporting to the EU for implementation of the own resources rules' (CEC 2006a).

In the Progress Reports, the Commission does not deal with the budgetary impact of the Turkish accession on EU resources. By virtue of the Negotiating Framework, the negotiations can be concluded only after the establishment of the Financial Framework for the period 2014–20, together with possible consequential financial reforms. It is clear that the EU fears the financial consequences of Turkey's accession to the EU: 'Any arrangements should ensure that the financial

Table 3.65 Impact on the EU of enlargement with Turkey, 2004

Impact	EU-27 +Turkey
Increase in surface (%)	18.0
Increase in population (%)	15.0
Increase in total GDP (%)	2.2
Change in per capita GDP (%)	–9.1
Average per capita GDP (EU-15=100)	79.4

Source: CEC (2004a: 38).

burdens are fairly shared among all member states' (Council of the European Communities 2006a).

Turkey will have to contribute to the EU budget in the form of VAT-based and GDP-based contributions. Financial and budgetary provisions are directly linked to the agricultural and structural appropriations Turkey will get. Several studies have tried to quantify Turkey's net receipts from the EU budget (see Table 3.66). The results differ in accordance with the assumptions put forward. Will the existing rules with respect to the CAP and Structural Policy be applied to Turkey or will budget appropriations be in the same order as the EU-12, irrespective of the appropriations Turkey would be entitled to in theory? As structural appropriations are related to economic growth, at what rate is the Turkish economy going to grow in years to come? How is the exchange rate of the Turkish lira going to evolve?

As for the EU readiness to pay, the 2007 budget foresees total revenue of about 126.5 billion Euros. Turkey's share in EU allocations would be between 7 and 18.50 per cent. As a share of the total EU budget, payments to Turkey will be substantial, almost equal to what all of the EU-12 combined will receive. Discussions among member states over whether the EU budget should be limited to 1 or 1.045 per cent of GDP show that even small sums can have a considerable political impact. In times of serious budget constraints and economic problems, it is almost certain that member states will not be ready to cough up an amount equal to 7 per cent let alone 18.50 per cent of the budget. Moreover, member states must comply with the Maastricht convergence criteria (Hillyard and Barclay 1998: 24) and in view of the EU's ambitious Lisbon strategy (March 2000) – becoming the world's most competitive knowledge economy in 2010 – they prefer to invest in R&D. Today only a tiny fraction of the EU budget is spent on projects that might further the Lisbon Agenda. Almost half of the budget is devoted to agriculture and one-third goes to structural policy (*The Economist* 2007a). The bottom line is that member states are selfish and want their contributions to the budget roughly to equalize their appropriations. This is contrary to the principle of solidarity: one of the core values on which the EU was founded. Since the accession of the UK to the EC, the budget has been one of the main bones of contention among member states. The net payers, the Netherlands, the UK, Germany, Austria, Sweden and France, want to revise the budgetary rules before any new (poor) member state joins the EU. Only significant reforms of the CAP and the Structural Funds could help finance the costs of accession within the present ceiling. It remains to be seen whether member states like France in the case of the CAP or Spain in the case of the Structural Funds will accept such reforms. These two countries will request

Table 3.66 Budgetary impact of Turkish accession on EU, 2015 (billion Euros)

Studies	Annual budget appropriations for Turkey
Hoekman and Togan (2005: 69)	7.756
Oskam *et al.* (2005a: 249)	10–26
Derviş *et al.* (2004a: 4)	15
Hughes (2004: 21)	13.63
Griffiths (2004: 189)	6.4–8.12

appropriate compensations and the Nice treaty requires unanimity in the Council for the CAP or Structural Policies to be fundamentally amended.

Still it is good to emphasize that prediction in the budgetary field is highly hypothetical. Budgetary appropriations in favour of Turkey will be calculated with the system existing at the time of accession, not with rules existing for the EU-27 (Kafyeke 2006: 13). Budgetary problems in the EU will complicate the possibility of Turkey receiving the kinds of pre-accession funds that the CEEC received. Without such funds, it will be much more difficult for the government to mobilize the public support that will be necessary for pushing through expensive reforms. When reforms do not take place, Turkey will be unable to harmonize its legislation in line with the *Acquis communautaire*. In case certain benchmarks are not met, EU member states will block negotiations on these chapters. This will play into the hands of those in Turkey who oppose membership (Kirişçi 2006: 55–6). It will put the Turkish government in an awkward position. One can only regret the way EU member states are behaving. Taken at face value, even the maximum EU payment (26 billion Euros) to Turkey is relatively small when compared to national budgets of EU member states. Take, for instance, Belgium, France and Italy. Government expenditures in 2005 were respectively: 149 billion Euros (50 per cent of GDP); 922 billion Euros (54 per cent of GDP); 688 billion Euros (48 per cent of GDP). The 26 billion Euros pale into insignificance when compared to the total of twenty-seven national budgets.

Foreign, security and defence policy

By virtue of the Negotiating Framework, Turkey has to align its policies progressively toward third countries with the policies and positions adopted by the EU. The opening statement with respect to the chapter on the Common Foreign and Security Policy (CFSP) in the 2006 Progress Report sounds upbeat: 'Turkey has broadly continued to align its foreign and security policy with that of the EU. The regular enhanced political dialogue established as part of the accession strategy with Turkey has continued' (CEC 2006a).

However, upon reading the rest of the chapter, it becomes clear that certain problems remain. We will first deal with the CFSP of the EU. Secondly, we will discuss the foreign policy of Turkey. In the third part, we will confront both.

The Common Foreign and Security Policy (CFSP)

Since the Treaty on the European Union entered into effect (1 November 1993), the EU has been able to assert its identity on the international scene. Article 11 of the Treaty reads as follows (EU 2002):

1   The Union shall define and implement a common foreign and security policy covering all areas of foreign and security policy, the objectives of which shall be:

- to safeguard the common values, fundamental interests, independence and integrity of the Union in conformity with the principles of the United Nations Charter;
- to strengthen the security of the Union in all ways;
- to preserve peace and strengthen international security, in accordance with the principles of the United Nations Charter, as well as the principles of the Helsinki Final Act and the objectives of the Paris Charter, including those on external borders;
- to promote international cooperation;
- to develop and consolidate democracy and the rule of law, and respect for human rights and fundamental freedoms.

2   The member states shall support the Union's external and security policy actively and unreservedly in a spirit of loyalty and mutual solidarity. The member states shall work together to enhance and develop their mutual political solidarity. They shall refrain from any action which is contrary to the interests of the Union or likely to impair its effectiveness as a cohesive force in international relations.

The Treaty gives the EU the opportunity to formulate common positions and to engage in joint actions. This has not always been easy, because intergovernmental cooperation still characterizes the so-called second EU pillar. Faced with a foreign-policy problem requiring quick action, a traditional state is more effective at reacting, given the greater simplicity in its policy-making process (Emerson and Tocci 2004: 8). Member states want to reach unanimous consensus. This leads to inefficient decision making whenever fundamental national issues are at stake – as, for example, in the 1990s with respect to the Balkans or in March 2003 with respect to the American invasion of Iraq. Nevertheless, progress has been made. It is generally agreed that the voting behaviour in the UN General Assembly (GA) is a clear expression of a given state's foreign policy orientation (Aral 2004: 138). Participation in the EU has led to an increasing Europeanization of member state foreign policies, as voting patterns in the General Assembly of the UN reflect. According to Young and Rees (2005: 206), cohesion among EU-15 member states has risen significantly since the early 1990s, following the Maastricht treaty and the introduction of the CFSP. Cohesive voting on average between 1990 and 2002 was at 68 per cent compared with 41 per cent for the 1980s.[25] This does not mean that EU member states are always on the same line as regards foreign policy. In matters where sovereignty is at stake they go their own way, without caring too much for common positions or joined actions.

The basic tenets of the gradually emerging CFSP seem to be the following:

- The EU relies far more on its economic and political influence and appeal than on its military powers (Park 2005: 133).
- The EU has a high esteem for international law, the UN and multilateral institutions (Tekin 2005: 290; Young and Rees 2005: 207).

- The EU considers conflict resolution and good neighbourly relations as prime security objectives.
- The EU believes in multilateral peaceful diplomacy based on voluntary cooperation between UN member states (for example, its two international pet projects: the Kyoto Protocol and the International Criminal Court statute).
- The doctrine of respect for human rights takes precedence over the doctrine of non-interference in domestic affairs.
- The EU offers its mediation services in international conflicts; in case of good behaviour, countries can count on EU economic help (for example, the Association and Stabilization Pacts with the Balkans countries or the Good Neighbourhood Policy devised for countries like Morocco, Israel, Georgia, Moldova and Ukraine that hope to but cannot join the EU).
- Accession candidates have to resolve outstanding difficulties with neighbours before they can accede to the EU.
- In case of violation of borders or infringement of human rights, military action is allowed but only under the auspices of the Security Council of the UN and after all diplomatic channels have been probed.
- In case of military conflicts, there has to be close cooperation between the EU, NATO and other international organizations in order to bring about the end of hostilities as quickly as possible.
- For its military operations, the EU will rely on NATO assets and capabilities.[26]
- The EU plays an active role in post-conflict peace-building efforts by giving aid to refugees, monitoring ceasefires, training police forces, organizing elections, setting up institutions, taking part in international peacekeeping forces, administrating areas, and so on (these are called the Petersberg tasks).

Turkey's foreign policy

Turkish foreign policy is based upon the following principles:

- opening up to the world as a result of the economic transformation Turkey has been through since the 1980s;
- non-interference in the domestic affairs and respect for the territorial integrity and national sovereignty of other countries;
- good neighbourly relations with countries in the Middle East and Central Asia;
- promotion of Western interests in the Eastern Mediterranean and Middle Eastern regions by portraying itself as a strategic corridor for the supply of energy and collective defence in the framework of NATO against common enemies.

In the following, we will deal with each of these basic tenets.

Under Turgut Özal Turkey has become an export-oriented economy. Therefore, good relations with surrounding regions have been of vital necessity. This open relationship with neighbouring countries – linked as it is to the increasing democratization process in Turkey itself – has needed a specific kind of foreign policy. In contrast with only a decade before, Turkish foreign policy has became less confrontational and less centred on national security (Kirişçi 2006: 16).

Secondly, it is clear that, throughout its voting patterns in the General Assembly of the UN, Turkey has demonstrated its attachment to the doctrine that states are the supreme sovereign in their territory. Turkey voted in favour of self-determination only in so far as it applied to colonial or foreign occupation regimes. Yet it did not favour self-determination to minorities in sovereign states (Aral 2004: 142). Whereas in the 1970s and 1980s Turkey condemned the violation of human rights in countries like Chile or South-Africa, in the 1990s condemnation of human-rights violations in most developing countries did not receive support from Turkey. Turkish delegates sometimes preferred not to vote at all on alleged human-rights violations in (Muslim) countries (see Table 3.67). Apparently, Turkey feared setting precedents for interference in its own domestic affairs. Claims of Turkish ill-treatment of the Kurdish minority might have led to the possibility of Turkey's own condemnation by the General Assembly. Notwithstanding its military alliance with Israel, Turkey voted in the UN for all the resolutions in favour of the Palestinians. It also supported countries favouring the Turkish occupation of Northern Cyprus (Müftüler-Bac 1996: 259).

As for the third objective, Turkey's geopolitical location determines its foreign and security policy choices. The end of the cold war opened up new horizons for Turkish foreign policy in the Caucasus, the Middle East and Central Asia. Turkey wants good relations with both the Middle East and Central Asia, thereby competing with both Iran and Russia. Turkey has economic interests in the Middle Eastern markets, both as a net importer of crude oil and as an exporter to the Middle Eastern countries. Since 1976 it has belonged to the Islamic Conference. However, its real influence in the Arab world should not be overrated. Its 1996 military alliance with Israel,[27] its particular brand of Islam, its different race and language, and the fact that it is the successor state of the Ottoman Empire – the erstwhile colonizer of the Arab world – are all factors that undermine its position. One of the reasons why part of the Turkish elite is keen on EU membership is to prove that Turkey is different from the Arab world. Nor are Arab countries altogether likely to regard Turkey as a model for their own development (*The Economist* 2004b). Turkey pursues an independent policy in the Middle East. In contrast with the USA, it favours cooperation with Iran and Syria, because these two countries also have to cope with a Kurdish minority that wants a Kurdish state.

Turkey's foreign and security policy also focuses on the South Caucasus and the Central Asian Republics. In the territory of the old Turkistan, which stretches from the Balkans to the Chinese province of Xingjian, live about 160 million people speaking languages related to Turkish. Turkey shares with these countries not only a common language, but also a common history, a common religion and a common culture. Yet irredentist Pan-Turkish feelings are weak in today's Turkey. Kemalism is polycentric in character, while Pan-Turkism is an essentially ethnocentric ideology. Modern Turkey opens up to the world, while Pan-Turks emphasize

Table 3.67 How UN member states voted on human-rights resolutions, 2005

Country	North Korea	Iran	Uzbekistan	Turkmenistan	Congo	Sudan*
Austria	Yes	Yes	Yes	Yes	Yes	No
Belgium	Yes	Yes	Yes	Yes	Yes	No
Bulgaria	Yes	Yes	Yes	Yes	Yes	No
Czech Republic	Yes	Yes	Yes	Yes	Yes	No
Cyprus	Yes	Yes	Yes	Yes	Yes	No
Denmark	Yes	Yes	Yes	Yes	Yes	No
Estonia	Yes	Yes	Yes	Yes	Yes	No
Finland	Yes	Yes	Yes	Yes	Yes	No
France	Yes	Yes	Yes	Yes	Yes	No
Germany	Yes	Yes	Yes	Yes	Yes	No
Greece	Yes	Yes	Yes	Yes	Yes	No
Hungary	Yes	Yes	Yes	Yes	Yes	No
Ireland	Yes	Yes	Yes	Yes	Yes	No
Italy	Yes	Yes	Yes	Yes	Yes	No
Latvia	Yes	Yes	Yes	Yes	Yes	No
Lithuania	Yes	Yes	Yes	Yes	Yes	No
Luxembourg	Yes	Yes	Yes	Yes	Yes	No
Malta	Yes	Yes	Yes	Yes	Yes	No
Netherlands	Yes	Yes	Yes	Yes	Yes	No
Poland	Yes	Yes	Yes	Yes	Yes	No
Portugal	Yes	Yes	Yes	Yes	Yes	No
Romania	Yes	Yes	Yes	Yes	Yes	No
Slovenia	Yes	Yes	Yes	Yes	Yes	No
Slovakia	Yes	Yes	Yes	Yes	Yes	No
Spain	Yes	Yes	Yes	Yes	Yes	No
Sweden	Yes	Yes	Yes	Yes	Yes	No
Turkey	Yes	Absent	Yes	Absent	Yes	Absent
United Kingdom	Yes	Yes	Yes	Yes	Yes	No

* A yes vote was a vote to block consideration of a resolution on the violation of human rights in Sudan.

Source: Democracy Coalition Project (2005).

the unification of all Turks in one state (Landau 1981: 182). Pan-Turkism has failed to engage state support and appeals only to extreme right-wing intellectuals. In contrast with other 'Pan' movements (like Zionism, Pan-German, Pan-Italian, Pan-Arab, Pan-African and Japan's Greater East Asia Co-prosperity Zone), it has never been a mass movement in Turkey. Its proponents are found in certain non-governmental organizations such as the Nurcu sect and in the National Action Party (Landau 1981: 185; Larrabee and Lesser 2003: 124). Turkey's links with former parts of the Ottoman Empire, such as the Balkans or along the shores of the Black Sea, are much stronger than those of the Central Asian republics. Because of the migration patterns of the last two centuries, nearly a third of the Turkish population has family roots in these areas (Zürcher 1997: 339).

This does not mean that Turkey did not see opportunities for special relations with the South Caucasus and Central Asia after the fall of the USSR. Communism had kept these countries away from Turkey. Some considered Trans-Caucasia and Central Asia as a power vacuum to be filled either by Iran or by Turkey (Faucompret 2002: 508). Turkey was the first country to establish diplomatic relations with Azerbaijan, Kazakhstan, Uzbekistan, Kyrgyzstan and Turkmenistan. In the excitement of the moment, President Özal talked about the coming of a 'Turkic century in an area stretching from the Adriatic to the Chinese Wall' (Zürcher 1997: 335; see also Krekeler-Joeris 1996: 1). Also some Central Asian politicians, like Askar Akajew, then president of dirt-poor Kyrgyzstan, favoured Turkey's presence – hoping to get large financial aid. (Turkey was called 'the morning star that showed the Turkic republics the right way' (Krekeler-Joeris 1996: 1).) In 1992 Prime Minister Demirel travelled to the region, thereby promoting Turkey's economic and political model. His aims were obvious: by appealing to common interests, Turkey could secure its supply of energy and bring these countries into the Western hemisphere away from Iran. Perhaps Turkey would be able to link Central Asia and the EU through technical, economic and financial assistance, thereby promoting Turkey's own chances for EU membership and enhancing its appeal to the USA. The US Congress even funded Turkish development projects in the Central Asian Republics. Turkey concluded over 300 military, technical, cultural and other agreements with these countries. Many joined business ventures set up by Turkish entrepreneurs. Turkey opened up cultural centres; it established scholarship programmes and it expanded its broadcast programmes (Larrabee and Lesser 2003: 100).

However, many of these initiatives came to nothing. Turkey does not have the necessary economic resources for this kind of policy. When a large number of people at home live below the minimum subsistence level, when social security is sub-par and when a country is beset with domestic problems, it is hardly feasible to invest in prestige projects abroad, the merits of which are highly debatable. Thus, Turkey is far from being a leader in the Turkic-speaking world of Central Asia. Turkey overestimated the economic potential of these new states, which were in the process of nation building and did not want to substitute one colonizing country for another. The Central Asian republics are coping with economic and political problems of their own, making them less reliable trading partners for Turkey. Moreover, the Turkish model of Muslim secular democracy did not appeal to authoritarian presidents who praise the nation state (Krekeler-Joeris 1996: 13–14; Larrabee and Lesser 2003: 101; Larrabee 2004: 127). Some of the leaders of the Central Asian republics have imperialistic designs. For instance, Islam Karimov, the ambitious president of Uzbekistan, considers his country to be the natural leader of the people living in Uzbekistan, Kyrgyzstan and Tajikistan (Faucompret 2002: 514). Finally, Russia perceived the Turkish (and Iranian) policy as a clear threat to its own interests. For Russia, the South Caucasus and Central-Asia are part of the so-called near abroad. Diplomatic relations with these countries are different from the ones between Russia and other countries. In Russia's view, international law does not govern relations with the member states of the Commonwealth of Independent States (CIS). They are too special for that. The economies and the transport and communication networks between Russia and the CIS members date from the past and are still very strong. Reliance on Russian imports, Russian minorities and Russian troops in certain countries remind the leaders of the Central Asian republics of their dependence on Moscow's goodwill. If their leaders do not behave, it is always possible that regions inhabited by Russian immigrants secede from the rest of the country and that Russian troops will protect them, as has happened with Moldova (Transdniestria) and Georgia (South Ossetia and Abkhazia). Russia remains a much greater economic and military power than Turkey ever hopes to be. Last but not least: some of these leaders wanted to create direct links with the USA without needing proxies like Turkey (Müftüler-Bac 1996: 265; Zürcher 1997: 337; Tibi 1998: 3–4; Wilkens 1998: 46–7). In case of trouble, Turkey can always be called in at a later stage.

Fourthly, Turkey's foreign policy aims at increasing the perception of its strategic value in the eyes of the West. It did so during the cold war (Zürcher 1997: 287). Now, with the cold war gone and the USSR disappearing from the geopolitical scene, Turkey's strategic value to the West has faded. Therefore, Turkey seizes every opportunity to show that it defends Western values in a dangerous environment. Under Özal's impulse – and contrary to the generals' wishes – Turkey was a member of the US-led coalition to liberate Kuwait in August 1990–February 1991,[28] and it played a critical role in launching Operation 'Provide Comfort' in April 1991, which made possible a speedy repatriation of almost two million refugees to Northern Iraq (Zürcher 1997: 333; Waxman 1998: 15). Before 1990 Iraq had been Turkey's first trading partner (Larrabee and Lesser 2003: 134). The UN embargo and the eventual removal of Saddam Hussein from power have cost Turkey a lot. It lost income from the pipelines, it had to accommodate refugees and, in the aftermath of the war, the Kurds rose up again. The West did not sufficiently appreciate Turkey's contribution to the war effort.

By the same token, Turkey emphasizes its strategic importance in the oil diplomacy of the West. It is sitting on pipeline connections between the EU and the gas- and oil-rich Caspian, thus opening up alternative routes for oil and gas producers to the routes through Russia. Therefore, Turkey was one of the driving forces behind the so-called International Energy Charter, signed in Lisbon on 17 December 1994 by EU member states, the members of the CIS (though not Russia and Turkmenistan) and some other Western states.[29] Two pipelines were opened: one linking Tabriz (Iran) with Erzurum (Turkey) and one linking Baku (Azerbaijan) and Ceyhan (Turkey). There are further plans on the drawing board: a Baku–Erzurum gas pipeline, a pipeline linking Italy to the Turkey–Greece pipeline, a pipeline linking Turkey and Greece to the Balkans and a pipeline linking Egypt to EU member states (CEC 2004a: 26; Roberts 2004: 19).

Last but not least, when dealing with Turkey's foreign policy, one should keep in mind that Turkey is not a politically stable country. Forming a government in Turkey has often involved as many as three parties, and it has always required the consent of the military. It is a common phenomenon in international relations that weak governments often screen their domestic problems outward in order to rally the nation behind the politicians. This is no different in Turkey. For instance, in 1998 Turkey threatened to declare war against Syria unless it gave up its decade-old support for the PKK, and it stopped providing its leader, Abdullah Öcalan, with accommodation. In 2000 Turkey prevented the US Congress from adopting a resolution condemning the Armenian genocide by threatening not to renew the mandate of Operation Northern Watch from the Inçirlik air base. On several occasions Turkey has successfully communicated to Greece that actions such as the deployment of Russian-made missiles in Cyprus (1998) or the extension of Greek territorial waters could provoke war. In the 1996 Imia/Kardak crisis, Turkey managed to challenge the Greek ownership of two uninhabited Aegean islets (Loizides 2002: 436).

Turkey and EU Common Foreign and Security Policy (CFSP)

Turkey straddles three areas of strategic importance to the EU: the Balkans, the Caspian region and the Middle East (Larrabee and Lesser 2003: 2). For the EU, an internally strong and confident Turkey could be a factor of stability and a positive counterbalance to the anti-Western mood in these unstable regions. A weak and divided Turkey is not in the interest of the EU: it might be caught up in border conflicts, thereby threatening the stability in the EU itself (Wilkens 1998: 15). There is no denying that an EU plus Turkey would increase the credibility of the CFSP. In the period 1995–2005 Turkey has emerged as an important regional actor in the Middle East. This growing involvement represents an important shift in Turkish policy. Under Atatürk – and for several decades after his death – Turkey avoided involvement in the Middle East, but since Erdoğan came to power Turkey has been engaged in the region (Larrabee and Lesser 2003: 3). Turkey played a moderating role in regional conflicts. It mediated between Israel and the Palestinians, between Israel and Syria and between Iran and EU member states in the nuclear crisis. It provided observers for the multinational force in Hebron and it contributed to the monitoring of elections in Palestine and elsewhere in the Middle East (Kirişçi 2006: 75, 87). In the Balkans Turkey took part in UN Peacekeeping Missions in Bosnia and Kosovo. In December 1992 it sent a military unit to support UN operations in Somalia. Because of Turkey's unique position, Israel, as well as Islamic and Western countries, requested its participation. Turkey cannot but enhance the EU reputation of being a soft power in the world trying to avoid conflicts. In the 2006 Progress Report the Commission noted with satisfaction that Turkey adopted the EU position in the following fields (CEC 2006a):

- the non-proliferation of weapons of mass destruction and the EU Codes on Arms Exports, Small Arms and Light Weapons;
- the Middle East peace process;[30]
- EU policy on Iraq, Iran, Lebanon and Afghanistan;[31]
- the EU Neighbourhood Policy versus Central Asia and the Southern Caucasus;
- the conventions on the suppression of terrorism.

However, in the Commission's view, Turkey aligns itself with significantly fewer EU declarations than other acceding and associated countries (CEC 2004a: 10–11). Turkey prioritizes regional and bilateral relations. Turkey does not like to delegate sovereignty to supranational EU organs in Brussels, for it has become independent less than a century ago in a bloody war of independence against some of the countries that are now EU members (Oğuzlu 2003: 293). Turkey has still not signed the Kyoto Protocol or the statute of the International Criminal Court. Many fear that a European Union with Turkey would be too diverse to act coherently on the world stage. The EU would become 'a colossus resting on clay footings': geographically large, but politically incapable of action (Murphy 2004: 586). We could ask ourselves whether this disadvantage would be compensated for by strategic advantages attached to EU membership of Turkey. We will first deal with the energy issue; next, we will discuss the security issue.

First, would Turkey's accession help to secure better energy supply routes for the EU? The EU currently imports more than 50 per cent of the energy it consumes (see Table 3.68) (Suárez de Vivero and Rodriguez Mateos 2006: 168–9). It is expected that in 2030 this share will increase to 70 per cent. The problem of EU security in energy supply is a matter of the availability of crude oil and gas. EU oil is almost exclusively imported from the Middle East and North Africa (45 per cent and from Russia (25 per cent) and the CIS (18 per cent). Natural gas is almost exclusively imported from Algeria (30 per cent), Russia (40 per cent) and Norway. In the future, Azerbaijan and the Central Asian Republics could play a role. In that case, the territory of Turkey could become important for the transport of crude oil and for pipelines to carry oil. Turkey is not itself a producer of oil or gas, but it is important for Western oil and gas companies. Pipelines running through Turkey could significantly reduce EU dependence on Russia (Wilkens 1998: 48; Mãné-Estrada 2006: 3783). Russian behaviour vis-à-vis other countries during the past few years (such as Ukraine, Georgia and Belarus) speak volumes in this respect. In the past Turkey has proved to be a far more reliable ally than Russia. Therefore, the EU would like to include Turkey in the Caspian–Europe Natural Gas Pipeline Project as well as in the South European Gas Ring. In late June 2006 the EU and a number of governments on the route of the pipeline signed a declaration

Table 3.68 Primary energy dependency, EU-25, 1990–2030

EU-25	1990	2030
Production (mtoe)	877.84	660.00
Total net imports (mtoe)	708.96	1,371.6
Oil imports (%)	71.65	48.26
Gas imports (%)	17.40	37.38
Total consumption (mtoe)	1,533.01	1,968.40
Oil consumption (%)	38.23	34.82
Gas consumption (%)	16.69	32.00

Source: Mãné-Estrada (2006: 3774).

Note
mtoe = million tons of oil equivalents.

of intent, lending political support to the eventual construction of the pipeline (Kirişçi 2006: 86).

Yet, though Turkey's importance in this should not be denied, neither should it be overrated. The development of pipelines requires significant investments. Oil companies are looking for the most profitable opportunities. For the time being Turkey cannot compete with Russia (Öğütçü 1995: 54, 58). European companies invest heavily in Russia's oil and natural-gas sectors, in exchange for guaranteed increased supplies to European markets. The Russian Federation is bound to become the first gas supplier of the EU (see Table 3.69).

Turkey's involvement in the Caucasus and Central Asia has complicated relations with Russia and has given the historical rivalry between the two countries new impetus (Larrabee and Lesser 2003: 5). Russia does not support any competition. From the four Caspian basin states, only Azerbaijan relies on Turkey (Roberts 2004: 20). Pro-Russian leaders rule most of Central Asia. Turkmenistan, Kazakhstan and Uzbekistan remain heavily dependent on existing Russian pipelines (Öğütçü 1995: 47). Russia's natural-gas monopoly, Gazprom, controls the gas pipelines that link Europe with Central Asia. When Turkmenistan signed a deal with Turkey to export natural gas to Turkey and from there to the West, Gazprom simply blocked the deal by cutting off gas exports to Turkmenistan (Wilkens 1998: 50). On the other hand, Turkey and Russia are important economic partners. Russia is Turkey's second trading partner. Turkish domestic oil production accounts for just 18 per cent of its demand. Natural gas accounts for only 3 per cent. Oil accounts for 65 per cent and gas for 20 per cent of domestic consumption (Larrabee and Lesser 2003: 129). To meet its energy needs, Turkey has, with Russia, constructed the Blue Stream gas pipeline under the Caspian. Turkey relies very heavily on third countries for its gas consumption: two-thirds is imported

Table 3.69 Gas export potential to EU, 2000–30 (%)

Country	2000	2010	2030
Russia	53.06	41.93	31.70
Norway	20.41	20.96	19.02
Algeria	24.49	18.87	18.23
Libya	0.41	2.31	5.55
Iran	0.00	2.10	4.75
Azerbaijan	0.00	3.14	4.75
Egypt	0.00	2.52	3.96
Nigeria	0.41	3.14	3.17
Iraq	0.00	2.10	3.17
Qatar/UAE/Yemen	0.82	1.89	2.54
Trinidad	0.41	1.05	1.58
Turkmenistan	0.00	1.05	1.58
Total (bcm)	245.00	477.00	631.00

Source: Mãné-Estrada (2006: 3783).

Note
bcm = billion cubic metres.

from Russia and the rest mostly from Iran. In the winter of 2006 Turkey had trouble with gas supplies from both Russia and Iran. Therefore, it decided to go nuclear. Turkey's first nuclear power plant will be constructed in Sinop on the Black Sea (Kirişçi 2006: 72). Turkey has opposed plans to expand trans-Russia pipelines to the Black Sea and it has obstructed any increase in supertanker traffic through the crowded Bosporus Strait (Öğütçü 1995: 54). In March 2007 an agreement was signed between Bulgaria, Greece and Russia to build the Burgas–Alexandroupolis pipeline, thereby avoiding Turkish territory. In conclusion, we can say that – although Turkey is not irrelevant – Russia seems more important for the EU to secure its energy supply. This is certainly not in the EU's long-term interests. A pro-Western Turkey, Georgia and Azerbaijan are far more advantageous to the EU than dependence on Russia.

Secondly, will Turkey make the EU Security Policy more credible? In the 2006 Progress Report the Commission notes the following (CEC 2006a):

- Turkey is strongly interested in the European Defence and Security Policy (EDSP).
- Turkey's participation in several UN and NATO peace missions in the Balkans continues.

Turkey occupies a strategic position in the Black Sea. Turkey is still able to contain Russia (Dahlman 2004: 568). It has the second largest standing army (after the USA) in NATO[32] with combat experience and the fourth largest military industry (after the USA, the UK and France). NATO, especially the USA, uses the Inçirlik Air Base (near Adana). Table 3.70 shows NATO military expenditure on equipment in 2005 and 2006. Turkey is the fifth largest spender on military equipment (after the USA, France, the UK and Germany). This is amazing in view of the fact that it is has by far the smallest GDP per capita of all NATO member states.

In December 2001 the EU decided to make operational the Political and Security Committee as well as the Military Committee, both core institutions of the future European Rapid Reaction Force.[33] The decision meant that the EU would have an authority and ability to launch humanitarian interventions and peace-keeping operations and to manage conflicts in low-intensity crises. The EU did not consider the creation of a European army with war-fighting capabilities and capable of being deployed in any part of the world. In the EU view, the sources of new threats to European security are in the unstable regions along the peripheries of Europe (Oğuzlu 2003: 288; Güney and Karatekelioğlu 2005: 454). Special modalities had to be worked out for cooperation with NATO in EU-led operations (Missiroli 2002: 10; Oğuzlu 2003: 289).

While other South European countries have welcomed the EU's development of a stronger security component, Turkey's attitude has been much more hesitant (Larrabee and Lesser 2003: 65). At first Turkey decided to block EU–NATO negotiations. It dreaded the idea of the EU playing a role in matters of defence if it was not included in the EDSP itself. Turkey fears the EU engaging in mili-

Table 3.70 NATO military expenditure on equipment, 2005–6 ($m.)

Country	2005	2006
Canada	1,563.0	1,779.0
USA	123,491.0	128,932.0
Belgium	268.0	234.0
Bulgaria	111.0	94.0
Czech Republic	258.0	248.0
Denmark	388.0	585.0
Estonia	24.3	32.6
France	11,285.0	12,556.0
Germany	5,396.0	5,550.0
Greece	1,032.0	1,050.0
Hungary	135.0	127.0
Italy	3,049.0	2,350.0
Latvia	17.6	35.9
Lithuania	46.6	59.0
Luxembourg	27.9	21.4
Netherlands	1,528.0	1,770.0
Norway	1,029.0	1,169.0
Poland	808.0	1,063.0
Portugal	280.0	378.0
Romania	394.0	468.0
Slovakia	122.0	134.0
Slovenia	48.6	70.4
Spain	2,880.0	3,255.0
Turkey	3,074.0	3,901.0
UK	11,149.0	11,859.0

Source: SIPRI (2007).

tary operations in neighbouring countries without (sufficiently) taking Turkey's geopolitical interests into account. Moreover, Turkey fears Greece and Cyprus influencing EU decision making contrary to its interests. The EU reassured Turkey that it would be brought into consultation at an early stage ('decision-shaping' process). In addition it would be an equal member of 'a committee of contributors' to any military operation. At first Turkey vetoed the EU use of NATO assets and capabilities unless it was included in the EU Security 'decision-making' process (*The Economist* 2000b). Since the European Council of Copenhagen (December 2002) and the so-called Berlin-plus-arrangement, Turkey has lifted its veto on EU recourse to NATO assets, and for Turkey to contribute to EDSP missions. Yet Turkey continues to block Cyprus and Malta participation in EU–NATO strategic cooperation. This is in clear violation of the Negotiating Framework:

> Turkey will be required to align its positions within international organiza-
> tions (including in relation to the membership by all EU member states of
> those organizations and arrangements) with the policies and positions adopted
> by the Union and the member states. (Council of the European Communities
> 2006a)

Sceptics believe that this episode demonstrates the scope for increased EU–Turkish tension. First, Turkey put no trust in the EU. It is hardly thinkable that other EU member states would not counteract Greece and Cyprus and explicitly act against Turkish security interests. Almost all the national forces and capabilities committed to the European Rapid Reaction Force are 'double-hatted' – that is, answerable both to the EU and to NATO (Missiroli 2002: 18). Secondly, Turkey's conduct has raised a problem of political style. European policy making requires a certain degree of willingness to compromise. Turkey has yet to deliver on this (Missiroli 2002: 19). Thirdly, Turkey made it explicitly clear that the EU's evolving security structure has to develop in close cooperation with NATO (Oğuzlu 2003: 297). Even if the US war on Iraq (2003) has pushed Turkey closer to the EU, it confirmed for the sceptics that Turkey would function as a new US 'Trojan horse' inside the EU if it were a member (Park 2005: 135; Önis and Yilmaz 2005: 266).[34] Turkey has always been a major and consistent strategic partner for the USA. Since 1969 the Defence and Cooperation Agreement has been renewed: Turkey's strong defence capacity has been acquired entirely with the help of the USA. Diplomatically the USA has supported Turkey in such important areas as its bid for EU membership, its struggle with the PKK, the construction of the Baku–Ceyhan pipeline and its financial needs during economic crises (Larrabee and Lesser 2003: 68, 164; Cohen 2004: 577–8; Önis and Yilmaz 2005: 271; Somer 2005: 112). You do not bite the hand that feeds you.

In February 2003 the latent divergence of views between the EU and Turkey came to a head. The USA and Turkey asked for the deployment of AWACS to protect Turkish territory against a possible Iraqi invasion. France, Germany and Belgium blocked this deployment – in clear violation of article 4 of the NATO Charter – fearing it could undermine UN efforts to avoid a war in Iraq. (In the end NATO did approve the deployment, but only for 'defensive purposes'.) One month later, EU leaders issued a stiff warning to Turkey not to dispatch troops to Northern Iraq. The EU spoke plainly: such an operation would further complicate Turkey's bid for EU membership (Tüsiad 2003). On the other hand, Turkey did play a significant role in the so-called Istanbul Cooperation Initiative launched by NATO in June 2004 (Kirişçi 2006: 80). The aim of the initiative was

> to enhance security and regional stability through a new transatlantic engagement with the region. This could be achieved by actively promoting NATO's cooperation with interested countries in the field of security, particularly through practical activities where NATO can add value to develop the ability of countries' forces to operate with those of the Alliance including by contributing to NATO-led operations, fight against terrorism, stem the flow of Weapons of Mass Destruction materials and illegal trafficking in arms, and improve countries' capabilities to address common challenges and threats with NATO. (NATO 2004)

If Turkey could play this role in the context of the EDSP, its inclusion into the EU would be a valuable asset. However, as long as Turkey is not included as a full partner in the EDSP, the USA will remain Turkey's key partner in the defence area (Larrabee and Lesser 2003: 170). One can hardly blame Turkey for this. The country is in a weak geo-strategic position. In an era of nuclear proliferation, with countries like Pakistan already having nuclear weapons and Iran wanting to acquire them – both of which are in Turkey's immediate neighbourhood – Turkey has to rely on the American nuclear umbrella for its protection. Turkey's difficult geographical situation is worsened by its internal domestic problems and the diverging views of politicians and generals on foreign policy. The EU's lukewarm support for its membership application does not help either. The alignment of Turkey with the EDSP will take time, but, if it succeeds, it will be one of the strategic advantages attached to Turkey's EU membership.

Justice, freedom and security

In the 2006 Progress Report the Commission concludes the following (CEC 2006a):

- Overall, some progress can be reported, particularly in the areas of asylum, border management and the fight against trafficking in human beings, customs and police cooperation.
- Alignment with the *Acquis* is under way but considerable and sustained efforts are required in areas such as migration, the fight against organized crime, money laundering and judicial cooperation in civil and criminal matters.

We will first deal with the growing *Acquis communautaire* in this field. Then we will discuss shortly problems typical of Turkey. Finally, we will evaluate progress made.

Growing Acquis communautaire

While Justice and Home Affairs were still called 'the third pillar' in the Maastricht treaty, the EU introduced the concept of the 'Area of freedom, security, and justice' in the Amsterdam Treaty. Certain issues linked to Justice and Home Affairs (external border controls, visas, free movement of persons, judicial cooperation in civil matters and fight against illegal immigration) were carried from the third pillar into the first (articles 61 to 69 of the Treaty Establishing the European Community), which made Community decision making possible. Other issues are not part of Community decision making: cross-border police cooperation, judicial cooperation in penal matters ... they are in part 6 of the Treaty on the European Union. At the European Council of Tampere (1999), EU member states recognized

> the need for approximation of national legislations on the conditions of admission and residence of third country nationals, based on a shared assessment of the economic and demographic developments within the EU, as well as the situation in the countries of origin. (Conclusions of the Presidency 1999a)

The key point is that EU member states cannot determine their own conditions for the admission of third-country citizens if they are operating in a single unified labour market (Piracha and Vickerman 2001: 2). Since 1999 EU decisions have been made in the fields of visa policy, political asylum and combating illegal immigration. In these areas, the *Acquis communautaire* is continuously growing:

- *the Schengen regulation*: entry into the Schengen zone constitutes admission into the whole Schengen territory and control is shifting to the EU outer borders;[35]
- *the Prüm treaty* (also called Schengen 2): police forces of participating countries exchange information;[36]
- *the Dublin treaty* (negotiated outside the EU framework): the first country into which asylum-seekers enter the EU (because they have a visa or they cross the border) has to deal with the asylum application;
- *judicial cooperation*: mutual confidence on the judicial systems of other member states;
- *the battle against corruption, fraud and drugs*: there has to be cooperation between police forces of participating member states.

EU standard policy is to require all newly acceding states to apply these arrangements in full upon accession. Opt-out clauses modelled on those for the UK, Ireland and Denmark are no longer available.

Problems for Turkey

Turkey has 2,627 kilometres of land borders and 8,333 kilometres of coastal borders. Only 475 kilometres of land borders would be internal EU borders after Turkish accession. Turkey also has several international airports and seaports. Turkey's geographical location between poor countries and Western Europe, accompanied by a relatively large informal economy, makes it an attractive country for illegal migrants and for traffickers in human beings (Apap *et al.* 2004: 17). Moreover, the absence of visa requirements and the practice of the so-called visa stickers[37] make it relatively easy to cross the Turkish borders, while Turkey denies non-European refugees the right of asylum.[38] Under growing EU pressure, and only in 2000, was Turkey ready to sign Readmission Agreements with certain third countries.[39]

Turkey attracts illegal immigrants from Afghanistan, Iraq, Iran, Sri Lanka, Pakistan, Egypt and Bangladesh (Laciner *et al.* 2005: 113; Oskam *et al.* 2005a: 221; see also Table 3.71).

Turkey and the area of justice, freedom and security

The Negotiating Framework stipulates the following:

Table 3.71 Illegal migrants captured in Turkey, most frequent countries, 2000–3

Nationality	2000	2001	2002	2003
Afghanistan	6,805	8,948	3,992	1,162
Bangladesh	2,910	1,438	1,782	954
Iraq	13,833	17,717	19,449	1,523
Iran	3,887	2,215	1,892	908
Pakistan	4,286	4,642	4,667	4,716

Source: Laciner *et al.* (2005: 120).

> With regard to the area of freedom, justice and security, membership of the EU implies that Turkey accepts in full on accession the entire *Acquis* in this area, including the Schengen *Acquis*. However, part of this *Acquis* will only apply to Turkey following a Council decision to lift controls on persons at internal borders, taken on the basis of the applicable Schengen evaluation of Turkey's readiness. (Council of the European Communities 2006a)

When will Turkey be ready? The EU is expecting Turkey to adopt a series of measures to enhance the protection of its borders, thereby disregarding particularities of the Turkish case (Apap *et al.* 2004: 23):

- Turkey has to sign a multilateral Readmission Agreement with the EU and bilateral Readmission Agreements with all relevant countries.
- Turkey has to intensify border controls and to adopt restrictive policies vis-à-vis illegal migrants.
- Turkey should put all the neighbouring countries on the EU 'negative visa list' and stop issuing 'visa stickers'.
- Turkey should lift the geographical limitation in the Geneva Convention on the Status of Refugees.
- The Commission makes it very clear that Turkey will have to finance these measures itself, since 'only minor parts can be financed by EU Funds' (CEC 2004a: 42). Turkey only gets EU financial and technical aid that is typically offered to 'third countries'.

Implementing these measures would represent a major shift in Turkey's immigration policy (Kirişçi 2003: 91; Özcan 2005: 95). After the two deadly terrorist attacks in Istanbul (November 2003) Turkey did adjust its visa policy to EU standards.[40] Other positive measures are mentioned in the 2006 Progress Report (CEC 2006a):

- A National Action Plan towards the implementation of Turkey's Integrated Border Management Strategy was adopted in March 2006.
- A National Action Plan on Asylum and Immigration is being implemented.
- Some progress has been achieved in the field of asylum.
- There is some progress in the field of police cooperation and the fight against organized crime.

- Progress has continued in the field of trafficking of human beings.
- Limited progress has been achieved in the fight against money laundering, the fight against drugs and the fight against terrorism.
- Some progress has been made in the field of customs cooperation.
- Limited progress has been made in the field of judicial cooperation in criminal and civil matters.

Overall, for the EU these measures do not go far enough. On the one hand, Turkey lacks the institutional and administrative capacity to go any further. On the other hand, Turkey does not seem ready to comply with all the EU demands. It wants the EU to take into account its specific geographical position and its economic, political and cultural interests in good neighbourly relations with other states. Irregular immigration involving nationals of befriended neighbouring countries and transit migrants is important for Turkey. A large number of people from Russia, Ukraine and Iran are involved in so-called suitcase trade,[41] business contacts, tourism or scientific contacts (Apap *et al.* 2004: 19, 28). The EU should not hinder the movement of persons with close cultural and linguistic ties between Turkey and its neighbours. Turkey points to the 2006 Progress Report: the Commission itself had to admit that, in 2005, Turkey apprehended 57,428 illegal immigrants (CEC 2006a). Moreover, Turkey is not the main entry point from the entire global south of Europe. Many Eastern European countries share borders with Russia; Greece is the traditional entry point for illegal immigrants arriving from the Middle East; France and Italy have settled illegal migration routes because of their former colonial ties. Turkey also refers to human-rights organizations that have repeatedly criticized EU member states for restrictive practices. EU policy acts as a barrier against asylum-seekers who have a valuable case. The main tendency has been to implement policies against illegal migration and human trading without presenting any legal alternatives, and, consequently, to violate the right of protection, transportation and 'non-refoulement',[42] which was given to asylum-seekers by the 1951 Geneva Convention (Özcan 2005: 107, 109). The conditions made by the Commission are, in Turkey's view, over the top. The twelve new member states did not have to sign multilateral Readmission Agreements with the EU before accession. Apparently, the EU's main concern is to keep illegal immigrants out and to shift the burden as much as possible to Turkey. Turkey could thus easily become a dumping ground for rejected asylum-seekers and economic refugees.

Unfortunately, the Commission does not see things eye to eye with Turkey. We think that here, as well as in the CFSP and in other areas, the Commission is too strict. Given time, technical assistance and money, Turkey will be better able to cope with the growing *Acquis communautaire* in this area.

Education and culture

In its 2006 Progress Report the Commission notes 'good' progress in the area of education, training and youth for the following reasons (CEC 2006a):

- Turkey has been participating successfully in Community Programmes such as Leonardo da Vinci, Socrates and Youth.
- Turkey has started to participate in the Education and Training 2010 Work Programme Coordination Group.
- Progress has been made in increasing enrolment ratios at all educational levels and a well-publicized girls' education campaign has had success.
- Revised curricula for primary as well as vocational education are being implemented, and Turkey is participating in the development of a European Qualifications Framework.
- Progress has continued in the implementation of the Bologna process in higher education.
- Turkey has started in the Community Programme 'Culture 2000'.

Unfortunately, one swallow does not make summer. People taking part in programmes such as those mentioned above are those who are cosmopolitan and in favour of EU membership. It is much more difficult to reach ordinary Turkish citizens. The hearts and minds of those Turkish citizens have yet to be converted to Europeanism. Opinion polls do not seem to justify entirely the Commission's optimism. Whereas 71 per cent of Turkish citizens think that EU membership is a good thing, only 48 per cent tend to put trust in the EU (see Tables 3.72 and 3.73).

EU opponents of Turkey's membership argue that Turkey is not of Europe: it does not share Europe's cultural identity. The Christian and the Renaissance ideals characterize Europe's cultural identity. According to the first, men live in accordance with the teachings of Jesus Christ to be rewarded in heaven. In accordance with the second, men try to reach the limits of their physical and mental abilities. Opponents of Turkey argue that Christian teachings and rationalist tradition are strange to Turks, who are Muslims (Littoz-Monnet and Villanueva Penas 2005: 7). Proponents ask for tolerance. Turkey is a proud country that has never been colonized and that in the recent past has not suffered military defeats. The state has never lost its legitimacy for the majority of its citizens. Turkey's independence was won in a struggle against the great powers of Europe (Keyder 2006: 74). Turks criticize their country but at the same time they take pride in what modern Turkey has realized (Wetenschappelijke Raad voor het Regeringsbeleid 2004: 161). For Turkish citizens it is not yet clear how they can reconcile their national identity with a European one that most of the population does not understand. But it also took time in EU member states for public opinion to become conscious of its European identity. One can even say that European integration has been very

Table 3.72 Support for EU membership, EU and Turkey, 2004 (%)

Support	EU-15	EU-10	Turkey
A good thing	48	43	71
A bad thing	17	16	9

Source: Eurobarometer (2004).

Table 3.73 Trust in EU membership, EU and Turkey, 2004 (%)

Trust	EU-15	EU-10	Turkey
Tend to trust	42	40	48
Tend not to trust	42	37	36

Source: Eurobarometer (2004).

much a matter that concerned only the cultural, political and economic elite of member states and that public opinion was left in the dark. When public opinion was asked to give its advice on a matter of European integration, the result was often negative, as in the French and Dutch rejections of the Constitutional Treaty, or the Danish rejection of the Maastricht treaty.

Table 3.74 shows that national pride is on average no stronger in Turkey than in other EU member states. However, in marked contrast to the EU-10, whereas 86 per cent of Turks feel very or fairly proud of Turkish citizenship, only 47 per cent feel very or fairly proud of European citizenship (Table 3.75). The three most widespread fears in Turkey with respect to the EU are abandoning the language, the end of national currency and loss of national identity and culture (see Table 3.76). This differs completely from the answers in other member states, where the problems for farmers, the increase in organized crime and the accession costs are the most frequently cited concerns. Turkish support for the Euro is weaker than it is in the EU-10, while – amazingly – support for the Constitutional Treaty is higher (see Tables 3.77 and 3.78).

Whereas the Central and East Europeans were driven by the desire to 'return to Europe' and feared return of Soviet domination, for most of the Turks membership is not about European identity. What Turks hope for are personal benefits, such as higher incomes, better jobs and the freedom to travel and to work in the EU (Barysch 2005: 3). As one would expect the opinions of the Turkish elite are different from those of average public opinion. Lauren McLaren (2000: 126) interviewed businessmen, academics, politicians and journalists. Tables 3.79 and 3.80 group the results of these interviews. To the question what would be the best thing about membership, the general emphasis in the responses was on economic and social development. The importance of the establishment of European credentials was the second most frequent response. Somewhat surprisingly, political and legal aspects of full membership were not emphasized very much. When interviewees were asked about the worst thing about being admitted, the most frequent response was that there would be no harm at all, followed closely by expressions

Table 3.74 National pride, EU and Turkey, 2004 (%)

Pride	EU-15	EU-10	Turkey
Very/fairly proud	85	85	86
Not very/not at all proud	11	12	8

Source: Eurobarometer (2004).

Table 3.75 European pride, EU and Turkey, 2004 (%)

Pride	EU-15	EU-10	Turkey
Very/fairly proud	62	79	47
Not very/not at all proud	27	11	42

Source: Eurobarometer (2004).

Table 3.76 Three most widespread fears connected to EU, Turkey and new member states, 2004

Country	Crime	Costs	Farmers	Loss of culture	Jobs	Currency	Language
Bulgaria	X	X	X				
Czech Republic	X	X	X				
Estonia	X	X	X				
Cyprus	X			X	X		
Latvia	X	X	X				
Lithuania	X	X	X				
Hungary		X	X			X	
Malta	X		X		X		
Poland	X	X	X				
Slovenia	X	X	X				
Slovakia	X	X	X				
Romania	X	X				X	
Turkey				X		X	X

Source: Eurobarometer (2004).

Table 3.77 Support for the Euro, Turkey and the new member states, 2004

Support	EU-10	Turkey
For	67	43
Against	18	50
Undecided	15	7

Source: Eurobarometer (2004).

Table 3.78 Support for the Constitutional Treaty, Turkey and the new member states, 2004

Support	EU-10	Turkey
For	63	70
Against	10	16
Undecided	27	14

Source: Eurobarometer (2004).

Table 3.79 Perceived benefits of Turkey's admission to the EU, 2000

Benefit	%
Economic/social development	49
European credentials established	23
Democratization/human-rights improvement	12
Legal system reorganized	5
Technological improvement	4
No benefit	4
Other	3
Total number of responses	77

Source: McLaren (2000: 126).

of concern for potential economic difficulties. Contrary to the public opinion, only a small minority expressed concern over the loss of national sovereignty and the traditional values and norms.

Before accession, there was in the CEEC strong cross-party consensus that EU membership was a good thing. In Turkey the consensus is much weaker and nationalist voices are much louder (Barysch 2005: 4). Results seem to indicate that Turkish public opinion is split on the EU accession. A recent survey of Turkish public opinion asked whether respondents belonged most to the East (Asia + Middle East) or the West (Europe + Balkans + Mediterranean): 40 per cent identified more with the East and 41 per cent with the West (Hughes 2004: 23). A recent study by Bosporus University found that more Turks are defining themselves by their religion than by their nationality; 45 per cent said they were 'Muslims first' and 19 per cent said they were 'Turkish first' (Matthews 2006). Apparently, there is, on the one hand, an intense desire to be part of the West, as Atatürk taught the population. On the other hand, there is a need to deny the common culture and to define its Turkishness (Keyder 2006: 75). A 2006 public-opinion survey showed 63.1 per cent of public opinion still in favour of membership, but at the same time 50.3 per cent believed that the EU aimed at harming Turkey by aspiring to split it up (Kirişçi 2006: 54).

Those in Turkey who are opposed to EU membership step up the nation-

Table 3.80 Perceived costs of Turkey's admission to the EU, 2000

Cost	%
No harm at all	29
No harm beyond the customs union	3
Economic harms	27
Loss of national sovereignty	17
Deterioration of traditional values and norms	6
Deterioration of religious values	5
Other	11
Total number of responses	63

Source: McLaren (2000: 126).

alist rhetoric: membership will imply the loss of national identity, of Islam, of Turkish dignity and even of Turkish soil. The EU requests Turkey to recognize the Armenian genocide, to grant independence to the Kurds and to get out of Cyprus. According to Devlet Bahceli, leader of the Nationalist Action Party, 'the EU project is a treacherous plan to weaken, divide, and disintegrate Turkey' (Matthews 2006).

The Nationalist Action Party promised its electorate to undo 'anti-Turkish' human-rights legislation pushed by Brussels when it comes to power. The nationalist civil movement has found its representative in Kemal Kerincsiz, a lawyer who opposes free speech. He has figured prominently in a number of high-profile free-speech cases, including the prosecution of Orhan Pamuk, Turkey's best-known author and Nobel Prize winner in literature. Commission Progress Reports and negative comments by conservative European politicians and scholars are playing into the hands of EU opponents. Since 2002 a stream of EU personalities have made it clear that they are against Turkey ever joining the EU. Take, for instance, Convention president Valéry Giscard d'Estaing's declaration (in November 2002): 'Turkish membership of the EU would spell the end of the European Union', or that of the president of the European People's Party, Wilfried Martens: 'Turkey has no place in Europe' (Müftüler-Bac 2005: 161).

Directly related to these declarations was the attempt by the Vatican and by Europe's Catholics to get a reference to the Christian values of European civilization into the EU Constitutional Treaty or the French parliament's action to make it a crime to deny the 1915 Armenian genocide. The perception in Turkey is that the EU is piling on big demands but offering little in return (*The Economist* 2006f).

Conclusion

The following conclusions can be drawn from the preceding:

- The EU wants Turkey to adopt the complete *Acquis communautaire* before its accession. This is a very harsh condition other candidates did not have to comply with in the past. Turkey has tried to comply, showing that its bid for membership is serious and that it realizes this is the price to be paid.
- Progress has been made in all the fields related to the customs union.
- In other areas, insufficient progress is caused mainly by the lack of administrative and institutional capacity. Turkey is doing its best to meet deadlines. Yet the lack of moral and material support from the EU does not make it easy for the Turkish government to comply with EU wishes.
- The integration of Turkey in the CFSP and in the Home Affairs and Justice Policy is important for the EU but at the same time it is made difficult because of conflicting visions.
- Public opinion in Turkey has not yet been sufficiently prepared for EU membership. Anti-Europeanism seems to be on the rise.

The Copenhagen economic criteria: general conclusions

From the preceding, we can draw the following conclusions:

- Turkey's market economy is functioning relatively well. The reform process has borne fruit: it has resulted in more liberalization, deregulation and privatization, less state intervention and more equal conditions of competition. A lot remains to be done, but Turkey is well on its way in transforming its economy. To solve problems like unemployment, inflation, exchange-rate fluctuations, state deficit and foreign debt, the government will have to commit itself to further reform, thereby taking the advice of both the IMF and the European Commission. This will not be easy for the government because it is consistently criticized by the opposition and because it has to retain the support of the electorate.
- In the medium run, Turkey will be able to cope with competition within the EU. Thanks to succeeding reform programmes its economy has become more robust during recent years. Its economy is well integrated with the EU. It will be better prepared for the EMU than some of the new member states.
- After a transition period Turkey will be able to adopt most of the *Acquis communautaire*. However, Turkey's inclusion in some chapters of the *Acquis* (free movement of workers, CAP and Regional Policy) might cause problems for member states, if not for Turkey. This is mainly due to financial aspects. Member states pursue selfish national objectives instead of helping other member states.

4 The Copenhagen political criteria

Accession into the EU enables candidate member states to democratize their political system and to introduce new laws on human rights. In fact, one of the political motivations of the CEEC for joining the EU was related to their desire to return to a West European model of democracy (Harun 2003: 23). Turkey was motivated by the same desire. Yet, in contrast with the CEEC, Turkey already had a pluralistic multi-party democracy. This was confirmed by the Council of Europe in 2004. Lifting the control mechanism on Turkey, this organization recognized that Turkey had become a functioning democracy with a multi-party system, free elections and separation of powers.[1] However, for the EU, Turkish democracy did not function sufficiently in accordance with West European practices, and human rights were not respected in the way that was common in the West. Therefore, at the end of the negotiating process, Turkey would have to comply with the political criteria set by the Copenhagen European Council, for the most part embodied in Article 6 (1 and 2) of the Treaty on the European Union and proclaimed in the Charter of Fundamental Rights (EU 2002):[2]

- The Union is founded on the principles of liberty, democracy, respect for human rights and fundamental freedoms, and the rule of law, principles that are common to the member states.
- The Union shall respect fundamental rights, as guaranteed by the European Convention for the Protection of Human Rights and Fundamental Freedoms signed in Rome on 4 November 1950 and as they result from the constitutional traditions common to the member states, as general principles of Community law.

The EU expects Turkey to sustain its process of reform and to work towards further improvement in the respect of the principles of liberty, democracy, the rule of law and respect for human rights and fundamental freedoms, including relevant European case law. In its Progress Reports the Commission breaks downs the Copenhagen political criteria into two fundamental categories: first, democracy and the rule of law; second, human rights and the protection of minorities. We will deal first with the democracy criterion and then discuss the human-rights issue.

Democracy and the rule of law

Table 4.1 shows the progress made by Turkey regarding the functioning of democracy and the rule of law, as registered by the Commission in the Progress Reports. For more than five decades, a parliamentary democracy with a competitive multi-party system has been in operation in Turkey. Parties include the centre-right-wing DP and its successors (including the Motherland Party), the centre-left-wing RPP and its successors and various Islamist and nationalist parties.

In the 2006 Progress Report the Commission thinks that parliamentary democracy works relatively well (CEC 2006a: 6–7):

* The Turkish Grand National Assembly, in which six parties are represented, has adopted 148 laws of a total of 429 draft bills submitted since October 2005.
* A public debate has developed over the need to change the electoral system, which currently requires political parties to reach a 10 per cent threshold at national level to achieve representation.
* The government has submitted a new reform package, covering a number of areas related to the Copenhagen political criteria. Parliament has passed several laws in this area.
* Parliament has adopted a law establishing an ombudsman. The ombudsman will handle petitions from natural and legal persons related to administrative acts.
* Turkey has made some progress regarding better regulation.

Yet the Commission also levels some criticism (CEC 2006a: 7–8):

* The devolution of central government powers to local government is hampered.
* Expenditure from local governments is exempt from the Court of Accounts Audit.
* There is no progress on the draft of the Civil Servant Law.

Table 4.1 shows that, in the view of the Commission, the main problems are related to the role that is played by the military and the judiciary and to corruption in the political system. We will deal with each of these in the following.

Table 4.1 Democracy and the rule of law, Turkey, 1998–2006

Criterion	Progress	No progress	Limited
Parliament	X		
Government	X		
Public administration	X		
Civil–military relations		X	
Judicial system			X
Anti-corruption measures			X

Source: CEC (1998, 1999, 2000, 2001, 2002, 2003b, 2004c, 2005, 2006a).

Civil–military relations

It seems a paradox: whereas the army has always favoured Turkish westernization, the role of this very organization is under pressure from the EU. The autonomous role played by the military in Turkish political life is seen as a major impediment to democratic consolidation (Tank 2001: 218; Güney and Karatekelioğlu 2005: 441). In the successive Progress Reports the role of the generals is criticized.

Since the establishment of modern Turkey, the army has been the major force in the state. It has both a moral and an institutional value. Despite its record of interfering with politics and forcing out democratic governments four times (see Chapter 1), the military remains extremely popular with the people (Aydinli *et al.* 2006: 77). The decisive victories at the end of the War of Independence made the establishment of modern Turkey possible (Önis 2000: 478; Tank 2001: 219). Although the generals preferred Atatürk's one-party rule, they supported the democratization process, but only as long as the government ruled in accordance with the army's convictions. The successful coup of 27 May 1960 against the DP marked the beginning of what was to become a tradition in modern Turkey (Karabelias 2003: 63).

Because of the ideological polarization of Turkish politics, infighting and endless disputes among the political parties, and the high level of corruption among politicians, public opinion considers the army to be the only institution in the country it trusts. Moreover, public opinion knows that in the past each time the army has been involved with political life the result has been the peaceful return of power to politicians. Turkey is not Chile or Pakistan. In the background, the generals – who consider themselves true heirs of Atatürk – exercise a significant influence. The chief of general staff is the second most powerful man next to the president, who himself – until 2007 – has always been a retired general or somebody close to the military. The chief of general staff reports not to the minister of defence but directly to the prime minister (Rouleau 2000: 102). According to the Constitution and the by-laws of the military, the generals have to intervene if vital interests of the country are at stake. They have the duty 'to defend the country against internal as well as external enemies' (Sozen and Shaw 2003: 110).

The generals have to protect the territorial and national unity of the state and the modernizing reforms of Atatürk. To achieve that aim they created several institutions which they dominate: the National Security Council (NSC), State Security Courts, the Council of Higher Education, the Radio and Television High Council and the Supreme Military Council. The latter is very important, for it is charged with the task of hiring, promoting and firing military personnel. The military creates a homogenous force. Cadets are trained in schools that are beyond the jurisdiction of the Ministry of National Education (Rouleau 2000: 104; Aydinli *et al.* 2006: 85). A 1989 survey showed that 22.2 per cent of the military cadets were sons of officers, while 22.4 per cent were sons of civil servants. In February 1997, 141 officers suspected of Muslim sympathies were dismissed (Bonner 2005: 57).

The National Security Council (NSC) plays a very important role. It is a shadow government through which the generals can impose their will on parliament and the government. Its influence does not go as far as that of the Council of Guardians in neighbouring Iran. Yet it should not be underestimated. The NSC steps in each time it thinks the unity of the country or its institutions is threatened (Mousseau 2006: 100). In normal times, the NSC keeps a low profile, for it knows that the government will think twice before it makes decisions that run counter to the NSC basic philosophy. Moreover, the political environment in Turkey is very volatile. Political parties come and go, while the NSC is a lasting and stabilizing force that can play a conciliatory role in the disputes among political parties. Strong prime ministers or presidents like Turgut Özal can resist the pressure of the NSC. Since Özal's death in 1993, the NSC has gradually won back the power lost during his tenure (Larrabee and Lesser 2003: 28). Moreover, the rise of political Islam and the resurgence of Kurdish nationalism have brought the NSC back to the forefront in Turkish politics (Aydin and Keyman 2004: 19). The NSC covers up illegal operations undertaken by the armed forces. According to the US Department of State (2004), Turkish armed forces must bear considerable responsibility for the sorry human-rights situation in Turkey:

> Torture and other cruel, inhuman, or degrading treatment or punishment: the Constitution prohibits such practices; however, members of the security forces continued to torture, beat, and otherwise abuse persons regularly, particularly in the southeast. Security forces most commonly tortured leftists and Kurdish rights activists.

The role of the military is very closely linked to its economic power. The military holding OYAK (the Armed Forces Pension Fund) is among the three or four largest in the country and is an important shareholder in a number of industrial sectors. It is exempt from duties and taxes and it cooperates with other powerful holding companies (Rouleau 2000: 109). OYAK's sister firm, TSKGV, is devoted exclusively to arms production (Larrabee and Lesser 2003: 28). The army's economic power goes even further. Many private firms depend on military orders. There is a kind of military-industrial complex with cosy little triangles between large Turkish corporations and the army brass.

The EU wants Turkey to redefine the constitutional role of the NSC as an advisory body to the government in accordance with the practice of EU member states. Until 2004 there had been no change in the role of the NSC, and its presence put serious limitations upon the functioning of the government. There was a great lack of parliamentary control over the issues related to defence and security. Another EU criticism was concerned with the status of the office of the chief of general staff (Güney and Karatekelioğlu 2005: 452). In response to EU criticism, the government passed its seventh reform package (Republic of Turkey 2003). It introduced some fundamental changes to the duties, functioning and composition of the NSC, and made several concessions:

- Military courts can no longer prosecute civilians in peacetime; nor for offences such as inciting soldiers to mutiny and disobedience or discouraging the public from military duty.

- The composition of the NSC changed: the generals would no longer have a majority vote.
- The post of Secretary General would no longer be reserved exclusively for a military person.
- The NSC budget was to be submitted to the Court of Auditors.
- Parliamentary supervision over military spending was established.
- Decisions of the NSC were no longer obligatory on the government: 'The NSC shall submit to the Council of Ministers its views on advisory decisions ...' and 'The Council of Ministers shall evaluate decisions of the NSC ...'.
- Army representatives were removed from civil bodies such as the Higher Education Council.

How far have these reforms been achieved in practice? The texts are sufficiently vague for them to be interpreted in different ways. The chief of general staff underplayed the significance of reform. Reminding Turks that NSC decisions are taken not by majority vote but by consensus, he declared 'that the Council could include one hundred civilians, if that is what they want' (Rouleau 2000: 106; see also Güney and Karatekelioğlu 2005: 456).

It is obvious that the armed forces are not ready to become a post-modern military yet. That is also the view expressed by the Commission in the 2006 Progress Report (CEC 2006a: 7–8):

- The Armed Forces have continued to exercise serious political influence.
- The Armed Forces Internal Service Law has not changed.
- No measures have been taken to establish civil control over the gendarmerie.
- A protocol allows for military operations to be carried out for internal security reasons without any civil control whatsoever.
- Most procurement projects are funded without parliamentary control.
- No internal audit of military property has taken place.

The army is divided about the benefits of EU membership. On the one hand, the military favours EU membership because of the economic benefits (Güney and Karatekelioğlu 2005: 455; Aydinli *et al.* 2006: 87). Moreover, the prospect of EU membership offers a welcome excuse to silence radicals.[3] On the other hand, for the generals, the EU is about economic integration. The nation cannot afford to follow the EU on 'civilization issues', because this would endanger its future as a secular democracy.[4] If – according to some generals – the EU had its way, an Islamic or truncated Turkey might see the light. The EU inspires the Kurds and the Islamists to use EU human-rights discourse to defend their own minority freedoms (Rumford 2002: 267). Further democratization, while favourable for Turkey's EU candidacy, is perceived by some of the brass as threatening the ideology of Atatürk's republic. Thus, the army rejects full civil control by the Defence Ministry. In domestic policy, the military will never accept that Kurds get regional autonomy in the south-east or that an Islamic government challenges the basic principles of secularism.

In March 2002 the Secretary-General of the NSC, General Tuncer Kilinç, declared that the EU was 'a Christian club and a neo-colonial force that wanted to divide Turkey' (Kirişçi 2006: 36). Yet a few days later the Chief of General Staff, General Hüseyin Kivrikoglu, retorted:

> The membership of the EU will assure so many benefits for Turkey. Turkey wants to increase its welfare, and this could be done much more easily in the EU. Turkish people and the bureaucracy will gain a discipline and dynamism and have to comply with many rules. However, what we say is that the critical position of Turkey, the geo-strategic position of Turkey that always creates problems, should be taken into consideration as the membership efforts are made. Do not ignore the secular character of Turkey. These are the main principles of the Republic of Turkey. Numerous freedoms will be available if Turkey becomes a member of the EU. However, these should not violate democracy and human rights. (Güney and Karatekelioğlu 2005: 455)

In foreign policy, the army will not tolerate the Turkish government making concessions on Cyprus, Armenia or the Aegean Sea conflict with Greece. Unhappy with the US kid-glove treatment of the 'Kurdish terrorists' operating in northern Kurdistan, the generals will not hesitate to invade Northern Iraq again should the Kurds there declare their independence or annex oil-rich Kirkuk.[5] According to foreign minister (now president) Abdullah Gül: 'Turkey will do everything necessary to fight the PKK … I want to give the message that if our friends don't help us, we will do the job ourselves' (Weymouth 2006).

There are also outspoken opponents to EU membership in the army. Take Tuncer Kilinc, former secretary-general of the NSC:[6] 'The EU will never accept Turkey … Thus Turkey needs new allies, and it would be useful if Turkey engages in a search that would include Russia and Iran' (Cizre and Çinar 2003: 315).

Retired General Suat Ilhan goes even further:

> The EU prepares the ground for the resolution of the Turkish–Greek dispute in favour of Greece … paves the way for carving out Turkish territories via endeavours in minority rights; and generates hope for the resolution of the Eastern Question by way of side-tracking Turkey. (Bilgin 2005: 185)

This is how the Commission concludes this chapter (CEC 2006a):

- Overall limited progress has been made in aligning civil–military relations with EU practices.
- Statements by the military should only concern military, defence and security matters and should only be made under the authority of the government.
- Civilian authorities should fully exercise their supervisory positions in particular as regards the formulation of the national security strategy and its implementation, including with regard to neighbouring countries.

We think that the Commission hits the nail on the head. The position of the military in the Turkish state is an established fact accepted by Turkish society. This position is not in accordance with Western democratic standards. However, we think that the solution of the problem can be found in the creation of a new political establishment. According to Sozen and Shaw (2003: 112):

> The transition from authoritarian one-party rule to a competitive multi-party system introduced a new pattern of dependency. Having affiliations with large groups such as families, religious groups, political parties, clan, and kinship provide security, and hence are seen as useful. Democratic norms and institutions cannot take root in a culture where leaders become more important than rules or institutions. The nature of the current Turkish political system is thus neither modern nor traditional, but something in between.

If the behaviour of the political establishment changes fundamentally, the military might perhaps be ready to loosen its grip on the political system.

Judicial system

According to the 1982 Constitution, the judiciary is guaranteed full independence and obeys the modern separation of powers in its ranks. It is divided into two entities: Administrative Justice and Judicial Justice. It allows for a Constitutional Court, which rules on the conformity of laws and regulations to the Constitution. However, according to many experts, the inefficient judicial system acts as a break on economic reform and market opening. According to the OECD (2006a: 81), the failing judicial system is one of the main reasons why Turkey could not ride the FDI wave of the late 1990s. In the 2006 Progress Report the Commission lists both qualities and shortcomings attached to the judicial system (CEC 2006a: 6–9). To start with the first:

- Courts apply the European Convention on Human Rights.
- 620 new judges were recruited; training activities continued to ensure implementation of the reforms.
- The authorities have been focusing on the implementation of the New Penal Code, the Code of Criminal Procedure and the Law on Enforcement of Sentences.
- 501 judges and prosecutors established an association called 'The Union of Judges and Prosecutors' (YARSAV). YARSAV's main objectives are to safeguard judicial independence, impartiality and security of tenure as well as professional rules and ethics.
- Judges and prosecutors can now access their appraisal files.
- Some progress has been achieved with regard to the impartiality of the judiciary (judges and prosecutors who leave their profession to become candidates in elections shall not be allowed to return to their profession; candidate

judges and prosecutors fall under the scope of the Law on the Ethical Board for Public Servants; salaries were increased by 40 per cent).

- The Ministry of Justice and the Justice Academy continued to provide extensive training on the new Penal Code and the Code of Criminal Procedure. Training is also provided on foreign languages, on the EU and on Human Rights Law. Opportunities were given to a number of judges and prosecutors to benefit from periods of training abroad.
- The budget of the Ministry of Justice was substantially increased and is now over 1 per cent of the overall state budget.
- The system of plea bargaining was recently introduced.

However, the judicial system is undermined by severe shortcomings (CEC 2006a 57–9; see also Aydin and Keyman 2004: 42; Barysch 2005: 7):

- There is a link between the judiciary and the executive. The High Council of Judges and Prosecutors – which is chaired by the Minister of Justice – decides on appointments, transfers and promotions of judges and prosecutors. Moreover, civil servants working with the Ministry of Justice system, regularly evaluate judges. The High Council has to obey orders of the Inspection Board of the Ministry of Justice. The Ministry tells public prosecutors how to interpret the law. At another level: there is close cooperation between judges and public prosecutors thereby (possibly) violating the rights of defendants.
- Judges are overloaded with administrative work and are underqualified. Judgments are slow and often inconsistent. Since Turks are quite litigious, everything from energy sector regulation to anti-trust rulings ends up in front of the courts.
- A number of cases have shown inconsistency in the judiciary approach to the interpretation of legislation.
- The shadow economy is beyond the reach of tax inspectors, officials and judges.
- Questions were raised on the independence of the High Council of Judges and Prosecutors in the aftermath of the publication in March 2006 of the indictment on the Semdlinli bombing.[7]

In conclusion, the Commission states the following (CEC 2006a 10): 'Overall, there was continued progress in the area of judicial reform. However, implementation of the new legislations by the judiciary presents a mixed picture so far and the independence of the judiciary still needs to be further established.'

According to the OECD (2006a: 81), the following reforms are urgently needed:

- simplification of legal codes;
- upgrading of professional training capacities for justice officials;
- provision of adequate wages to judges;
- abolishment of optional or mandatory contributions by the users of the justice system because of low central budget allocations;

- modernization of the legal and judicial codes, of methods of administration of the justice system and of its physical and human infrastructures.

Anti-corruption measures

Since 1995 Transparency International has published its annual Corruption Perceptions Index (CPI). The CPI ranks 158 countries by their perceived levels of corruption, as determined by expert assessments and opinion surveys. It is important to emphasize that CPI scores relate to perceptions of the degree of corruption as seen by business people and country analysts. Yet, they reflect accurately the real situation. The score ranges between 10 (highly clean), and zero (highly corrupt). Table 4.2 shows that Turkey ranks 65 among 163. If we compare Turkey's record with that of most EU member states, Turkey compares poorly. Its ranking is 18 places below Greece, the Czech Republic and Slovakia, 14 places below Latvia and 10 below Bulgaria, but 5 places above Poland and 20 above Romania.

There was a lot of corruption in Turkey in the 1980s and 1990s. However, until

Table 4.2 Corruption Perceptions Index, EU and Turkey, 2005

Country	Rank	CPI
Austria	10	8.7
Belgium	19	7.4
Bulgaria	55	4.0
Czech Republic	47	4.3
Cyprus	37	5.7
Denmark	4	9.5
Estonia	27	6.4
Finland	2	9.6
France	18	7.5
Germany	16	8.2
Greece	47	4.3
Hungary	40	5.0
Ireland	19	7.4
Italy	40	5.0
Latvia	51	4.2
Lithuania	44	4.8
Luxembourg	13	8.5
Malta	25	6.6
Netherlands	11	8.6
Poland	70	3.4
Portugal	26	6.5
Romania	85	3.0
Slovenia	31	6.1
Slovakia	47	4.3
Spain	23	7.0
Sweden	6	9.2
Turkey	65	3.5
United Kingdom	11	8.6

Source: Transparency International (2005).

the mid-1990s, either it was covered up or it was related to lower levels of government. Many of Turkey's economic problems were due to government corruption. Many private enterprises depended on the state for orders. The links between the state, banks and business in Turkey have been at the centre of allegations of crony capitalism (Larrabee and Lesser 2003: 24). In order to build electoral coalitions, the government used secret funds that did not appear in the official budget (Eder 2003: 223–4). Between 1995 and 2002 cases of high-level corruption emerged, resulting in several ministerial resignations (*The Economist*, 2006f). According to the World Bank, Turkish economic and social fragility was partially due to corruption. Corruption has also radicalized the Turkish electorate. Nationalistic and Islamic parties have focused on public cynicism about Turkey's political class and have taken a strong stance against corruption. Moreover, in recent years Turkey has seen a general expansion of the illegal sector, above all drug trafficking, smuggling of people and money laundering. The unstable situation in the south-east, with its own war economy surrounding the battle with the PKK, has contributed a great deal to the Turkish illegal sector (Larrabee and Lesser 2003: 24).

In the 2006 Progress Report the Commission reports some very limited progress on the fight against corruption. The Law on Access to Information (amended in 2006) enables citizens to dispute all decisions of state agencies regarding denials of requests for information. Turkey has signed several international conventions on the battle against corruption and passed laws thereon. It has set up several parliamentary committees of inquiry. In January 2003 it approved an emergency anti-corruption plan and it ratified the Council of Europe Criminal and Civil Law Conventions on Corruption. In 2006 it ratified the UN Convention on Fight against Corruption. Yet there is still no overall strategy and action plan to fight corruption, and Turkey lags in implementation of laws (CEC 2006a: 59):

- The efficiency and effectiveness of the various governmental, parliamentary and other bodies established to combat corruption are weak and the degree of coordination amongst these bodies is inadequate.
- An anti-corruption law has been shelved.
- Stronger action is required to raise public awareness of corruption as a serious criminal offence.
- The Ethical Board for Public Servants established in 2004 is not operating efficiently because of the lack of human and financial resources.
- The Law on Public Financial Management and Control adopted in 2003 has not been implemented properly.
- The Turkish Court of Auditors lacks the power to audit military expenses.
- Despite the fact that the application of parliamentary immunity has been identified as a significant problem in the context of corruption in Turkish public life, nothing has been done on it.
- No progress can be reported regarding the financing of political parties.

Bryane (2004: 6) notes that 'Turkey has no independent institutions to fight corruption at the local level', and thinks that it is unfair to blame only Turkey for this situation (2004: 9). Part of the blame must be allocated to the tepid support given by international organizations. In most of the EU-10 one or more of the international donors has been involved in anti-corruption work. Lejour, de Mooij and Capel find that an improvement in the Turkish position from its current place on the CPI to place 25 might have important implications for the Turkish economy. Turkey's GDP would increase by 5.6 per cent and its consumption by 8.9 per cent (Lejour *et al.* 2004: 45).

Human rights and the protection of minorities

In the Negotiating Framework heavy emphasis is placed on human rights (see Table 4.3). To ensure the irreversibility of progress and its full implementation by Turkey, the Commission closely monitors progress in the field of human rights. The Commission has to report regularly to the European Council, and, in case of a serious breach by Turkey, it has to recommend the suspension of the negotiations. Amnesty International (2005), as well as other human-rights organizations, tends to agree with the Commission that, overall, human-rights violations have decreased on the ground across Turkey:

> Turkish citizens are becoming aware of their rights even in remote areas of the country. Turkey made some progress in the field of legislative protection of human rights. However, implementation of the reforms was uneven and it was too soon to evaluate the significance of the progress made. Changes were made to laws but the reforms consisted of amendments to articles of these laws rather than the fundamental redrafting of the laws that human rights lawyers had asked for. There was also concern that despite amendments to and repeal of certain articles of the Turkish penal code and Anti-Terror Law, the lack of a global approach means that similar articles to those repealed were retained in other laws.

The following rights and freedoms are explicitly mentioned in the Turkish National Action Programme (Republic of Turkey 2003):

- freedom of thought and expression;
- freedom of association and peaceful assembly;
- protection of civil society;
- independence of the judiciary;
- limited pre-trial detention and improving detention conditions in prisons;
- the fight against torture;
- the fight against human rights violations;
- training of law-enforcement personnel and other civil servants on human rights issues;
- decreasing regional disparities.

Between 2002 and 2004 substantial legislative improvement was realized, but

Table 4.3 Copenhagen criteria: human rights and the protection of minorities, Turkey, 1998–2006

Criterion	Progress	No progress	Limited
Observance of international law	X		
Torture and ill-treatment	X		
Freedom of expression (and media)		X	
Freedom of assembly	X		
Freedom of association	X		
Freedom of religion		X	
Women's rights			X
Children's rights		X	
Trade unions' rights		X	
Minority rights		X	
Cultural rights		X	
Protection of minorities		X	

Source: CEC (1998, 1999, 2000, 2001, 2002, 2003b, 2004c, 2005, 2006a).

progress has been limited since the end of 2004. In addition, implementation of reforms has been slow and erratic. To a large extent this has been attributed to conservative members of the judiciary 'who tend to put their ideas of the state ahead of individual rights' (Economist Intelligence Unit 2007). There is no chapter in the 2006 Progress Report on which the Commission spends more attention than that on human rights and the protection of minorities (CEC 2006a: 10–23). The chapter is broken down as follows:

- observance of human-rights law;
- civil and political rights;
- economic and social rights;
- minority rights, cultural rights and the protection of minorities.

In the following, we will comment on each of these topics and we will focus on the shortcomings by Turkey.

Observance of human-rights law

In the 1980s several European states raised human-rights concerns regarding Turkey through the Council of Europe. Under pressure from Denmark, France, the Netherlands, Norway and Sweden – who had initiated state complaints against Turkey in 1983 – Turkey signed the European Convention against Torture and it recognized Turkish citizens' right to make individual petitions to the European Court of Human Rights (1989). Turkey also ratified UN treaties and protocols to the European Convention on Human Rights. However, four additional protocols to the European Convention remain to be ratified. The first optional protocol to the UN Treaty on Civil and Political Rights and the Optional Protocol to the UN Convention against Torture also await ratification. Both protocols add legal force to the treaties by allowing an independent commission to investigate and judge complaints of human-rights violations from individuals. Their ratification is for the EU a priority in the Accession Partnership.

The European Court handed down its first judgments against Turkey from mid-1995 on. By mid-1996 they were piling up (Sugden 2003: 248). In 2005 Turkey accounted for 290 of the judgments (26.24 per cent) handed down by the Court.[8] The bulk of these cases were related to:[9]

- the right to life (art. 2);
- the right to liberty and security (art. 5);
- the right to a fair trial (art. 6);
- the right to respect for private and family life (art. 8);
- freedom of expression (art. 10);
- freedom of association (art. 11);
- the right to own property (art. 1, protocol 1).

In 2006 there was not much change, as the 2006 Progress Report makes clear (CEC 2006a: 11):

- During the first eight months of the year 2006, the European Court for Human Rights delivered 196 final judgments finding that Turkey had violated at least one article of the European Convention on Human Rights. In five cases, the Court ruled that there was no violation.
- From 1 September 2005 to 31 August 2006, one hundred new applications were lodged. More than two thirds of the applications refer to the right to a fair trial, and protection of property rights. The right to life and prohibition of torture are referred to in 78 and 142 cases respectively.

Even if Turkey still scores highly as far as the number of judgments is concerned, the situation has improved a lot. Judgments are mainly the result of cases introduced in the early 1990s. Nowadays, complaints lodged by Turkish citizens have become 'lighter'. In the view of Erik Fribergh, registrar with the Court: 'There is a remarkable reversal in the attitude of the Turkish legal world with a lot of attention for human rights' (*De Standaard*, 2007a).

The legal reforms undertaken by Turkey in the preceding years have had positive consequences on the execution of judgments of the Court. However, Turkish cases still represent about 14 per cent of cases pending before the Committee for execution control. Restrictions in Turkish legislation prevent the reopening of domestic proceedings following a violation found by the Court under certain circumstances.

To promote and enforce human rights Turkey set up a Human Rights High Council with the task of acting upon the reports submitted by the Human Rights Advisory Council. Regional Human Rights Boards were set up and entered into dialogue with Human Rights Organizations. A special Reforming Monitoring Group was established with a view to ensuring effective implementation of all political reforms (Aydin and Keyman 2004: 22–3). The Human Rights Presidency and the 931

District Human Rights Boards continued to provide training on human rights and on process applications on alleged human-rights violations. Unfortunately, the Human Rights Presidency lacks independence from the government, is understaffed and has a limited budget. The Parliamentary Human Rights Committee continued to play an active role in collecting complaints on human-rights violations and conducting fact-finding visits to the regions. However the Committee should be consulted on legislation affecting human rights.

The conclusion drawn by the Commission is moderately positive (CEC 2006a: 13): 'Overall, Turkey has made progress on the ratification of international human rights instruments and in the execution of judgments of the European Court for Human Rights. However, there is need to further upgrade the human rights institutional framework.'

Civil and political rights

Under EU pressure, a lot has changed in Turkey in the field of civil and political liberties. First, we will briefly summarize the conclusions drawn in the 2006 Progress Report. Secondly, we will elaborate a bit further on the most sensitive of these rights: the freedom of religion.

Summary of conclusions

- *Regarding torture and ill-treatment*: because of a comprehensive legislative framework, there is a downward trend in the number of cases of torture and ill-treatment. However, implementing the legislative reforms remains a challenge, especially in the south-east of the country. The Human Rights Boards have yet to assume a more prominent role in the on-site monitoring of law enforcement establishments. Areas of concern are the new anti-terror bill and the fight against impunity.[10]
- *Regarding justice and right of defence*: there is a considerable increase in the appointment of legal-aid lawyers; the prison system is being reformed. Yet, the new anti-terror law bill has reintroduced jail sentences, denied suspects' access to a lawyer for the first twenty-four hours of detention, and licensed security forces to shoot anybody who does not surrender on first command. Cases of ill-treatment and other abuses in prisons have been reported.
- *Regarding freedom of expression*: as asked for by the Commission in its 2005 Report, the Ministry of Justice has requested public prosecutors to take into consideration the relevant provisions of the European Convention on Human Rights. However, article 301 of the New Penal Code is a cause for serious concern. This article penalizes insulting 'Turkishness', the Republic as well as the organs and institutions of the state. (When a Turkish citizen in a foreign country commits this crime, the penalty to be imposed is to be increased by one-third.)[11] In July 2006 the final ruling of the Turkish Court of Cassation established jurisprudence on Article 301 that violated European standards.[12]

- *Regarding freedom of assembly*: public demonstrations are subject to fewer restrictions than in the past. However, in some cases security forces have used excessive force, especially when the demonstrations were carried out without permission.[13]
- *Regarding freedom of association*: the legal framework is generally in line with international standards. Civil society organizations have become relatively more vocal and better organized. There is an increasing variety of organizations in Turkey, including approximately 80,000 registered associations, and several hundred unions and chambers. Unfortunately, non-governmental organizations (NGOs) must notify the authorities in case of receipt of finances from abroad. Foundations need permission before applying for projects that are outside Turkey and funded by international organizations. Initially the state looked with suspicion on some NGOs, and some of their activists were prosecuted for violations of law. In recent years the state and the NGOs have begun to cooperate. Yet there has been no progress aligning the Turkish Law on Political Parties with EU practice. Since the founding of the republic more than twenty parties that were established by Islamists and separatists have been outlawed. Seven such dissolved parties brought cases before the European Court on Human Rights, and three of them won their case (Gündüz 2001: 23).

Freedom of religion

Regarding freedom of religion the 2006 Progress Report mentions the following (CEC 2006a: 17): 'Overall freedom of worship is respected. However, no progress can be reported as to difficulties encountered by non-Muslim religious and Alevi[14] communities on the ground.'

We think the problems mentioned by the Commission are related to the position Islam occupies in modern Turkey. People often call Turkey a secular state whose citizens are Muslim and refer to France, whose constitution was Turkey's model. This picture is not entirely correct. Article 24 of the Turkish Constitution guarantees personal religious freedom, and in Turkey the clergy does not rule the state, as in theocracies such as Iran or Saudi Arabia. Turkey is governed by a secular regime that derives its authority from the constitution, not from Islamic law. Yet, contrary to France, there is no strict separation between church and state. Religion has always played a very important role in the life of the Turkish people. In the Ottoman Empire religion was removed from political but not from family and personal life (Karpat 1974: 81, 82). Atatürk's basic ideal was a modernized Turkey. The West had reached its high level of modernization thanks to the Renaissance, the Reformation and the industrial and the democratic revolution. For Atatürk, 'a natural religion must be compatible with reason, technology, science and logic' (Karpat 1968: 325).

Atatürk did not want the government to interfere with the faith and worship of the people, but at the same time he did not want religion to interfere with the government of the state. Thus Kemalism did not remove religion from the state.

Atatürk wanted to use the state to interpret, control and manage religion (Davison 2003: 338; Larrabee and Lesser 2003: 61).

There is no state religion in Turkey. The constitution does not include a statement to this effect. Yet – although the debate is still going on – there is a kind of semi-official religion that is supported by the government: the mainstream Hanafi school of Sunni Islam. The Ministry of Religious Affairs – which is led by an Islamic theological scholar – hires and pays imams, determines the content of sermons and runs religious schools. Only teachers who have studied at secular universities are in charge of religious education. The Ministry bans headscarves from both schools and state premises. State-sponsored religious training and national education fit like a hand in glove. Friday sermons are used to invite citizens to engage in acts supportive of government (Davison 2003: 339–41). The law prohibits mystical Sufi and other religious-social orders and lodges.

Muslim minorities are in principle not recognized: Alevi and Shia Muslims are assumed to follow the Sunni form of Islam. Yet in today's Turkey there is a lively debate unfolding on the issue. In the Treaty of Lausanne (1923) Turkey had to recognize three non-Muslim minorities: Greek Orthodox, Jewish and Armenian. Religion (non-Muslim) is mentioned on the identity card of Turkish citizens. Members of non-Muslim minorities can practise their religion freely. Yet, their freedom is sometimes restricted. Under Turkish law, religious minorities do not have legal personality. Training clergy, owning property, forming associations, opening schools or building churches or synagogues requires prior authorization from the state. This direct state interference violates the Treaty of Lausanne, as it restricts the right of non-Muslim minorities to manage and control their institutions (Aydin and Keyman 2004: 33). In the past, property worth hundreds of millions of dollars – schools, hospitals and orphanages, for example – has been appropriated from non-Muslim religious communities, and in particular from the Greek Orthodox Church in Istanbul (*The Economist* 2006h). Police occasionally prohibit Christians from holding religious services in private places, and prosecutors sometimes open cases against Christians for holding unauthorized gatherings. Those indicted of proselytizing activities face heavy fines or even imprisonment. Christian missionaries, especially Protestants, complain that the authorities do little to protect them from Muslim vigilantes. Legally, non-Muslims are not barred from holding positions in state institutions, such as the armed forces, the Ministry of Foreign Affairs, the National Police and the National Intelligence Agency. Still there is a widespread practice of security checks being used as a mechanism to withhold employment (US Department of State 2004: 13–15). Orthodox priests and bishops have to be Turkish citizens by birth.[15] The Turkish state is opposed to reopening the theological school of Halki, near Istanbul. Upon EU pressure, Turkey has amended the legislation on religious foundations and on constructions, which now allows the bodies concerned to buy and sell property and build new places of worship.[16] Thanks to the EU, these are not closed chapters but ongoing debates. Yet we think that this chapter in the accession file is one of the most difficult.

Economic and social rights

The 2006 Progress Report mentions the following (CEC 2006a: 18–19):

- *Regarding women's rights*: overall, attention has been growing and the legal framework is satisfactory, but implementation is slow. The Law on the Protection of the Family has been applied only partially. Despite the provisions in the new Penal Code, the sentences issued with respect to 'moral killings' are sometimes too light. Crimes in the name of honour continue to exist, especially in the regions in the east and south-east of the country. There is a lack of reliable data on such events, and crimes are not sufficiently investigated. The provision of shelters for women subjected to domestic violence needs to be increased further. Women remain vulnerable to discriminatory practices largely because of illiteracy and a lack of education. As regards institutional capacity, the Directorate General for the Status of Women still suffers from a lack of staff.
- *Regarding children's rights*: the Law on the Protection of Children (2005) offers a legal framework. The right to education, especially for girls, remains a problem in some areas. With the 'cash transfer programme', the government has tried to encourage parents to send their children to school. The Turkish Labour Law prohibits the employment of children under the age of 15, yet there are problems implementing the law.
- *Regarding disabled people*: several regulations were adopted when the Law on People with Disabilities (2005) came into force.
- *Regarding trade unions' rights*: Turkey still falls short of several ILO conventions, especially with respect to the freedom of association, the right to collective bargaining, the right to set up organizations and to strike.

Minority rights, cultural rights and the protection of minorities

Turkey does not recognize Muslim minorities. This is a legacy of the strong assimilation policies pursued by Atatürk. He was determined to create a new Turkish nation state based on a Turkish identity. Turkey should not become a new Ottoman Empire: that Empire perished because of its multicultural composition. It had given international status (through so-called capitulations[17]) and extensive self-rule to religious (non-Muslim) minorities (Gündüz 2001: 25). Some of these minorities, such as the Armenians and the Kurds, collaborated with the occupying powers after the First World War. Nevertheless, Atatürk's concept was generous: all immigrants could apply for Turkish citizenship. But on one condition: Turkish citizens had to give up their previous ethnic identity. Out of the melting pot has emerged a society in which an overwhelming majority of individuals feel a strong attachment to a Turkish identity (Cornell 2001: 34; Larrabee and Lesser 2003: 58–9). In the Turkish context the issue of minority rights is very much – but not exclusively – linked to the treatment of the Kurds[18]. A great number of Kurds migrated to the west of the country and integrated successfully into Turkish society. Yet a significant part of the Kurdish population in the south-east is not assimilated, not only because of language, but also because of its clan-based feudal social structure (Faucompret 1999: 423; Cornell 2001: 34).

Turkey's human-rights record is poor, mostly because of measures taken to fight Kurdish separatism. Turkey has been among the top three sources of those seeking asylum in Europe since 1980. Political demands for recognition of a Kurdish identity did not arise until the emergence of a college-educated generation. In 1978 the PKK was established as a Marxist-Leninist Kurdish political party advocating the creation of a separate socialist republic. In 1984 the PKK showed its dirty hands for the first time, when its militants seized towns in the east (Cornell 2001: 34; Bonner 2005: 60). The Turkish establishment considered the Kurds' demand for the recognition of their identity a threat to the territorial integrity of the state, the more so because the PKK was supported by countries hostile to Turkey: the Soviet Union, Greece, Cyprus, Iran and especially Syria (Rochtus 2002: 172). Syria hosted the organization and its leader for twenty years, and it provided training facilities in the Beka'a Valley of Syrian-controlled northern Lebanon (Cornell 2001: 41). While there is no doubt that violations of humanitarian law have occurred on both sides in the conflict between the Turkish armed forces and the Kurds, NGOs report that the vast majority of these violations have been committed by the army in its efforts to put down the Kurdish insurgency (Domke 1997: 2). Between 1984 and 1999 the military turned much of the Kurdish region in south-east Anatolia into a militarized zone, spending some $2 billion there each year (Rochtus 2002: 176). Kurds were expelled from their villages;[19] prisoners were tortured; a Village Guards system was set up.[20] According to an official report, between 1984 and 1996 about 23,000 individuals were killed in the conflict, including about 13,878 PKK members, 4,310 civilians and 2,917 government soldiers (Aydin and Keyman 2004: 22; Bonner 2005: 60). The PKK lost much of its élan when its leader Abdullah Öcalan was arrested in February 1998. Since then the PKK has dissolved itself and changed its name into KADEK. Its new aim is to strive for regional autonomy within the Turkish state. However, on 1 June 2004 the PKK lifted its unilateral ceasefire because the government did not want to offer amnesty to PKK leaders.

For Turkey, combating the PKK has often been an excuse to repress peaceful representatives of the Kurdish cause. Under the Anti-Terror Law pro-Kurdish newspapers were closed, political parties were banned; politicians, journalists and human-rights activists were jailed.[21] Under EU pressure (and because of the PKK's defeat by the Turkish military) the state of emergency in the south-east was lifted and certain articles of the Anti-Terror Law were abolished. The most notable of these reforms were the right to broadcast in Kurdish by national radio and television stations,[22] the right to learn the Kurdish language[23] and the right to name children in Kurdish. Implementation of the 'Return to Village and Rehabilitation Project' led to the reopening of more than 400 villages in the southeast (Aydin and Keyman 2004: 35). However, most of these reforms are cosmetic operations. Between 2000 and 2004 only 5 per cent of the applications for pecuniary compensation were honoured. Kurdish language training in public schools is illegal, while television and radio in Kurdish is limited to a few hours per week and under the monopoly of the state broadcasting cooperation TRT. Educational programmes teaching the use of the Kurdish language are forbidden. The use of a language other than Turkish in political life is illegal. There is intense opposition in Turkey to any adoption of more mainstream EU approaches to minority rights and identity politics (Park 2005: 136). Whereas aspirations for religious freedom had become more or less part of the political system, Kurdish nationalist aspirations have not. The renewed fighting in the south-east has enhanced the position of hardliners in the military and the nationalist movement who argue that further liberalizations – as asked for by the EU – would endanger the territorial integrity of the country. In the event of a permanent ceasefire, it will become increasingly difficult for the government and the military establishment to justify repressive measures against Kurdish citizens.

In the 2006 Progress Report the Commission mentions the following:

- The visit of the OSCE High Commissioner on National Minorities to Ankara has not been followed up and no progress has been made in starting a dialogue on the situation of national minorities in Turkey. It needs to include minority education, minority languages, the participation of minorities in public life and broadcasting in minority languages. This would facilitate Turkey's further alignment with international standards and best practice in EU member states.
- Turkey's reservation towards the UN Covenant on Civil and Political Rights regarding the rights of minorities and its reservation to the UN Covenant on Economic, Social, and Cultural Rights regarding the right to education are not acceptable. Turkey refuses to sign the Council of Europe Framework Convention for the Protection of National Minorities[24] or the European Charter for Regional or Minority Languages.[25]
- After the resumption of violence by the PPK, the situation in the south-east has deteriorated. There are many reports of widespread and arbitrary violence by the security forces. There is insufficient compensation for lost property. The overall economic situation in the south-east is bad, and there is no plan to address this issue. Elected politicians face court charges. Refugees are given no opportunity to return to their villages.

The Commission draws three important conclusions in this chapter (CEC 2006a: 23):

- Overall Turkey has made little progress on ensuring cultural diversity and promoting respect for and protection of minorities in accordance with international standards.
- A return to normality in the south-east can only be achieved by opening a dialogue with local counterparts.
- A comprehensive strategy should be pursued, to achieve the socio-economic development of the region and the establishment of conditions for the Kurdish population to enjoy full rights and freedoms.

According to Human Rights Watch, there are four strong forces at work in Turkey. First, there is pressure for reform coming from Turkish civil society. Secondly, there are the incentives provided by the EU through Turkey's candidacy for membership. Thirdly, there is the resistance to change presented by the powerful sectors within the military, security forces and state apparatus. Fourthly, there are the destructive effects of political violence (Human Rights Watch 2000). It remains an open question whether Turkey is willing to abide completely by EU standards in terms of human rights. According to Mousseau (2006: 104), EU-led changes in the legal framework are insufficient to liberalize Turkish society and politics and produce a stable and liberal democracy. There is no guarantee that these laws will be widely followed. To achieve a real democratic transition, Turkish citizens must develop a desire for the rule of law to protect individual rights, civil, political and socio-economic. For this they must have greater opportunities in the market than in the earlier state-oriented and patronized economy. This means the emergence and the expansion of jobs in the market, a reduction in state jobs in bureaucratic institutions obtained through social connections and a reduction in dependency on traditional and kinship leaders in rural areas. Individuals dependent on a market for economic security will want a neutral state that respects the rule of law. Thus, there is a close link between the economic and the political Copenhagen criteria.

Conclusions

From the preceding, the following can be concluded:

- With respect to the first Copenhagen political criterion – democracy and the rule of law – we found that progress has been made in the field of parliament, government and public administration. More remains to be done with respect to the judiciary and anti-corruption measures. However, the most serious divergence from the EU system is in the relation between the military and civil society. It remains to be seen whether progress is possible here, given the nature of the Turkish political system and the forces of resistance not only in the army but also in public opinion and in the civil establishment.
- With respect to the second Copenhagen political criterion – human rights and the protection of minorities – progress has been made in the area of (some) political and civil rights and in the area of economic and social rights. Much remains to be done with respect to the freedom of expression, cultural rights and religious rights. As in the case of civil–military relations, we seriously doubt whether the progress required by the EU as to freedom of religion and cultural autonomy for the Kurds is possible in the short run in centralized Muslim Turkey.

5 Other conditions

Apart from the Copenhagen economic and political criteria, the Negotiating Framework (Council of the European Communities 2006a) requires from Turkey the following:

- Turkey's unequivocal commitment to good neighbourly relations and its undertaking to resolve any border disputes in conformity with the principle of peaceful settlement of disputes in accordance with the UN Charter; including, if necessary, jurisdiction of the International Court of Justice.
- Turkey's continued support for efforts to achieve a comprehensive settlement of the Cyprus problem within the UN framework and in line with the principles on which the Union is founded, including steps to contribute to a favourable climate for a comprehensive settlement, and progress in the normalization of bilateral relations between Turkey and all EU member states, including Cyprus.
- The fulfilment of Turkey's obligations under the Association Agreement and its Additional Protocol extending the Association Agreement to all new EU member states, in particular those pertaining to the EU–Turkey Customs Union, as well as the implementation of the Accession Partnership, as regularly revised.
- Moreover, in the Negotiating Framework there is one final condition: enlargement should strengthen the process of continuous creation and integration in which the Union and its member states are engaged. Every effort should be made to protect the cohesion and effectiveness of the Union. In accordance with the conclusions of the Copenhagen European Council in 1993, the Union's capacity to absorb Turkey, while maintaining the momentum of European integration is an important consideration in the general interest of both the Union and Turkey. The Commission will have to report to the European Council in order to ascertain whether this condition has been met.

In the following, we will deal with each of these conditions: good neighbourly relations, the Cyprus problem and the EU absorption capacity.

Good neighbourly relations

Outside the immediate framework of the accession negotiations, Turkey is expected by the EU to normalize its ties with neighbouring countries, before joining the EU. The EU does not want Turkey to import new territorial conflicts into the Union. The Progress Reports deal in essence with Greece and Cyprus. We will first mention three other neighbouring countries.

Iraq, Syria and Armenia

Turkey has territorial border disputes with Syria, Iraq and Armenia. Syria has never relinquished its claim on the Hatay province (now Alexandretta), which was annexed by Turkey in the waning days of the French mandate in Syria (Wilkens 1998: 36). Turkey, on the other hand, claims sovereignty over the Northern Iraqi (Kurdish) cities of Mossul and Kirkuk, which were annexed by the UK in the final days of the British mandate. Moreover, Turkey has conflicts with Iraq as well as with Syria on the water reserves of the rivers Tigris and Euphrates. Its 'South-East Anatolia' project – a massive hydroelectric-irrigation complex with twenty-one large dams and seventeen hydroelectric power stations along the Euphrates and Tigris headwaters – will benefit the south-east of Turkey (Liel 2001: 21). For Syria and Iraq, the same project is a cause for concern. They argue that it is ecologically and financially unsound, that it displaces many communities whose valley homes will be flooded and that it will further increase tensions among the three countries (Dahlman 2004: 567; Przewieslik 2005: 26). In accordance with the UNCLOS 3 treaty on the international law of the sea, each riparian state is entitled to a fair share of the water of an international river. Yet, for Turkey, the Euphrates is a Turkish river (Liel 2001: 21).

In the past Turkey claimed that Syria supported Kurdish insurgents in Turkey's south-east provinces and even Armenian terrorists in order to extract concessions on the water issue. Syria, on the other hand, said that it felt threatened by the close Turkish–Israeli military and intelligence cooperation (Wilkens 1998: 37). In 1998 both countries came close to war. Yet relations have improved since the Adana Accords were signed on 20 October 1998. By the terms of this agreement, Syria agreed to expel PKK leader Abdullah Öcalan, arrest PKK militants active on its territory, cease providing weapons and logistical and financial support to the PKK and forbid it to use Syrian soil. Nowadays relations have further improved. Since the end of the cold war Syria's ally, the Soviet Union, has disappeared. Moreover, under American pressure, the Syrian army has had to leave Lebanon (2006). Therefore, Syria has been keen to normalize its relations with its neighbours, including Turkey (Kirişçi 2006: 76). Yet the USA has not been very happy about the recent rapprochement between Turkey and Syria, and the latter has been labelled a rogue nation by Washington (Kirişçi 2006: 77).

Notwithstanding the fact that Turkey was an important ally of the USA in the liberation of Kuwait in 1991, it shared common interests with Saddam Hussein's Iraq.[1] Before the Gulf War one-third of Iraqi oil was exported by Turkey through two pipelines linking Mossul and the Turkish port of Ceyhan. The UN oil embargo against Iraq was a major blow to the Turkish economy, but the international community took no notice of this. Turkey also shared with Saddam Hussein's Iraq the interest in limiting self-determination of the Kurds in Northern Iraq. In 1994 the Turkish army even supported one of the two major Kurdish factions (the Kurdish Democratic Party (KDP) of Massoud Barzani) against the other (the People's Union of Kurdistan (PUK) of Jalal Talabani). In 1997 the military openly fought the PUK for several days (Wilkens 1998: 40). Whereas Turkey supported the December 2001 American-led invasion of Afghanistan, it was opposed to the March 2003 intervention in Iraq. The attack on Iraq as well as the failure of the American government to ensure stability in Iraq has made Turkish public opinion – like that in Western Europe – anti-American. Turkey fears that the break-up of Iraq into its three constituent parts jeopardizes Turkey's own territorial integrity (Kirişçi 2006: 79–80). How could Turkey further restrain Turkish–Kurdish aspirations for independence in the event that an independent Kurdistan is established in the north of Iraq? Moreover, Turkey says it wants to protect the Turkmen community in northern Iraq and it may well be interested in the oil resources (Kazancigil 1986: 140). The USA is blamed for threatening Turkey's territorial integrity, the main objective that has been pursued since independence. In spite of this, the Turkish government has tried to play a constructive role, and has mediated between the Sunni community in Iraq and the USA (Kirişçi 2006: 80).

Since 1992 Turkey has maintained an economic embargo against landlocked Armenia, and land border crossings have been closed. Nevertheless, direct flights between Istanbul and Yerevan are permitted, and Armenians may enter Turkey on a facilitated visa arrangement (Kirişçi 2006: 51). Armenia's three million citizens depend largely on the generosity of the rich five million-strong Armenian Diaspora. Turkey and Armenia do not have diplomatic relations, and they came close to war in 1993.[2] In the dispute over Nagorno Karabakh with Armenia, Turkey has sided unconditionally with the authoritarian Aliev regime of Azerbaijan. Karabakh – an Armenian enclave created by the former USSR in Azerbaijan – proclaimed its independence in 1991. The Azeri army attacked it, while Armenia and Russia came to its help. After many atrocities committed by both sides in the conflict, an uneasy ceasefire was reached in 1994. The war left 30,000 death and about one million refugees. Since then Armenia has occupied the enclave and the territory surrounding it (about one-third of Azeri territory). There are no peacekeepers in the area, and the truce is regularly violated. Azerbaijan is investing its oil dollars in rebuilding its army. With Turkish military support, it prepares to recuperate Karabakh. Since 1996 Turkey has been actively engaged in the training of Azerbaijan's military officers; it has also helped to modernize the Azerbaijani army (Larrabee and Lesser 2003: 105). Mediation efforts by the OSCE-sponsored Minsk Group (Russia, USA, France) have failed. The Minsk Group favoured a three-staged solution:

- first, the Armenian troops leave the Azeri territory surrounding Karabakh;
- then a referendum is held on the status of the enclave;

- finally, an international peacekeeping force is sent and financial aid is given to resettle the refugees and to rebuild the economy.

As long as Turkey supports Azerbaijan unconditionally, and Russia supports Armenia, it is difficult to see how the conflict can be solved. Moreover, Armenia–Turkey relations are burdened by the past. As a prelude to establishing diplomatic relations, Turkey has requested the following from Armenia:

- unconditional recognition of its eastern border;
- cessation of attempts at seeking international recognition as genocide of the 1915 Ottoman pogrom (which might have caused the death of 1,500,000 people);[3]
- total withdrawal of Armenian troops from Karabakh and unconditional recognition of Azeri sovereignty over the area.

Given that these conditions are completely unacceptable to Armenia, it is difficult to see how in the not too distant future these neighbouring countries can live together in peace, as is being asked by the EU in the Negotiating Framework.

Greece

Like Indian and Pakistani or Israeli and Palestinian, Greek and Turkish nationalism has for the most part developed during conflicts with the other side. Internal cohesion was the result of hostility vis-à-vis the neighbouring country. For Turkey, Greek nationalism destroyed the Ottoman Empire from within. Moreover, in 1919 Greece tried to annex all the remaining European territory of the Empire. For Greece, Turkey is the successor state to the Ottoman Empire, which suppressed their national identity and which tried to eliminate its national existence (Faucompret 2001b: 831; Larrabee and Lesser 2003: 73). Relations between Greece and Turkey have always remained frosty, especially when the military have been in power. The Cyprus conflict has made things worse. Yet there have been attempts at improving relations. The latest date from 1999, when the two countries rushed to each other's aid after earthquakes had struck İzmir and Athens. In January 2000 the first reciprocal visits of ministers of foreign affairs took place in almost four decades (Kirişçi 2006: 20). Two years later, exploratory talks were initiated between the two governments. Both countries also signed a draft agreement to build a pipeline to take gas from Iran and Central Asia through Turkey to Greece and then on to markets in Western Europe. Greek companies are investing in Turkey (*The Economist*, 2002). In 2006 a new package of confidence building measures was agreed. The package included the building of a new bridge over the border river Evros/Meriç and the establishment of a joint civilian task force on natural disaster prevention. Direct hotlines were established between the respective chiefs of general staff. These developments were also accompanied by an increase in private relations. Trade between Greece and Turkey increased more than fourfold between 1995 and 2005. In April 2006 the National Bank of Greece acquired a Turkish bank (Kirişçi 2006: 21, 58–61).

There have been attempts at improving relations in the past. Therefore, the question is whether the recent rapprochement between Greece and Turkey is different. There is at least one important new element: if Turkey wants to join the EU, it has to improve relations with its neighbour, who happens to be a member state of the EU. Still the improvement of relations has been limited to issues that do not touch upon national sovereignty, such as trade, the environment and tourism (Larrabee and Lesser 2003: 6). Notwithstanding the cooperation in the economic field, there are still a number of unsolved political disputes burdening relations between Greece and Turkey:

- *The Aegean Sea and its continental shelf*: according to the UNCLOS 3 treaty on the international law of the sea, Greece is allowed to extend its territorial waters from 6 to 12 miles. Yet Turkey argues that this treaty is not part of customary law, since it has not been signed by some countries, including Turkey itself. In 1982 both countries started exploration for oil in disputed waters both protected by their naval forces (Zürcher 1997: 333). Five years later there was belligerent talk when Turkey sent an oil-drilling ship into the disputed areas of the Aegean Sea. The same happened again in 1996 over a disputed uninhabited islet in the Aegean. One year earlier the Turkish Grand National Assembly had decreed that, if Greece extended its territorial waters, Turkey would consider this to be a *casus belli*.
- *The airspace*: Greece extended its airspace to 10 miles outside its borders. Turkey recognizes only 6 miles. There are daily incidents between jetliners of these two NATO member states. In May 2006 there was a serious accident involving a Greek aircraft and a Turkish plane (Kirişçi 2006: 58).
- *Militarization of Greek islands in the Eastern Aegean and the Dodecanese*: Turkey wants the Greek islands off the Turkish coast to be completely demilitarized. Greece argues that the Turkey's Fourth Aegean army has its headquarters in İzmir, just a few miles from the islands (Larrabee and Lesser 2003: 75), and thus threatens them.
- *Minorities*: both countries occasionally accuse each other of ill-treating minorities of the other side.

Geopolitical interests also differ. Whereas, since the end of the cold war, Turkey has created a network of relations with countries surrounding Greece, like the FYR Macedonia, Albania, Bulgaria and Bosnia-Herzegovina, Greece has concluded agreements with Syria and Armenia (Larrabee and Lesser 2003: 93–5). Because of these disputes, Greece and Turkey are engaged in an arms race, whereby increases in defence expenditure on one side engender increases on the other side (Dritsakis 2004: 264; Özdemir 2004: 148). On several occasions, Greece has misused its EU membership to hinder Turkey. It blocked EU financial aid to Turkey on the ground of Turkey's failure to maintain good relations. For Turkey, this is blackmail: Greece wants to score diplomatic victories at its expense (Harun 2003: 91). Greece has suggested submitting the bilateral disputes with Turkey to the UN International Court of Justice. However, a fundamental principle governing the settlement of international disputes is that the jurisdiction of an international tribunal depends in the last resort on the consent of the states concerned. Accordingly, no state can be made party in proceedings before the International Court of Justice unless it has in some manner consented thereto. In contrast to Greece and many other EU member states,[4] Turkey has not recognized the compulsory jurisdiction of the Court.

It is also possible for states that have not recognized the compulsory jurisdiction of the Court to submit a specific dispute before the Court and thus to recognize its authority in that particular case. Yet Turkey is also opposed to this procedure. Turkey considers its bilateral disputes with Greece of a political not of a legal nature. The Aegean Sea commands access to the Black Sea through the Turkish-controlled Dardanelles Strait. International law regarding territorial sea, air and drilling rights cannot be applied to disputes with Greece, because of the special circumstances that prevail in the Aegean Sea (Wilkens 1998: 28). Therefore, in Turkey's view the appropriate political procedures provided for in the UN Charter (UN n.d.: art. 33) should be used:

> The parties to any dispute, the continuance of which is likely to endanger the maintenance of international peace and security, shall, first of all, seek a solution by negotiation, enquiry, mediation, conciliation, arbitration, judicial settlement, resort to regional agencies or arrangements, or other peaceful means of their own choice.

Unfortunately, by excluding the International Court of Justice's jurisdiction, Turkey is violating one of the conditions for membership, as laid down in the Negotiating Framework and reiterated by the Brussels European Council in December 2004: 'The Council reaffirmed its view that unresolved disputes having repercussions on the accession process should if necessary be brought to the International Court of Justice for settlement' (Conclusions of the Presidency 2004).

In its National Programme for the adoption of the *Acquis communautaire* Turkey commits itself only to 'undertaking initiatives and efforts towards the settlement of bilateral problems with Greece through dialogue' (Republic of Turkey n.d.).

Since its bid for EU membership, Turkey has moderated its stance somewhat. In January 2002 Greece agreed to open a bilateral dialogue with Turkey on the Aegean seabed. Turkey wanted the dialogue to extend to other issues. It will be difficult for both sides to reach a solution.

The Cyprus file

The problem of Cyprus raises passions in Greece as well as in Turkey. In July 1974 the Turkish army occupied the northern part of Cyprus. Since then, the government has controlled 60 per cent of the territory, the Turkish army 36.3 per cent, with the neutral zone with UN peacekeepers constituting the remaining 3.7 per cent (Faucompret 2001b: 828; Üçer 2006: 203). The division of the island caused a massive migration: 200,000 Greek Cypriots and 60,000 Turkish Cypriots left their ancestral homes. In November 1983 Turkish Cypriots proclaimed their independent 'Turkish Republic of Northern Cyprus', which was recognized only by Turkey. The UN Security Council called upon all states not to recognize the breakaway state and not to facilitate or in any way assist it. Similarly, by declarations of 16 and 17 November 1983, the European Parliament, the Commission and the foreign ministers of EU member states rejected the Turkish Cypriot declaration of independence and expressed their continued recognition of the Greek Cypriot Government. In 1994 the European Court of Justice ruled that EU member states should not accept certificates required under EC law for the import of goods originating in Cyprus under the Association Agreement signed with Cyprus (Talmon 2001: 1–2). Preferential tariff treatment was ended for Northern Cyprus, although there was no formal EU or international embargo on trade. Most trade is indirect with Turkey and via Turkish ports (Hughes 2006: 20).

Whereas in the past Turkey mainly put emphasis on the protection of the Turkish Cypriot community, since the end of the 1990s the focus has shifted to security issues. Thus, recently Cyprus has become a cornerstone for the defence of Anatolia (Larrabee and Lesser 2003: 79). Under the influence of nationalists, the issue has also become very much linked to sovereignty: no part of the motherland will be sacrificed. While Northern Cyprus is integrated more and more with Turkey economically, politically and militarily, numerous attempts have been undertaken by various international organizations and envoys[5] to find a solution. The latest attempt dates back to April 2004. In December 2003 national elections had been held in Northern Cyprus. The results indicated a divided community, with a slight majority of votes in favour of negotiations with the Greek side and EU membership, but with twenty-five seats for the opponents (led by Rauf Denktas) and twenty-five for the proponents (led by M. Mehmet Ali Talat) of a negotiated solution (Kirisçi 2006: 46). In January 2004 the new government of Ali Talat showed itself ready to negotiate with the Greek Cypriots. Thereupon the Erdoğan government seized the initiative and succeeded in convincing the Turkish military to support a solution based on the peace plan worked out by UN Secretary-General Kofi Annan, in close cooperation with the EU. The plan provided for three stages: first, negotiations were to be held between the two Cypriot communities under UN auspices. Then a conference was to be organized in which the Greek and Turkish Cypriots and Greece and Turkey were to take part. Finally, a referendum would be held on the plan in both communities. Whereas in the past Turkey had always supported the intransigent Denktas, in the course of these negotiations it played a very constructive role, referring to the UN for solving the issues on which parties did not agree (Kazangicil 1986: 138). Of course, the timing was important: Cyprus was about to join the EU on 1 May 2004 and Turkey was waiting for a positive outcome of the December 2004 EU Council, which was going to decide on its membership application.

From Table 5.1 we learn that the Annan Plan was as far as possible a balanced compromise between the contradictory points of view of both parties. However, Greeks and Turks have a completely different conception of the problem. The Greek Cypriots want a solution based on the *status quo bellum ante*. The occupation should be lifted and the Greek Cypriot government should extend its control

Table 5.1 Opinion of Greek and Turkish governments on solution of the Cyprus conflict, 1974–2008

Issue	Greece	Turkey	Annan Plan (April 2004)
State structure	Federation or unitary state	Loose confederation	Confederation
Greek refugees	Complete return to the North or full compensation	No return; no compensation	Limited phased-out return or (small) compensation
Turkish troops	Complete removal	No removal	Partial phased-out removal
Turkish settlers in the north	Have to leave immediately	Will stay unless full compensation is paid for those willing to leave	Not clear
Borders between north and south	Significant rectifications	No rectifications	Significant rectifications

Source: Faucompret (2001b: 832–34); Annan (2002).

over the whole island. At the most, some rights could be accorded to the Turkish minority. For the Turkish Cypriots a return to the situation from before 1974 is totally out of the question. The Makarios regime had not treated the Turkish minority on the island well. Never again should Greeks rule the Turkish Cypriot community (Faucompret 2001b: 833). Therefore, the Annan Plan came to nothing. Seventy-five per cent of the Greek Cypriot community rejected the plan on 24 April 2004, while 65 per cent of the Turkish Cypriots were in favour.[6] Since then the issue has been blocked again, and the prospects for a solution look grim. In the Negotiating Framework and the Accession Partnership, Turkey is expected to ensure continued support for efforts to find a comprehensive settlement of the Cyprus problem, in line with the principles on which the EU is founded, whilst contributing to a better climate for a comprehensive settlement. In its National Programme for the adoption of the *Acquis communautaire* the government (Republic of Turkey n.d.) commits itself only to

> supporting the efforts of the UN Secretary General, in the context of his good-offices mission aiming at a mutually acceptable settlement with a view to establishing a new partnership in Cyprus based on the sovereign equality of the two parties and the realities on the island.

Turkey has dropped the reference to 'the principles on which the EU is founded': military occupation certainly violates one of these principles. While one can understand Turkey from a moral point of view, from a legal point of view it is wrong. There is no sovereign equality between the two governments on the island: Northern Cyprus is part of the Republic of Cyprus and is occupied by a foreign power. The 'realities on the island' refer to the Turkish occupation army and the Turkish citizens having settled in the houses of Greek Cypriot refugees.

On 1 May 2004 Turkey suffered a serious diplomatic setback when a divided

Cyprus entered the EU. President Tasos Papadopoulos made it very clear that Cyprus as an EU member state would block any decision regarding Turkey's EU membership, until a solution for Cyprus had been reached on better terms for the Greek Cypriots than the Annan Plan (Güney 2005: 310). Yet, wanting to recompense the Turkish Cypriots for their yes vote in the referendum, on 26 April 2004 the EU Council had declared its intention to end Turkish Cypriot isolation. The Council went on rapidly – in advance of Cyprus accession – to adopt the so-called Green Line regulation, which deals with movement of goods and people across the UN-patrolled Green Line (Hughes 2006: 19).[7] The Commission also put forward two other draft regulations: one on opening Turkish Cypriot ports and airports to direct trade and another on providing 250 million Euros of aid. Only in February 2006 did the EU finally adopt the regulation on financial assistance. Cyprus boycotts the execution of the second regulation.

Although Turkey signed the Additional Protocol to the Ankara Agreement in July 2005, the government did not submit it to Parliament. In a separate declaration, it made clear its signature did not imply recognition of the Republic of Cyprus. It also announced Turkey was not going to open its seaports and airports to Cyprus-registered ships and aircraft. Turkey hoped to use these issues to extract concessions from Cyprus with respect to the economic isolation of the north and diplomatic recognition of the Turkish Republic of Northern Cyprus. Moreover, it wanted new international efforts to find a diplomatic solution for the island. Turkey does not comply with the conditions made in the Negotiating Framework. By virtue of international law, northern ports and airports can be blockaded until the Turkish occupation is lifted. The government of Cyprus represents both communities and rules (in theory) over the whole of Cyprus. It is entitled to require that the customs union agreement of which it is now part is implemented. Free movement of goods is one of the fundamental principles of the European Community. The European Court of Justice supports this theory: 'The principle of free movement of goods must be understood to eliminate all barriers whether direct or indirect, actual or potential to intra-Community trade' (ECJ, 12 June 2003 (case C-112/00); 9 December 1997 (case C–265/95).

In its 2006 Progress Report the Commission almost stated the same: 'Restrictions on shipping often preclude the most economical way of transport and therefore result in a barrier to free movement of goods and to trade. They infringe the customs union' (CEC 2006a: 24).

In the view of the Commission, Turkey's behaviour is not right: a candidate country has to recognize all EU member states. EU representatives have frequently reminded the Turkish government that implementing the Additional Protocol and normalization of relations between Turkey and Cyprus are legal obligations as such, which Turkey on its own initiative should not link to the situation of the Turkish Cypriot community. The Commission takes the interest of this community to heart, but for the time being both Cyprus and Turkey make it very difficult for the Commission to deploy new initiatives on their behalf.

Because of the foregoing, the European Council decided to suspend eight of the thirty-five chapters on the agenda of the accession negotiations (15 December

2006): chapters 1, 3, 9, 11, 13, 14, 29 and 30. No chapter will be provisionally closed until the Commission has confirmed that Turkey has fully implemented its commitments with respect to the Additional Protocol. The European Council's position was a compromise between the hardliners (Austria, France, the Netherlands, Greece and Cyprus), who wanted negotiations to be broken off right away, and member states who did not want to apply any sanction at all (mainly the UK and the Scandinavian countries).

Absorption capacity of the EU

In light of its relatively large size and population, Turkey's accession would raise a number of institutional, financial and policy-based issues for the EU. It is clear that, compared to the EU-12, Turkey will have a more significant influence on the deepening process of the EU (Harun 2003: 35). According to Olli Rehn (2006a: 3), EU absorption capacity is determined by two factors. First, there is the transformation of the applicants into member states. Secondly, there is the development of the EU functional capacity: 'The EU's integration capacity is primarily about the EU's institutions, budget and policies' (Rehn 2006d).

It is the Commission's philosophy that, if member states think the EU does not function well, it is up to them to do something about it. They could have restructured the institutional framework a long time ago if only they had agreed among themselves. Since the intergovernmental conference leading to the Treaty of Amsterdam (EU 1997), member states have been trying to reach a consensus. Instead, they have been improvising. They failed to find a consensus at the two following intergovernmental conferences (2000 and 2004). Confronted with the negative French and Dutch referenda on the Constitutional Treaty and a growing discontent among EU public opinion regarding enlargement, the European Parliament and the Council charged the Commission with writing yet another report, this time on the absorption capacity of the EU. The Commission accepted the task grudgingly and dealt with the request only partially. It decided to write a new report on enlargement issues. In an annex to the report, the Commission deals with the more positive and future oriented notion of EU 'integration capacity' instead of the pejorative Copenhagen notion 'absorption capacity'. Still this annex is interesting, for it shows where the Commission stands in this phase of EU–Turkey negotiations. In addition, it is a balanced report, for it compares advantages and disadvantages attached to EU enlargement. Here are its main findings (CEC 2006b):

- The capacity of the EU to maintain the momentum of European integration has three main components: institutions, common policies, and budget.
- The EU does not need new institutional arrangements simply for the sake of enlargement, it also needs them for the EU to function better.
- The two latest enlargements (2004 and 2007) were preceded by institutional reforms: the Nice treaty provided rules for up to 27 member states. This is no longer the case for the following enlargements.

- The allocation of seats in the European Parliament and the weighting of votes in the Council are central to the EU capacity to make decisions. Therefore, before any further enlargement, the EU will have to decide on those institutional reforms.
- Past enlargements have strengthened EU policies, as new member states have brought their own national expertise to the EU. The present *Acquis* reflects, in part, the impact of past enlargements. Some EU policies would bring even greater benefits if expanded to more countries under the right conditions, for example the internal market or the area of justice, freedom, and security.
- The EU needs to be in a position, as it enlarges, to continue developing common policies in all areas. Therefore, assessment of the impact of enlargement on EU policies will take place at all key stages of the enlargement process.
- The negotiation frameworks for Croatia and Turkey envisage a set of measures to enable their smooth integration in EU policies. They also lay down measures to ensure the proper functioning of EU policies after enlargement, such as transition periods, derogations, specific arrangements, and permanent safeguards.
- The Commission will examine the impact of future enlargements on agriculture and cohesion policies when assessing the budgetary impact of enlargement. This will take into account the future evolution of these policies.
- In the course of accession negotiations, the Commission will provide substantial assessments of the impact of accession on key policy areas, including the movement of persons, border management, agriculture, cohesion policy, and transport. Similar assessments will be conducted in the areas of energy policy and foreign and security policies, also taking into account EU strategic motives to enlarge in terms of increased stability, foreign and security policy assets, or secure energy supply.
- The EU needs to be in a position to continue financing its policies. The impact of enlargement on the EU budget will be carefully assessed throughout the enlargement process. Before any further accession, the EU will need to decide on the overall budgetary means required. The Commission's analysis will take account both of the budgetary aspects and of the increased economic dynamism generated by accessions.
- Conditionality is one of the pillars of the Commission's enlargement strategy. Good preparation by candidate countries facilitates their smooth integration into the EU. Monitoring will be based on the political, economic and *Acquis* criteria for membership. The Commission will pay particular attention to the establishment of the structures needed to ensure the rule of law. This includes administrative and judicial capacity and the fight against fraud and corruption.
- Candidate countries will be expected to demonstrate success in meeting precise benchmarks before a negotiation chapter can be opened or closed. Failure to meet a benchmark could lead to negotiations on the chapter concerned being suspended or reopened.
- The Commission wants greater transparency: screening reports, benchmarks for opening negotiation chapters as well as EU negotiation positions should

be made public. It is in the interest of all stakeholders in this process to avoid a gap between policymakers on the one side and the public on the other side.

- Democratic legitimacy means that the EU should listen to the expectations of its citizens. For any of its policies, including enlargement, the EU has to win the support of its citizens. Maintaining strict conditionality is essential to safeguard this support. So is confidence in the EU's integration capacity. In addition, better communication is an essential part of EU's enlargement policy. The EU, member states, and candidate countries need to intensify their efforts to foster mutual knowledge. The Civil Society Dialogue established with Turkey in 2004 and extended to the Western Balkan countries in 2006 should be further developed. It is important to involve the citizens in this dialogue and to address anxieties and misapprehensions.

Conclusion

From the preceding, we can conclude the following:

- The EU wants Turkey to settle border disputes with neighbouring countries peacefully. Whereas in the past Turkey pursued a rather assertive policy, in recent years this has changed for the better. Turkey shows itself more in favour of a policy of reconciliation with neighbours. This is partially due to domestic stability and Turkey's wish to join the EU. Relations with Syria have improved a lot, but relations with Northern Iraq and Armenia remain tense. Turkey should restrain itself if, for instance, Azerbaijan decides to recuperate its lost territory from Armenia or when the Kurds proclaim their independent state in Northern Iraq.
- Economic relations with Greece are improving; yet there is no framework available for settling disputes. The disagreement on the definition of whether conflicts between Turkey and Greece are of a legal or a political nature makes them almost insolvable.
- Regarding the Cyprus conflict, there is no progress; this conflict risks becoming one of those eternal conflicts for which the international community cannot find a solution.
- Turkey has not implemented the Additional Protocol extending the Association Agreement to the ten new member states. This is a serious situation and it looks as if Turkey does not recognize the impact of its behaviour on the EU sufficiently.
- As far as the so-called absorption capacity of the EU is concerned, this is a matter the EU has to solve for its own benefit. If the EU wants to become more than a Common Market, it first has to reform its internal decision-making process.

6   Final conclusion

In this last chapter we will try to answer the two following questions:

- Does Turkey satisfy the Copenhagen criteria?
- What are the costs and benefits linked to membership for the EU as well as Turkey?

Turkey, the EU and the Copenhagen criteria

Table 6.1 summarizes our findings. We conclude that from an economic point of view in the medium run Turkey does qualify for membership. It has made progress in economic reform, while some macroeconomic imbalances have remained. Thanks to the IMF, it has also taken steps towards macroeconomic stability and structural reforms, which will enhance its capacity to cope with competitive pressure and market forces within the EU. Harrison, Rutherford and Tarr state that even at the beginning of the 1990s Turkey was a more open economy than either Greece or Spain at the start of their accession to the EU. All three economies experienced the problem of excessive state involvement in their domestic economies. Although Greece, like Spain, adopted the external trade policies of the EU, Greece continued to support its state-owned enterprises to a much greater degree. Its fiscal deficit crowded out private investment and contributed to stagnant growth. As a result, between 1980 and 1992 Spain grew at over twice the rate of Greece. If Turkey wants to boost the growth of its economy still further, it should follow the example of Spain (Harrison *et al.* 1996: 10).

Despite the problems in the Turkish economy and Turkey's inability in adopting some chapters of the *Acquis communautaire*, the most important obstacles to membership are related to the Copenhagen political criteria. In recent years, Turkey has made important progress. Yet there still needs to be further improvement in this field. There is not enough freedom of religion. At any time, the military can intervene and push aside a democratically elected government. The Kurds do not enjoy local autonomy. These three elements are closely linked to the constitutional basis of the Turkish state, and it does not look as though this is going to change fundamentally in the near future.

Table 6.1 Does Turkey satisfy the Copenhagen criteria, 2008?

Copenhagen criteria	Yes	No
Functioning market economy	X	
Capacity to compete	X	
Acquis communautaire	X	
EMU	X	
Rule of law		X
Human rights		X
Good neighbourly relations		X
Cyprus		X

However, we think that the Copenhagen economic criteria are more important than the political ones in an essentially economic organization like the EU. By continuously absorbing new member states that were obviously not in favour of European political integration (the UK, Denmark, Austria, Sweden, Finland, Poland, the Czech Republic, Hungary, and so on) the EU implicitly decided to abandon the federalist model that had been conceived by its founding fathers.[1] While they pay lip service to the ideal of a united Europe, member states do not want to give up their own nations' distinctiveness. Governments will not say so explicitly – let alone the Brussels bureaucracy – because the EU integration process serves domestic purposes. By rallying political parties and the nation behind a common ideal, it creates cohesion in the economic, cultural and political field. The large majority of EU member states prefer a loose confederation of independent states, joined in a common currency area, with coordinated macroeconomic policies, in addition to a free trade area supplemented by a harmonization of regulations and standards (Alesina *et al.* 2000: 1293). In this context, enlargement should be seen in a different perspective. According to Alesina, Angeloni and Schuknecht, one should observe either small unions in which many prerogatives are centralized, or large unions in which few prerogatives are delegated above the national governments. This implies that the enlargement of the EU and the deepening of coordination of policies are contradictory, if the new members and the incumbents are heterogeneous (Alesina *et al.* 2005: 278). Instead of adapting the decision-making process, as the EU is now trying to do, it might even be feasible to reduce the legislative burden of the EU. According to Alesina *et al.*, in the past too many legislative areas have been transferred from national levels to EU level. Policies where economies of scale and/or externalities are predominant should be allocated at EU level (Alesina and Wacziarg 1999: 28; Alesina *et al.* 2005: 276). *The Economist* (2007a) echoes the same theme:

> The EU should scrap such pointless bodies as the Economic and Social Committee and the Committee of Regions; it should replace the European Parliament that cannot win legitimacy with a European Senate made up of national parliaments, and it should repatriate more powers back to nation-states.

Even in a large economic union like the EU-27 there are minimum political standards to be met by future member states as regards democracy, rule of law and respect of human rights. Yet, in such a union, the economic criteria assume more importance than the political ones. Negotiations with a view to enlarging the EU should concentrate on the Copenhagen economic criteria and on what is essential in the enlargement process: international trade, common market and business relations, and, in second order, environment and monetary matters. The number of chapters in the *Acquis communautaire* could easily be reduced from thirty-five to ten. If the EU is committed to turning Turkey into a workable democracy with respect for human rights, we think the EU should encourage this process. Doing otherwise might hurt EU economic, political and security interests. Moreover, it will hurt the global image of the EU, as a moral arbiter on the world stage. Most certainly, there is in Turkey a progressive trend towards more democratic openness, inclusion of diversified class structures in mainstream politics, social justice and respect for human rights. The EU should not create the illusion that Turkey is treated differently from the South European countries and the CEEC.

Benefits and burdens

By way of conclusion, one can justifiably ask oneself whether it is worthwhile to putting so much energy into this enlargement process when the outcome is – to put it mildly – very doubtful. What are the benefits and burdens for both parties? Although assessing them is like reading tea leaves, we have tried to do so. Table 6.2 summarizes our findings. We will look first at the benefits and burdens for the EU; then we will concentrate on Turkey.

Benefits and burdens for the EU

Table 6.2 shows that immediate economic benefits will be very limited for the EU, because of both the modest size of the Turkish economy and the degree of economic integration that existed before accession. Political benefits are more tangible but depend on Turkey's goodwill. On the one hand, enlargement is the essence of the EU soft power: its power to transform its neighbours into functioning democracies and market economies (Rehn 2006c). By exporting European laws and values, the EU can expand a zone that is committed to prosperous and peaceful coexistence and the rule on law (*The Economist* 2004a). On the other hand, after the stillborn Constitutional Treaty and the commotion surrounding it, the EU finds itself in a serious political crisis. Many see Turkey's membership aspirations as complicating things at a time when the EU agenda is already so intricate. Many also suffer from enlargement fatigue. The EU is still struggling to come to terms with the increase in membership from fifteen to twenty-seven countries (Centre for European Reforms Essays 2004: 2). Finally, yet importantly, European public opinion is vehemently opposed to further enlargement. It still doubts the appropriateness of previous enlargements. French and Dutch citizens rejected the Constitutional Treaty because they were concerned about job losses,

Table 6.2 Possible benefits and burdens for Turkey and the EU, 2008

Benefits and burdens	Turkey	EU
Possible economic benefits	• free movement of workers • agricultural and structural subsidies • increased trade • increased investment • productivity growth because of reallocation • macroeconomic stability	• in the long run: increased trade and investment opportunities • security of energy supplies
Possible political benefits	• consolidation of reforms • better protection of human rights • solution of the Kurdish problem • political stability and harmony	• credible commitment and 'soft power' • anchoring Turkey to the West • EU opening to the Muslim world • increase in political clout • more credible defence capacity • better relations with the USA • solution of the Cyprus problem • better control of illegal immigration
Possible economic burdens	• farmers and industries squeezed out of market • significant financial transfers to farmers • new institutions require financial means	• budget appropriations for Turkey • loss of structural subsidies for regions • complication of CAP and structural reforms
Possible political burdens	• disagreement among military and government • manifestation of Islamists • regional autonomy requests from Kurds • deterioration of relations with neighbours • necessary fiscal reforms might cause political unrest	• membership is unacceptable to public opinion • complicated decision-making • new stand-still in European integration process • Morocco, Russia, Georgia and Ukraine will use Turkish example as precedent

immigrants, globalization, delocalization of national companies towards cheaper Eastern European markets and the possible accession of Turkey to the EU (Traser 2005: 30).

Table 6.3, based on the *Eurobarometer* survey of March–May 2006, shows that – even if Turkey should meet all the Copenhagen criteria – 49 per cent of EU-25 citizens are against Turkey joining the EU, while about 38 per cent are in favour. Citizens from the EU-10 are slightly more in favour of Turkey joining (44 per cent) than the EU-15. The country whose population most strongly opposed Turkish membership was Austria (81 per cent), while Sweden was the current member state most in favour (61 per cent). Austrian chancellor Wolfgang Schüssel and French president Nicolas Sarkozy have said that they may hold a referendum on the issue, an unprecedented approach to EU enlargement. These figures suggest that referenda would be lost in a number of member states, by wide margins. EU

Table 6.3 Question: 'Once Turkey complies with all the conditions set by the EU, would you be in favour of or opposed to the accession of Turkey in the EU?', 2006 (%)

Reply	EU-15	EU-10	Turkey
In favour of	38	44	54
Opposed to	49	40	22

Source: Eurobarometer (2006: 255).

public opinion seems to reject overwhelmingly Turkey's bid for membership for different reasons. Those on the right are opposed to a 'more Muslim' Europe. They argue that – because of higher birth rates of Muslims linked to further immigration – in twenty to fifty years Muslims might come to power in some EU member states. European federalists fear for the further dilution of the European project. Proponents of this view argue that, if Turkey joins the EU, there is no logical basis for denying membership to Ukraine, Russia, Israel, Morocco, and so on. Yet, some delimitation of Europe is necessary if the idea of Europe is to retain meaning and practical utility (Murphy 2004: 585). It is no coincidence that countries such as the UK or Spain, preferring a looser form of integration, are emerging as the active supporters of Turkish membership, while countries such as France and Germany seem to be having second thoughts (Önis 2004: 508).

Benefits and burdens for Turkey

For Turkey, the economic benefits are real, but, if the EU – as is generally expected – excludes Turkey from the CAP, structural policy and the free movement of workers, EU membership becomes a lot less attractive. In the end, Turkey might get new opportunities for increased trade, higher investment and higher growth of productivity. The development of negotiations with the EU will help the continued efforts of Turkey to liberalize trade and ensure macroeconomic stability. Yet, taken at face value, these benefits could also be reached without EU membership if the will existed to go down the chosen path. More and more Turkish citizens are asking themselves whether the adoption of the *Acquis communautaire* – the Maastricht criteria, rules on competition and state aid, expensive environmental rules, hygiene standards on food production, industrial and social policy, designed as they are for countries at a higher stage of economic and social development – is the most appropriate strategy for Turkey's development. An institutionally weak country like Turkey may have to reverse the sequence of reforms against its own interests (Esfahani 2003: 824; Burrell 2005b: 284).

It is even more difficult to say something meaningful about political benefits and burdens. Most certainly, without the incentive of EU membership, political liberalization might go backwards. Yet for many Turks the reforms induced by the political Copenhagen criteria are dangerous. Compared to the CEEC, the elites within Turkish society are divided on the issue of EU-related reforms. EU aspirations have created a kind of cohesiveness that links some of Turkey's key groups in the establishment: the Muslim democrats, secularists, part of the armed forces and the business community represented by Tüsiad.[2] They see EU norms, such as the Copenhagen criteria, as crucial for the realization of basic human rights and freedoms in Turkey (Taniyici 2003: 479). However there seems to be no strong political commitment from Turkish grassroots society (Centre for European Reforms Essays 2004: 3). In Turkey legal reforms are not the result of a well-devised strategy but they come about haphazardly because of negotiations with the EU. Additionally, the objectives of key players are contradictory. While Islamists and Kurds hope for the EU to promote more religious-inspired legislation and regional autonomy, the army wants the EU to defend Atatürk's Western modernization dream against what it sees as the combined attack of Islamists, Kurds and other leftist separatists (Hughes 2006: 8). While the AKP government refers to the Copenhagen criteria to ease restrictions on expressions of religious identity, the secular establishment calls on the European Court of Justice to suppress them. As long as it believes Kemalism is under threat, the Turkish establishment will be very reluctant to relax restrictions by giving in to the Copenhagen political criteria for EU membership. Similarly it will be difficult to know whether the Islamists' support for EU membership is real or whether it is just a means to introduce the Shari'a into Turkey (Jenkins 2003: 61). Finally, there seems to be a fundamental lack of confidence between Turkey and the EU, which is based on history. The issue of EU membership is closely intertwined with the nature of Turkish society. Turkey seems to be increasingly polarized along religious and secular lines. Like the EU, Turkey is coping with an identity crisis. Negotiations between Turkey and the EU have come too soon. Perhaps both the EU and Turkey should first solve their identity crises.

Notes

Introduction

1 The budget foreseen for Turkey in the revised Accession Partnership was 149 million Euros in 2002, 144 million Euros in 2003, 250 million Euros in 2004, 300 million Euros in 2005 and 500 million Euros in 2006. The amount offered to the EU-12 in their Accession Partnerships was significantly higher: 3.12 billion Euros annually (Harun 2003: 100).
2 The Maastricht criteria were also used by some EU member states eager to join the Economic and Monetary Union to justify budget cuts.

1 Short survey of the history of Turkey

1 Many years later, young Iranians were going to do the same, eventually bringing down the repressive regime of the Shah in 1979.
2 Precisely the opposite was going to happen: after the First World War the positions of France and the UK in the Middle East would be stronger than ever before.
3 Since then, the United Nations, as successor to the League of Nations, has often been confronted with the same kinds of tragedy.
4 Kurds were reclassified as 'Mountain Turks', and evidence to the contrary was to be erased (Bonner 2005: 48).
5 According to Zürcher (1997: 197), this explains why illiteracy has remained relatively high in Turkey, even compared with other developing countries.
6 Islamic law, for example, forbids a Muslim woman from marrying a non-Muslim man unless he converts to Islam. Islamic law allows husbands to divorce their wives if there is a justifiable reason, by clearly saying 'I divorce you' in the presence of witnesses. Conversion by Muslims to other religions is strictly forbidden and is punished by death.
7 Turkey imported 57.2 per cent of its oil from Iran and Iraq (Liel 2001: 109).
8 Out of this initiative grew the Black Sea Economic Cooperation Organization (1998). Its aim was to promote private-sector activity and encourage the free movement of goods and services among the eleven member states (Albania, Armenia, Azerbaijan, Bulgaria, Georgia, Greece, Moldova, Romania, Russia, Serbia, Turkey and Ukraine). Because of rivalries and diverging interests between member states, this organization does not play any significant role in today's international relations (Larrabee and Lesser 2003: 122).

2 History of Turkey–EU relations

1 This was unfair. During the Second World War Turkey had adhered to the neutral status of the sea lanes as laid down in the Convention of Montreux. It had even granted Soviet warships the right to sail through the straits.

2 At first the West European countries did not favour Turkey's membership of the OEEC and NATO, because it would create an overextension of West European commitments. Before Korea, Turkey's application for NATO membership had been turned down three times.

3 Apart from Turkey, the Baghdad Pact also encompassed the UK, Iran, Iraq and Pakistan. After the 1958 coup in Baghdad it changed its name to the Central Treaty Organization (CENTO). In 1979 Iran withdrew from it, and the organization – which had never properly functioned – was abolished. The Balkan Pact encompassed Greece, Turkey and Yugoslavia.

4 Skilled workers emigrated from the German territory occupied by the Soviet army. Unskilled workers were found in Turkey; Germany was among the first European countries to import *Gastarbeiter* (guest workers).

5 Birkelbach said 'they should not pick the raisins out the cake'.

6 In accordance with its Association Agreement, Greece had the right to veto reductions in the common external tariff levied on some imports. This right did not hold if the EC signed Association Agreements.

7 The Fourth Protocol was blocked in the Council of Ministers by Greece.

8 The proposals were named after Abel Matutes Juan, the Spanish commissioner in charge of Mediterranean Affairs.

9 Since Maastricht it has been common to refer to the European Union (EU) instead of the European Community. The EU encompasses the three so-called pillars: EC matters, foreign and security policy, and home affairs and domestic security. The EU does not have legal personality. If the Reform Treaty takes force, this will change.

10 Decisions have to be taken at the lowest possible level, as close as possible to the citizen. The EC only takes decisions that affect the citizens of all member states.

11 The European Economic Area (EEA) Agreement was negotiated between the EC, the then member states, and seven member states of the EFTA and was signed in May 1992. Subsequently, Switzerland decided not to participate following a referendum, and Finland, Austria and Sweden joined the EU. The EEA agreement came into force on 1 January 2004. The EEA was maintained because of the wish of the three remaining countries – Norway, Iceland and Liechtenstein – to participate in the internal market, while not assuming the full responsibilities of EU membership.

12 *Paragraph 4*: 'In this respect the European Council stresses the principle of peaceful settlement of disputes in accordance with the United Nations Charter and urges candidate states to make every effort to resolve any outstanding border disputes and other related issues. Failing this, they should within a reasonable time, bring the dispute to the International Court of Justice.'
Paragraph 9a: 'The European Council welcomes the launch of the talks aiming at a comprehensive settlement of the Cyprus problem on 3 December in New York and expresses its strong support for the UN Secretary-General's efforts to conclude the process.'

13 Austria's favoured alternative to Turkish membership – privileged partnership – was rejected, but Austria got what it wanted in that accession negotiations with Croatia were going to start soon.

14 These six pieces are: the law on associations, the new penal code, the law on intermediate courts of appeal, the code of criminal procedure, the legislation establishing the judicial police and the law on execution of punishments (CEC: 2004b).

15 This happened on 29 July 2005. However, Prime Minister Erdoğan made it very clear that this did not imply diplomatic recognition of Cyprus.

3 The Copenhagen economic criteria

1 This prediction has been extensively confirmed by empirical work.

2 A treasure bill is a short-term debt obligation backed by the US government with a

maturity of less than one year. Treasury bills are issued through a competitive bidding process at a discount from par, which means that, rather than there being fixed-interest payments as with conventional bonds, the appreciation of the bond provides the return to the holder.

3 The Central Bank could also have sterilized its foreign-exchange operations: in the case of foreign capital inflows, it could have sold domestic assets with domestic currency. In that case, the increase in foreign reserves would have been exactly offset by a decrease in domestic assets. In that way the expansion in the money supply and the associated effects (drop in the interest rate, increase in consumption) might have been avoided.

4 The crisis erupted when Prime Minister Ecevit stormed out of a meeting with President Sezer because the President criticized the government for failing to fight corruption.

5 Until then Turkey had had a crawling peg system, under which the Turkish lira was allowed to slide down by about 15 per cent against a currency basket comprising the American dollar and the Euro.

6 COFACE is a private international organization active in the field in facilitating business-to-business trade worldwide: business information (marketing and financial), credit insurance, credit management and factoring.

7 The specialization index in a specific sector: the minimum figure of exports or imports in that sector multiplied by 2, divided by exports + imports in that sector.

8 The revealed comparative advantages index: the share of the exports of a specific sector in total exports divided by the share of the imports of that sector in total imports.

9 These services mainly comprise computer and information services; 'merchanting' and other trade-related services; operational leasing services; legal, accounting, management consulting, professional and technical services; advertising, market research and public-opinion polling services; research and development services; architectural, engineering and other technical services; agriculture, mining and on-site processing services (Amiti and Wei 2005: 318). 'Merchanting' is defined as the purchase of a good by a resident of the compiling economy from a non-resident and the subsequent resale of the good to another resident; during the process the good does not enter or leave the compiling economy.

10 Sweden did not join the EMU either. The legal basis for this is shaky, to say the least. From the new member states, Slovenia joined the EMU on 1 January 2007. Malta and Cyprus joined on 1 January 2008.

11 The Commission considers 'Foreign, security and defence policy', 'Justice, freedom and security' and 'Education and culture' as part of the *Acquis communautaire* and thus of the economic Copenhagen criteria. One could also argue that they are already part of the Copenhagen political criteria (see next chapter).

12 The USA puts Turkey on the list of 'risky countries' as far as protection of intellectual property rights is concerned.

13 HS: Harmonized Commodity Description and Coding System.

14 By imposing identical EU rules in all free trade agreements, EU corporations will get a competitive advantage in international trade and investment if these rules eventually become universally accepted (François *et al.* 2005: 1552).

15 For agricultural products, the position of Turkey is close to that of the 'G20' developing countries.

16 Turkey argued that, in accordance with the customs union agreement, the product could have been re-exported to the EU and thus Turkey had to prohibit its imports into the country. Yet, the WTO Panel ruled that Turkey could have prevented the product from being re-exported to the EU by other means – e.g. rules of origin. The case was solved by mutually satisfactory compensation (see WTO 2001: 25).

17 Turkey was a founding member of the ECO, which encompasses Turkey, Iran, Afghanistan and seven CIS member states.

18 The mark-up is defined as:

$$\frac{\textit{Sales minus labour costs minus material costs}}{\textit{Sales}}$$

19 Even under the prevailing strict regime, there is, as a result of family integration and family formation, an annual net migration from Turkey to the EU-15 in the order of 35,000 people (Erzan *et al.* 2004: 11).

20 In a country like Austria the share of the Islamic population might grow from 4 per cent to as much as 26 per cent by 2050 (Kaufmann 2006: 4).

21 Predictions suggested a net inflow of only 13,000 workers a year up until the end of the decade. Instead figures released on 22 August 2006 showed that 427,000 migrants from Eastern Europe had registered for work between May 2004 and June 2006. These figures do not include the self-employed. Allowing for that, the true figure might be nearly 600,000 (*The Economist* 2006e).

22 According to Buğra (2003:459), Turkey is one of the few countries in the world where there were no productivity improvements in agriculture between the early 1980s and the late 1990s.

23 In the EU-10 member states, average agricultural prices were lower than EU-15 prices, so in principle no compensation for income losses was due. However, on the insistence of some new member states, compensation will be given. This could also play into Turkey's hands: part of the direct payments would be paid from the EU budget post-accession.

24 Some member states favour re-natoinalising the CAP.

25 France and the UK were the two countries that voted differently from the rest of the member states most frequently.

26 There are different views in this field. France – not a member of NATO's Integrated Military Command – prefers an independent stance towards the USA, while the UK favours close cooperation with the USA. Belgium prefers Community decision making in the military field (with roles to play for the Commission, the European Parliament and the European Court).

27 This alliance serves three purposes: counterbalancing Syria, which used to support the PKK; getting weapons denied by the USA and the EU because of the resistance of the US Congress and European parliaments; strengthening the alliance with the USA (Larrabee and Lesser 2003: 140–4).

28 Afterwards relations soured. Although the USA had first called upon the Kurds to rise up against the Iraqi regime, the advance of coalition troops was called to a halt under pressure from the Arab allies and Turkey, which did not want to see Iraq dismembered or a Kurdish state being established in the north of Iraq. Kurdish refugees were not allowed to enter Turkish territory (Zürcher 1997: 334).

29 The USA refused to ratify the treaty.

30 The Erdoğan government performs a difficult balancing act. For instance, Erdoğan visited Israel in the spring of 2005, while a few months later the Hamas representative, Khaled Mashal, visited Turkey (Kirişçi 2006: 89).

31 Like the EU, Turkey thinks that the American policy versus the Middle East – inspired as it is by the American Enterprise Institute ('Project for a New American Century') – will have dire consequences. It is impossible to impose democracy by force. Like the EU, Turkey favours a slow evolution towards democracy and therefore supports the EU policy of dialogue and constructive engagement (Kirişçi 2006: 82).

32 Turkey has 514,000 troops enrolled. This compares with 210,000 from the UK; 260,000 from France; 296,000 from Germany (Emerson and Tocci 2004: 32).

33 In 2008 the objective to make operational a Rapid Reaction Force of 60,000 by the end of 2003 has yet to be realized.

34 The old one was apparently the UK. The Turkish media reported US support during EU–Turkey negotiations culminating in the October 2005 Negotiating Framework. Foreign Minister Gül thanked Condoleezza Rice in person for this (Kirişçi 2006: 84).

35 The UK and Ireland stay completely out of Schengen, while Denmark has an opt-out

clause. Norway, Iceland and Switzerland are in the Schengen zone. Some of the twelve new member states are not yet in the zone.
36 In 2007 only seven EU member states had signed this treaty: Belgium, France, Germany, Luxemburg, Netherlands, Spain and Austria.
37 Visas are easily obtained at airports or other entry points.
38 Turkey has entered a reservation into the Geneva Convention on the Status of Refugees: only European refugees and people of Turkish descent and culture can apply for asylum.
39 In a Readmission Agreement, the state declares itself ready to take back illegal refugees having the nationality of that state or having stayed or transited through its territory.
40 Turkey itself is still on the negative EU list.
41 Goods are purchased by visitors in Turkey and are then transported as luggage for resale in the home countries. The OECD calculates that these exports represent almost 20 per cent of total Turkish exports (Lohrman 2002: 46).
42 According to the right of 'non-refoulement', asylum-seekers are not to be sent back to countries where their lives are in danger.

4 The Copenhagen political criteria

1 The frequency with which political parties were dissolved was nevertheless a real source of concern, and the Council of Europe hoped that in future the constitutional changes would limit the use of such extreme measures as dissolution. (Since 1982 the Turkish Supreme Court has dissolved eight political parties.)
2 This Charter is not legally binding. This will change once the Reform Treaty takes effect. Yet two member states (Poland and the UK) have entered a reservation in the treaty with respect to the legally binding nature of the Charter.
3 When on 28 February 1997 the military stepped in to remove the Islamist Welfare Party from power, it justified its action by arguing that it upheld Turkey's commitment to full EU membership (Cizre and Çinar 2003: 314; Tekin 2005: 296).
4 General Yasar Buyukhanit, the new chief of general staff, echoes this theme (Baran 2006).
5 In March 1995 the Turkish army intervened on its own initiative in Northern Iraq with the clear aim of 'putting an end to terrorism'. Germany, Norway and the Netherlands imposed an arms embargo, while the European Parliament and the Parliamentary Assembly of the Council of Europe threatened to impose sanctions on Turkey (Müftüler-Bac 1996: 261–2). On 1 March 2003 the Turkish Parliament refused to approve the deployment of American troops on Turkish soil destined to invade Iraq. In October 2003 the Parliament authorized the deployment of Turkish troops to join the American forces in Iraq. However, because of Iraqi Kurdish opposition and apparent American reluctance, the offer was repealed (Somer 2005: 115).
6 In 2004 the NSC was for the first time led by a civilian, Mehmet Yigit Alpogan, the son of a famous general (Bonner 2005: 58).
7 In November 2005 security forces allegedly perpetrated a bombing against a Kurdish bookshop in the city of Semdlinli. The prosecutor charged high-ranking military commanders with involvement. Yet, upon insistence of the general staff, the High Council of Judges and Prosecutors applied the highest disciplinary sanction against the prosecutor: dismissal from office.
8 Five member states of the Council of Europe accounted for over 60 per cent of the judgments in 2005: Turkey: 290 (26.24 per cent); Ukraine: 120 (10.86 per cent); Greece: 105 (9.5 per cent); Russia: 83 (7.5 per cent); Italy: 79 (7.15 per cent).
9 It is important to mention that the Court did uphold the ban on the Refah (Welfare) Party (February 2003) and the ban on headscarves in Turkish universities (June 2004) (European Court of Human Rights).

10 Amnesty International has also welcomed the Turkish government's declared commit-ment to a zero tolerance for torture policy. Amnesty International has noted that there are fewer reports of torture and ill-treatment in police custody and that the safeguards in the protection of suspects against ill-treatment have been improved. Yet the govern-ment's commitment to a zero tolerance for torture can never be regarded as a sincere and fully effective policy until real steps have been taken to ensure that officials who violate the absolute prohibition on torture and other ill-treatment are brought to justice (Amnesty International 2007).

11 It gives fanatics the chance to take to courts some of Turkey's finest journalists, including Hrant Dink, as well as writers and scholars. Prosecutions have exposed many people to the rage of nationalistic and religious fanatics. Hrant Dink was assassinated in January 2007 by such a fanatic.

12 This was sharply criticized by Mr Olli Rehn (2006b), European commissioner in charge of enlargement.

13 In March 2005 there were serious incidents during a demonstration promoting women's rights.

14 The Alevi maintain that their religion is separate from Islam, and that it is a purely Anatolian faith based on Shaman and Zoroastrian beliefs going back 6,000 years. Christian, Jewish and Islamic influences were added later, though the Alevi accept that the Islamic influence is the strongest (*The Economist* 2005a).

15 Other churches do appoint foreign-born missionaries and priests.

16 The law allows 161 recognized minority foundations to acquire property. However, the legislation does not allow the foundations to reclaim hundreds of properties expropri-ated by the state over the years (US Department of State 2004: 14).

17 Foreigners resident in the Ottoman Empire were subject to the laws of their respec-tive countries. Various non-Muslim minorities were allowed semi-autonomy in matters affecting their personal status. The capitulations were abolished by the Treaty of Lausanne (1923).

18 The Greek minority also encounters problems with respect to education and property.

19 According to human-rights organizations, there are about 4.5 million 'internally displaced persons'. This figure is disputed by the Turkish government.

20 Village Guards are paramilitary troops that assist the regular army in suppressing the Kurdish rebellion. Human-rights organizations have criticized their activities.

21 One of the most famous of them is Leyla Zana, who was sentenced to fifteen years in prison for having spoken Kurdish at the inauguration ceremonies in Parliament. The European Parliament awarded her the 1995 Sakharov Peace Prize. Under EU pressure, she was released in 2002.

22 In March 2006 local television stations began broadcasting in Kurdish (*The Economist* 2006a). Ironically, it was in the interest of the Turkish government itself to allow this: until recently the PKK-aligned channel MED-TV had – via satellite from Europe – a virtual monopoly on Kurdish-language programming (Cornell 2001: 44).

23 The changes do not cover the use of Kurdish as a teaching medium.

24 France has also refused to sign the convention, while Belgium and Luxembourg refuse to ratify it.

25 Belgium and Portugal have refused to sign this convention, while France and Poland have not ratified it.

5 Other conditions

1 The army was opposed to taking part in the operation but the government had its way.

2 Some refer to Turkey and Azerbaijan as 'one nation, two states'. Some also call Azerba-ijan 'Turkey's East Germany' because of investments by Turkish firms in low wage sectors in that country (Hughes 2004: 12).

3 On 28 February 2002 the European Parliament stated that Turkey must recognize the Armenian genocide before it could join the EU. The Turks deny there was genocide. They insist that Armenians – who had collaborated with the invading Russian forces in eastern Turkey – died from hunger and disease during their mass deportation to Syria. This theory does not find much support with historians outside Turkey. In contrast with its predecessors, the AKP government has declared its readiness to have the issue debated. To this end, a conference was organized in September 2005 (Kirişçi 2006: 50).

4 Austria, Belgium, Bulgaria, Cyprus, Denmark, Estonia, Finland, Greece, Hungary, Luxembourg, Malta, Netherlands, Poland, Portugal, Slovakia, Spain, Sweden and the UK.

5 In June 1997 President Clinton sent Richard Holbrooke, the architect of the Dayton Peace Accord for Bosnia, to Cyprus.

6 The Turkish military voiced its support for the Turkish Cypriot president Rauf Denktas, who opposed the Annan Plan.

7 While the movement of persons is encouraging (some 40,000 Turkish Cypriots now have Cypriot passports), Green Line trade remains very limited, amounting to approximately 160,000 Euros per month (CEC, n.d.).

6 Final conclusion

1 Even then, countries like France did not favour this supranational approach.

2 Tüsiad played an important role on the road from Luxembourg (1997) to Helsinki (1999), particularly in terms of influencing the decisions of the two key countries, Germany and Greece (Önis 2000: 474).

References

Akgüngör, S., Barbaros, F. and Kumral, N. (2002), 'Competitiveness of the Turkish Fruit and Vegetable Processing Industry in the European Market', *Russian and East European Finance and Trade*, 38(3): 34–53.

Akyüz, Y. and Boratav, K. (2003), 'The Making of the Turkish Financial Crisis', *World Development,* 31(9): 1549–66. Online: <http://www.econturk.org/Turkisheconomy/boratav.pdf#search=%22allintitle%3A%20korkut%20boratav%22> (accessed 2 September 2007).

Alba, J. D. and Park, D. (2005), 'An Empirical Investigation of Purchasing Power Parity for Turkey', *Journal of Policy Modelling*, 27(8): 989–1000.

Alesina, A. (2002), 'The Size of Countries: Does it Matter?', Discussion Paper No. 1975, Harvard Institute of Economic Research.

Alesina, A. and Perotti, R. (2004), 'The European Union: A Politically Incorrect View', *Journal of Economic Perspectives*, 18(4): 27–48.

Alesina, A. and Wacziarg, R. (1999), 'Is Europe going too far?', NBER Working Papers 6883, National Bureau of Economic Research; Carnegie–Rochester Conference Series on Public Policy, Elsevier Science, 51.

Alesina, A., Spolaore, E. and Wacziarg, R. (2000), 'Economic Integration and Political Disintegration', *American Economic Review*, 90(5): 1276–96.

Alesina, A., Angeloni, I. and Schuknecht, L. (2005), 'What Does the European Union Do?', *Public Choice*, 123: 275–319.

Aleskerov, F., Avci, G., Iakouba, V. and Türem U. Z. (2002), 'European Union Enlargement: Power Distribution Implications of the New Institutional Arrangements', *European Journal of Political Research*, 41: 379–94.

Allemand, F. (2006) 'Le Poids de la Turquie en Europe', *Futuribles: Analyse et Prospective*, 18: 13–29.

Amadeus (n.d.), 'Database'.

Amiti, M. and Wei, Shang-Ji (2005), 'Fear of Outsourcing: Is it Justified?', *Economic Policy*, 20(42): 309–47.

Amnesty International (2005), 'Report on Turkey'. Online: <http://web.amnesty.org/report2005/tur-summary-eng> (accessed 2 September 2007).

—— (2007), 'Report on Turkey'. Online: <http://web.amnesty.org/library/Index/ENGEUR440132007> (accessed 2 September 2007).

Andrews, C. (1998), 'EU Enlargement: The Political Process', Library Research Paper 98/55, House of Commons.

Annan, K. (2002), 'Plan for Cyprus Settlement'. Full Text. Online: <http://www.tcea.org.uk/Annan-Plan-For-Cyprus-Settlement.htm> (accessed 12 December 2007).

Apap, J., Carrera, S. and Kirişçi, K. (2004), 'Turkey in the European Area of Freedom, Security and Justice', EU–Turkey Working Papers, 3.

Aral, B. (2004), 'Fifty Years on: Turkey's Voting Orientation at the UN General Assembly, 1948–97', *Middle Eastern Studies*, 40(2): 137–60.

Atici, C. and Kennedy, P. L. (2005), 'Tradeoffs between Income Distribution and Welfare: The Case of Turkey's Integration into the European Union', *Journal of Policy Modelling*, 27: 553–63.

Augier, P. and Gasiorek, M. (2003), 'The Welfare Implications of Trade Liberalization between the Southern Mediterranean and the EU', *Applied Economics*, 35: 1171–90.

Axt, H.-J. (2002), 'Selbstbewusstere Türkei: Worauf sich die EU einstellen muss', *Internationale Politik*, 57(1): 45–50.

Aydin, S. and Keyman, E. F. (2004), 'European Integration and the Transformation of Turkish Democracy', EU–Turkey Working Papers 2.

Aydinli, E., Özcan, N. A. and Akyaz, D. (2006), 'The Turkish Military's March toward Europe', *Foreign Affairs*, 85(1): 77–90.

Balasubramanyam, V. N. and Corless, N. (2001), 'Foreign Direct Investment in Turkey and the Transitional Economies of Eastern Europe', in S. Togan and V. N. Balasubramanyam (eds), *Turkey and Central and Eastern European Countries in Transition*, Basingstoke and New York: Palgrave, 51–64.

Baldwin, R. and Widgrén, M. (2004), 'Winners and Losers under Various Dual-Majority Voting Rules for the EU Council of Ministers', Centre for European Policy Studies Policy Brief, 50.

—— (2005), 'The Impact of Turkey's Membership on EU Voting', Centre for European Policy Studies Policy Brief, 62.

Baran, Z. (2006), 'The Coming Coup d'Etat?', *Newsweek*, 4 December.

Barysch, K. (2005), 'The Economics of Turkish Accession', Essays Centre for European Reform. Online: <http://www.cer.org.uk.> (accessed 2 September 2007).

Bekmez, S. (2002), 'Sectoral Impacts of Turkish Accession to the European Union', *Eastern European Economics*, 40(2): 57–84.

Berument, M. H., Malatyali, N. K. and Neyapti, B. (2001), 'Turkey's Full Membership to the European Union', *Russian and East European Finance and Trade*, 37(4): 50–60.

Bilgin, P. (2005), 'Turkey's Changing Security Discourses: The Challenge of Globalisation', *European Journal of Political Research*, 44: 175–201.

Boel, M. F. (2006), 'Simplification of the CAP: Meeting the Challenge', paper presented at 'A Single CAP for Europe' conference in Brussels, 3 October.

Boeri, T. and Brücker, H. (2001), 'Eastern Enlargement and EU–Labor Markets: Perceptions, Challenges and Opportunities', *World Economics*, 2(1). Online: <http://www.lavoce.info/news/attach/immigration.doc.> (accessed 2 September 2007).

Bonner, A. (2005), 'Turkey, the European Union and Paradigm Shifts', *Middle East Policy*, 12(1): 44–71.

Boratav, K. and Özugurlu, M. (2006), 'Social Policies and Distributional Dynamics in Turkey: 1923–2002', in Massoud Karshenas and Valentine M. Moghadam (eds), *Social Policy in the Middle East. Economic, Political and Gender Dynamics*, United Nations Research Institute for Social Development; New York: Palgrave MacMillan, 156–89.

Bourrinet, J. (2005), 'Les Coûts de l'élargissement de l'UE de mai 2004', in J.-C. Vérez (ed.), *D'un élargissement à l'autre, la Turquie et les autres candidats*, Paris: l'Harmattan, 75–107.

Bryane, M. (2004), 'Anti-Corruption in the Turkey's EU Accession', *Turkish Policy Quarterly*, 3(4). Online: <http://www.turkishpolicy.com> (accessed 2 September 2007).

Buğra, A. (2003), 'The Place of the Economy in Turkish Society', *South Atlantic Quarterly*, 102(2/3): 453–70.

Buğra, A. (2004), 'Crise économique et transformations sociales', in Ali Kazancigil (ed.), *La Turquie au tournant du siècle*, Paris, Budapest and Turin: L'Harmattan, 53–62.

Buğra, A. and Keyder, C. (2006), 'The Turkish Welfare Regime in Transformation', *Journal of European Social Policy*, 16(3): 211–28.

Burrell, A. (2005a), 'Turkey's Foreign Trade Position', in Alison M. Burrell and Arie J. Oskam (eds), *Turkey in the European Union: Implications for Agriculture, Food and Structural Policy*, Wallingford and Cambridge, MA: CABI, 149–68.

—— (2005b), 'Opportunities, Threats and Challenges', in Alison M. Burrell and Arie J. Oskam (eds), *Turkey in the European Union: Implications for Agriculture, Food and Structural Policy*, Wallingford and Cambridge, MA: CABI, 279–86.

Cakmak, E. H. (2004), 'Structural Change and Market Opening in Turkish Agriculture', EU–Turkey Working Papers, 10.

CEC (Commission of the European Communities) (1989) *Bulletin of the European Commission*, 18 December.

—— (1997), *Agenda 2000. Voor een sterkere en grotere Unie*, Brussels: COM.

—— (1998), 'Regular Report from the Commission on Turkey's Progress towards Accession'. Online: <http://www.ec.europa.eu/enlargement/archives/pdf/key_documents/1998/turkey_en.pdf> (accessed 2 September 2007).

—— (1999), 'Regular Report from the Commission on Turkey's Progress towards Accession'. Online: <http://www.ec.europa.eu/enlargement/archives/pdf/key_documents/1999/turkey_en.pdf> (accessed 2 September 2007).

—— (2000), 'Regular Report from the Commission on Turkey's Progress towards Accession'. Online: <http://www.ec.europa.eu/enlargement/archives/pdf/key_documents/2000/turkey_en.pdf> (accessed 2 September 2007).

—— (2001), 'Regular Report from the Commission on Turkey's Progress towards Accession'. Online: <http://www.ec.europa.eu/enlargement/archives/pdf/key_documents/2001/turkey_en.pdf> (accessed 2 September 2007).

—— (2002), 'Regular Report from the Commission on Turkey's Progress towards Accession'. Online: <http://www.ec.europa.eu/enlargement/archives/pdf/key_documents/2002/turkey_en.pdf> (accessed 2 September 2007).

—— (2003a), 'CAP Reform'. Online: <http://www.ec.europa.eu/agriculture> (accessed 2 September 2007).

—— (2003b), 'Regular Report from the Commission on Turkey's Progress towards Accession'. Online: <http://www.ec.europa.eu/enlargement/archives/pdf/key_documents/2003/turkey_en.pdf> (accessed 2 September 2007).

—— (2004a), *Issues Arising from Turkey's Membership Perspective*, Brussels: COM.

—— (2004b), *Communication from the Commission to the Council and the European Parliament: Recommendation of the European Commission on Turkey's Progress towards Accession 2004*, Brussels: COM.

—— (2004c), 'Regular Report from the Commission on Turkey's Progress towards Accession'. Online: <http://www.ec.europa.eu/enlargement/archives/pdf/key_documents/2004/turkey_en.pdf> (accessed 2 September 2007).

—— (2005), 'Regular Report from the Commission on Turkey's Progress towards Accession'. Online: <http://www.ec.europa.eu/enlargement/archives/pdf/key_documents/2005/turkey_en.pdf> (accessed 2 September 2007).

—— (2006a), 'Regular Report from the Commission on Turkey's Progress towards Accession'. Online: <http://www.ec.europa.eu/enlargement/archives/pdf/key_documents/2006/package/sec_1426_final_progress_report_tr_en.pdf> (accessed 2 September 2007).

—— (2006b), 'Communication from the Commission to the European Parliament and the

Council: Enlargement Strategy and Main Challenges 2006–2007', including annexed special report on the EU's capacity to integrate new members, Brussels: COM.

—— (n.d.), 'Turkish Cypriot Community'. Online: <http://www.ec.europa.eu/enlargement/turkish_cypriot_community/index_en.htm> (accessed 2 September 2007).

Centre for European Reform Essays (2004), 'From Drift to Strategy: Why the EU should Start Accession Talks with Turkey'. Online: <http://www.cer.org.uk>.

Chaponnière, J.-R. and Vérez, J.-C. (2005), 'Analyse économique des échanges extérieurs de la Turquie et des Peco dans le contexte de l'élargissement', in Jean-Claude Vérez (ed.), *D'un élargissement à l'autre, la Turquie et les autres candidats*, Paris: l'Harmattan, 13–47.

CIA (2007), 'The World Factbook'. Online: <https://www.cia.gov/library/publications/the-world-factbook/> (accessed 12 September 2007).

Cizre, U. and Çinar, M. (2003), 'Turkey 2002: Kemalism, Islamism and Politics in the Light of the February 28 Process', *South Atlantic Quarterly*, 102(2/3): 309–31.

Claeys, P. and Dillen, K. (2004), *Een brug te ver: Turkije in de Europese Unie*, Brussel: Egmont, 2004.

COFACE Belgium (2006), '@ ratings EU and Turkey'. Online: <http://www.coface.be/CofacePortal/redirection.jsp?pageID=pages/home&site=BE/en_EN> (accessed 2 September 2007).

Cohen, S. B. (2004), 'The Geopolitics of Turkey's Accession to the European Union', *Eurasian Geography and Economics*, 45(8): 575–82.

Common Market Law Review (2005), 'Turkey's Quest for Membership of the European Union', 42: 1561–6.

Conclusions of the Presidency (1993), Copenhagen, DN: Doc/93/3; 22 June.

—— (1994a), Corfu, DN: Doc/94/1; 25 June.

—— (1994b), Essen, DN: DOC/94/4; 12 October.

—— (1995), Cannes, DN: Doc/95/6; 27 June.

—— (1997), Luxembourg, DN: DOC/97/24; 13 December 1997.

—— (1999a), Tampere, Online: <http://www.europarl.europa.eu/summits/tam_en.htm> (accessed 2 September 2007).

—— (1999b), Helsinki, Online: <http://europa.eu.int/council/off/conclu/dec99/dec99_en.htm#enlargement> (accessed 2 September 2007).

—— (2000), Nice, Online: <http://europa.eu.int/council/off/conclu/dec2000/dec2000_en.htm#2> (accessed 2 September 2007).

—— (2002), Copenhagen, Online: <http://www.gumruk.gov.tr/english/Gumruk/DosyaUpload/ab/haberler/copenhagen.pdf> (accessed 2 September 2007).

—— (2004), Brussels, Online: <http://www.abgs.gov.tr/index.php?p=300&l=2> (accessed 2 September 2007).

Constitution of Turkey (1961). Online: <http://www.anayasa.gen.tr/1961constitution-text.pdf> (accessed 2 September 2007).

Cornell, S. E. (2001), 'The Kurdish Question in Turkish Politics', *Orbis*, 45(1): 31–46.

Council of the European Communities (2003), 'Directive 2003/109/EC of 25 November 2003 Concerning the Status of Third-Country Nationals who are Long-Term Residents', *Official Journal of the European Union*, L 16, 23 January 2004. Online: <http://www.europa.eu.int/eur-lex/pri/en/oj/dat/2004/l_016/l_01620040123en00440053.pdf> (accessed 2 September 2007).

Council of the European Communities (2006a), 'Council Decision of 23 January 2006 on the Principles, Priorities, and Conditions Contained in the Accession Partnership with Turkey', *Official Journal of the European Union*, L 22/34, 26 January. Online: <http://www.eur-ex.europa.eu/smartapi/cgi/sga_doc?smartapi!celexplus!prod!DocNumber&lg=en&type_doc=Decision&an_doc=2006&nu_doc=35> (accessed 2 September 2007).

Council of the European Communities (2006b), 'Regulation 2006/1083/EC of 11 July Concerning General Principles on the EFRD, the ESF and the Cohesion Fund'. Online: <http://www.eur-lex.europa.eu/LexUriServ/LexUriServ.do?uri=OJ:L:2006:210:0025:01:NL:HTML> (accessed 2 September 2007).

Dahlman, C. (2004), 'Turkey's Accession to the European Union: The Geopolitics of Enlargement', *Eurasian Geography and Economics*, 45(8): 553–74.

Davison, A. (2003), 'Turkey, a "Secular" State? The Challenge of Description', *South Atlantic Quarterly*, 102(2/3): 333–50.

Democracy Coalition Project (2005),. 'Campaign for a United Nations Democracy Caucus'. Online: <http://www.demcoalition.org/2005_html/commu_cdm00.html> (accessed 2 September 2007).

Deringil, S. (2000),. *The Ottomans, the Turks, and World Power Politics*. Collected Studies, Istanbul: Isis Press.

Derviş, K., Gros, D., Öztrak, F., Bayar, F. and Işik, Y. (2004a), 'Turkey and the EU Budget: Prospects and Issues', EU–Turkey Working Papers, 6.

—— (2004b) 'Relative Income Growth and Convergence', EU–Turkey Working Papers, 8.

De Santis, R. A. (2003), 'The Impact of a Customs Union with the European Union on Internal Migration in Turkey', *Journal of Regional Science*, 43(2): 349–72.

De Standaard (2007a) 'Turkije succesverhaal ondanks lang strafblad', 5 February.

—— (2007b), 'Erdoğan: respect voor de seculiere staat', 24 July.

Diez, T., Stetter, S. and Albert, M. (2006), 'The European Union and Border Conflicts: The Transformative Power of Integration', *International Organization*, 60: 563–93.

Domke, D. M. (1997), *Turkey's Human Rights Record Impedes European Integration*, Washington, Center for Human Rights and Humanitarian Law, College of Law, American University, 4(2). Online: <http://www.wcl.american.edu/hrbrief/v4i3/index43.htm> (accessed 12 December 2007).

Dritsakis, N. (2004), 'Defense Spending and Economic Growth: An Empirical Investigation for Greece and Turkey', *Journal of Policy Modelling*, 26: 249–64.

EBRD (European Bank for Reconstruction and Development) (2005), 'Countries and Topics'. Online: <http://www.ebrd.com/country/index.htm> (accessed 2 September 2007).

EC–Turkey Association Council (1995), 'Decision No 1/95 on implementing the final phase of the Customs Union'. Online: <http:www.abmankara.gov.tr/ab/001e.html> (accessed 2 September 2007).

ECJ (European Court of Justice), 11 July 1974 (case 8/74); 20 February 1979 (case 120/78); 30 November 1995 (case C-55/94); 23 January 1997 (case 171/95); 9 December 1997 (case C-265/95); 4 December 2001 (case C-465/01); 18 March 2003 (case C-136/03); 12 June 2003 (case C-112/00). Online: <http://www.curia.europa.eu/en/content/juris/index.htm> (accessed 2 September 2007).

The Economist (2000a), 'Turkey: Uppity Soldiers', 7 September.

—— (2000b), 'Turkey: Not Yet Slotted in', 21 December.

—— (2001), 'Special: Turkey's Future. On the Brink Again', 22 February.

—— (2002), 'Turkey and Greece: Let's be Friends', 11 April.

—— (2004a), 'Charlemagne: Wider Still and Wider', 11 March.

—— (2004b), 'Charlemagne: Turkish Tales', 9 September.

—— (2004c), 'Human Rights in Turkey: Haunted by the Past', 11 November.

—— (2005a), 'Surveys: A Turkey. Which Turkey?', 17 March.

—— (2005b), 'Charlemagne: When to Talk Turkey', 15 September.

—— (2006a), 'Sheikh, Rattle and Roll; Turkey and Islam', 11 February.

—— (2006b), 'Turkey and its Kurds: Fighting on', 12 April.

—— (2006c), 'Emerging Market Indicators: Overview', 6 July.

—— (2006d), 'Turkish Education: School Scandals', 27 July

—— (2006e), 'Second Thoughts; Migration from Eastern Europe', 24 August.

—— (2006f), 'Turkey: Troubles Ahead', 19 October.

—— (2006g), 'Charlemagne: The Turkish Train Crash', 30 November.

—— (2006h), 'Tiptoeing through a Spiritual Minefield: The Pope in Turkey', 2 December.

—— (2007a), 'Europe's Mid-Life Crisis: The European Union', 15 March.

—— (2007b), 'Turkish Politics: Erdogan's Dilemma', 29 March.

—— (2007c), 'Turkey's Presidency: Erdogan's Presidential Gamble', 19 April.

—— (2007d), 'Turkey: Election Fever', 14 June.

—— (2007e), 'Turkey's Election: A Battler for the Future', 19 July.

—— (2007f), 'Turkey and Free Speech: Flying Insults', 27 July.

—— (2007g), 'The European Union in the World: Abroad be Dangers', 24 August.

Economist Intelligence Unit (2007), 'Country Report Turkey'. Online: <http:www.economist. com/countries/turkey> (accessed 2 September 2007).

Eder, M. (2003), 'Implementing the Economic Criteria of EU Membership: How Difficult is it for Turkey?', *Turkish Studies*, 4(1): 219–43.

Emerson, M. and Tocci, N. (2004), 'Turkey as a Bridgehead and Spearhead: Integrating EU and Turkish Foreign Policy', EU–Turkey Working Papers, 1.

Erzan, R., Kuzubas, U. and Yildiz, N. (2004), 'Growth and Immigration Scenarios for Turkey and the EU', EU–Turkey Working Papers, 13.

Esfahani, H. S. (2003), 'Fatal Attraction: Turkey's Troubled Relationship with the European Union', *Quarterly Review of Economics and Finance*, 43(5): 807–26.

EU (European Union) (1992), 'Treaty of Maastricht'. Online: <http://www.europa.eu.int/ eur-lex/en/treaties/dat/EU_treaty.html> (accessed 2 September 2007).

—— (1997), 'Treaty of Amsterdam'. Online: <http://www.europarl.europa.eu/topics/ treaty/pdf/amst-en.pdf> (accessed 2 September 2007).

—— (2001), 'Treaty of Nice'. Online: <http://www.ec.europa.eu/comm/nice_treaty/ summary_en.pdf> (accessed 2 September 2007).

—— (2002), 'Consolidated Version of the Treaty on the European Union'. Online: <http:// www.europa.eu.int/eur-lex/en/treaties/dat/EU_consol.html> (accessed 2 September 2007).

—— (2004), 'Treaty Establishing a Constitution for Europe', *Official Journal of the European Union*, No. C 310/01, 16 December.

—— (n.d.), 'Treaty Establishing the European Community'. Online: <http://www.europa. eu.int/eur-lex/en/treaties/dat/EC_consol.html> (accessed 2 September 2007).

Eurobarometer (2004), 'Recent Standard Eurobarometer'. Online: <http://www.ec.europa. eu/public_opinion/index_en.htm> (accessed 2 September 2007).

—— (2006), 'Attitudes towards European Union Enlargement', special volume, 255. Online: <http://www.mobility-migration.net/documents/attitude_towards_enlargement. pdf> (accessed 2 September 2007).

European Communities (1973), 'Texts of the Agreement Establishing an Association between the European Economic Community and Turkey and the Additional Protocol', *Official Journal of the European Communities*, No. C 113/16, 24.12.1973.

—— (1987), 'Single European Act'. Online: <http://www.europa.eu.int/eur-lex/en/treaties/ selected/livre509.html> (accessed 2 September 2007).

—— (2006), 'Council Regulation (EC) No 1083/2006 of 11 July 2006 Laying down General Provisions on the European Regional Development Fund, the European Social Fund and the Cohesion Fund and Repealing Regulation (EC) No. 1260/1999', *Official Journal of the European Union*, No. L 210/25, 31.7.2006.

European Court on Human Rights and Fundamental Freedoms, Council of Europe (2006), 'Case Law'. Online: <http://www.echr.coe.int/ECHR> (accessed 2 September 2007).

Eurostat (2006a), 'Data Navigation Tree'. Online: <http://www.epp.eurostat.ec.europa.eu/> (accessed 2 September 2007).

—— (2006b), News Release, 19 May. Online: <http://www.epp.eurostat.ec.europa.eu/portal/page?_pageid=0,1136107&_dad=portal&_schema=portal> (accessed 2 September 2007).

Faivre, E. (2004), 'Une restructuration salvatrice du système bancaire turc', in Didier Billion (ed.), *La Turquie vers un rendez-vous décisive avec l'Union Européenne*, Paris: Institut de Relations Internationales et Stratégiques, PUF, 103–8.

FAO (1999), Food and Agricultural Organization, *The Potential Extension of the Customs Union between Turkey and the EU: A Report on the Impact of Including Agricultural Products in the Customs Union on the Turkish Agricultural Sector*, Rome: FAO.

Faucompret, E. (1979), *Een politiek-economische studie van de relaties tussen de staten van de Europese Gemeenschap en de landen van het Middellands Zeegebied en het Nabije Oosten*, Antwerpen: UFSIA.

—— (1999) 'Volk zonder staat: De Koerden', *Streven*, 66: 412–24.

—— (2001a), 'European Political Integration: A Historical Perspective', Research Paper 2001–017, Antwerp, Faculty of Applied Economics.

—— (2001b), 'Cyprus: Het verdeelde eiland', *Streven*, 68: 825–36.

—— (2002), 'Het nieuwe grote spel: Centraal-Azië als geostrategische regio, *Streven*, 69: 508–22.

Faucompret, E. and Konings J. (2002), 'Het Poolse lidmaatschap van de Europese Unie', *Economisch en sociaal tijdschrift*, 56: 193–215.

Faucompret, E., Konings, J. and Vandenbussche, H. (1999), 'The Integration of Central and Eastern Europe in the European Union: Trade and Labour Market Adjustment', *Journal of World Trade Law*, 33: 121–45.

Findikçi, A. (1997), *Handelspolitische Auswirkungen der gemeinsamen Auszenhandelspolitik der Europäischen Gemeinschaft gegenüber assoziierten Drittstaaten am Beispiel der Türkei*, Frankfurt: Peter Lang.

François, J.-F., McQueen, M. and Wignaraja, G. (2005), 'European Union-Developing Countries FTAs: Overview and Analysis', *World Development*, 33(10): 1545–65.

Friends of Europe (2004), *Turkey's EU End-Game? European Policy Summit*, La Bibliothèque Solvay Brussels. Online: <http://www.friendsofeurope.org/Adv_Board_Netherlands_HCSS/2004/335/tabid/868/Default.aspx.

Furceri, D. and Karras, G. (2006), 'Are the New Members Ready for the Euro? A Comparison of Costs and Benefits', *Journal of Policy Modelling*, 28: 25–38.

Gönel, F. D. (2001), 'How Important is Intra-Industry Trade between Turkey and its Trading Partners?', *Russian and East European Finance and Trade*, 37(4): 61–76.

Grabbe, H. (2004), 'From Drift to Strategy: Why the EU should Start Accession Talks with Turkey', Centre for European Reforms Essays. Online: <http://www.cer.org.uk> (accessed 2 September 2007).

Grethe, H. (2004), 'De Integratie van de Turkse Landbouwsector: Twee scenario's', in R. T. Griffiths and D. Özdemir (eds), *Turkije in Europa: Turkije en het lidmaatschap van de Europese Unie*, Utrecht: Lemma, 155–75.

Griffiths, R. T. (2004), 'Turks Lidmaatschap: Implicaties voor de Begroting', in R. T. Griffiths and D. Özdemir (eds), *Turkije in Europa: Turkije en Lidmaatschap van de Europese Unie*, Utrecht: Lemma, 177–92.

Gültekin, N. B. and Yilmaz, K. (2005), 'The Turkish Economy before the EU Accession Talks', in M. Lake (ed.), *The EU and Turkey: A Glittering Prize or a Milestone?*, London:

Federal Trust for Education and Research, 61–77.

Gündüz, A. (2001), 'Human Rights and Turkey's Future in Europe', *Orbis*, 45(1): 15–30.

Güney, A. (2005), 'The Future of Turkey in the European Union', *Futures*, 37: 303–16.

Güney, A. and Karatekelioğlu, P. (2005), 'Turkey's EU Candidacy and Civil–Military Relations: Challenges and Prospects', *Armed Forces & Security*, 31(3): 439–62.

Gürsel, S. (2004), 'Du gouffre à la reprise', in D. Billion (ed.), *La Turquie vers un rendez-vous décisive avec l'Union Européenne*, Paris: Institut de Relations Internationales et Stratégiques, PUF, 109–14.

Hagemann S. and De Clerch-Sachsse, J. (2007), 'Decision-Making in the enlarged Council of Ministers: Evaluating the Facts', Centre for European Policy Studies Policy Brief, 119. Online: <http://shop.ceps.eu/BookDetail.php!item_id=1430> (accessed 2 September 2007).

Hale, W. (2003), 'Human Rights, the European Union and the Turkish Accession Process', in A. Carkogly and R. M. Rubin (eds), *Turkey and the European Union: Domestic Politics, Economic Integration and International Dynamics*, London and Portland, (Or.): Frank Cass, 107–26.

Harrison, G. W., Rutherford, T. F. and Tarr, D. G. (1996), 'Economic Implications for Turkey of a Customs Union with the European Union', Policy Research Working Paper, 1599, The World Bank, International Economics Department.

Hartler, C. and Laird, S. (1999), 'The EU Model and Turkey: A Case for Thanksgiving?', World Trade Organization Staff Working Paper.

Harun, A. (2003), *Turkey and the EU: An Awkward Candidate for Membership,* Aldershot and Burlington: Ashgate.

Heritage Foundation (2006), 'Index of Economic Freedom'. Online: <http://www.heritage.org/index/countries.cfm> (accessed 2 September 2007).

Hillyard, M. and Barclay, C. (1998), 'EU Enlargement: The Financial Consequences', Library Research Paper, 98/56, House of Commons.

Hoekman, B. M. and Togan, S. (2005) (eds), *Turkey: Economic Reform and Accession to the European Union*, World Bank.

Hughes, K. (2004), 'Turkey and the European Union: Just Another Enlargement? Exploring the Implications of Turkish Accession', A Friends of Europe Working Paper.

—— (2006), 'Turkey and the EU: Four Scenarios: From Train Crash to Full Steam Ahead', A Friends of Europe Working Paper.

Human Rights Watch (2000), 'Turkey: Human Rights and the European Union Accession Partnership'. Online: <http://www.hrw.org/reports/2000/turkey2/> (accessed 2 September 2007).

—— (2006), 'Report on Turkey'. Online: <http://www.hrw.org/wr2k/Eca-20.htm> (accessed 2 September 2007).

Huntington, S. P. (1996), *The Clash of Civilizations and the Remaking of the World Order*, New York: Simon & Schuster.

ILO (International Labour Organization) (2006), 'Laborsta Database'. Online: <http://www.laborsta.ilo.org/> (accessed 2 September 2007).

IMF (International Monetary Fund) (2006), *Balance of Payments Yearbook*, Washington: IMF.

Insel, A. (2004), 'La Turquie à l'horizon de 2020', in A. Kazancigil (ed.), *La Turquie au tournant du Siècle*, Paris, Budapest and Turin: L'Harmattan: 113–25.

Jenkins, G. (2003), 'Muslim Democrats in Turkey?', *Survival*, 45(1): 45–66.

Jones, E. and van der Bijl, N. (2004), 'Public Opinion and Enlargement: A Gravity Approach', *European Union Politics*, 5(3): 331–51.

Kafyeke, C. (2006), 'L'Adhésion de la Turquie à l'Union Européenne: Enjeux et état du débat', *Courrier Hebdomadaire,* Centre de Recherche et d'Information Sociopolitiques, 28/29 (1933–1934). Online: <http://www.cairn.info/resume_p.php?ID_ARTICLE=CRIS_1933_0005.

Karabelias, G. (2003), 'A Brief Overview of the Evolution of Civil–Military Relations in Albania, Greece and Turkey during the Post-WWII Period', *Journal of Political and Military Sociology*, 31(1): 57–70.

Karpat, K. H. (1968) (ed.), *Political and Social Thought in the Contemporary Middle East*, London: Pall Mall.

—— (1973a), 'Structural Change, Historical Stages of Modernization, and the Role of Social Groups in Turkish Politics', in K. H. Karpat (ed.), *Social Change and Politics in Turkey: A Structural Historical Analysis*, Leiden: E. J. Brill, 11–92.

—— (1973b), 'Ideology in Turkey after the Revolution of 1960: Nationalism and Socialism', in K. H. Karpat (ed.), *Social Change and Politics in Turkey: A Structural Historical Analysis*, Leiden: E. J. Brill, 317–66.

—— (1973c), 'Social Groups and the Political System after 1960', in K. H. Karpat (ed.), *Social Change and Politics in Turkey: A Structural Historical Analysis*, Leiden: E. J. Brill, 227–81.

—— (1974), 'The Stages of Ottoman History: A Structural Comparative Approach', in K. H. Karpat (ed.), *The Ottoman State and its Place in World History*, Leiden: E. J. Brill, 79–98.

Kaufmann, E. (2006), 'Breeding for God', *Prospect*, 128: 26–30. Online: <http://www.population-growth-migration.info/index.php?page=population.html> (accessed 2 September 2007).

Kazancigil, A. (1986), 'Paradigms of Modern State Formation in the Periphery', in A. Kazancigil (ed.), *The State in Global Perspective*, Paris: Unesco; London and Vermont: Gower, 119–42.

—— (2004), 'Du coup d'état militaire à l'Union Européenne, 1980–2004', in A. Kazancigil (ed.), *La Turquie au tournant du siècle*, Paris, Budapest, and Turin: L'Harmattan, 15–44.

Keyder, C. (2006), 'Moving in from the Margins? Turkey in Europe', *Diogenes*, 53: 72–81.

Khan, M. R. and Yavuz, H. M. (2003), 'Bringing Turkey into Europe', *Current History*, 101 (653): 119–23.

Kirişçi, K. (2003), 'The Question of Asylum and Illegal Migration in European–Turkish Relations', in A. Carkoglu and B. Rubin (eds), *Turkey and the European Union: Domestic Politics, Economic Integration and International Dynamics*, London and Portland, OR: Frank Cass, 79–126.

—— (2006), 'Turkey's Foreign Policy in Turbulent Times', Chaillot Paper No. 92; Paris: EU, Institute for Security Studies.

König, H. and Sickiry, M. (2005) (eds), *Gehört die Türkei zu Europa? Wegweisungen für ein Europa am Scheideweg*, Bielefeld: Transcript Verlag.

Konings, J. and Murphy, A. P. (2006), 'Do Multinational Enterprises Relocate Employment to Low-Wage Regions? Evidence from European Multinationals', *Review of World Economics*, 142(2): 267–86.

Konings, J. and Vandenbussche, H. (2005), 'Antidumping Protection and Markups of Domestic Firms', *Journal of International Economics*, 65: 151–65.

Konings, J., Van Cayseele, P. and Warzynski, F. (2005), 'The Effects of Privatization and Competitive Pressure on Firms' Price–Cost Margins: Micro Evidence from Emerging Economies', *Review of Economics and Statistics*, 87(1): 124–34.

Kotan, Z. and Sayan, S. (2002), 'A Comparative Investigation of the Price Competitiveness of Turkish and Southeast Asian Exports in the European Union Market, 1990–1997', *Emerging Markets and Trade*, 38(4): 59–85.

Krekeler-Joeris, A. (1996), *Turkey: A Bridge to Central Asia? Aspects of a Foreign Policy between Megalomania and Inability*, Leuven: KULeuven.

Laciner, S., Oezcan, M. and Bal, I. (2005), *European Union with Turkey: The Possible Impact of Turkey's Membership on the European Union*, Ankara: ISRO.

Landau, J. M. (1981), *Pan-Turkism in Turkey: A Study of Irredentism*, London: C. Hurst.

Lannon, E. and Lebullenger, J. (2006) (eds), *Les Défis d'une adhésion de la Turquie à l'Union Européenne*, Brussels: Bruylant.

Larrabee, S. F. (2004), 'Die Türken vor Brüssel: Eine Amerikanische Sicht der Beziehungen zwischen der Türkei und der EU', *Internationale Politik*, 59(11/12): 125–33.

Larrabee, S. F. and Lesser, I. O. (2003), *Turkish Foreign Policy in an Age of Uncertainty*, Santa Monica, CA, Arlington, VA, and Pittsburgh, PA: Rand.

Latham and Watkins (2003), Client Alert, Global Antitrust and Competition Practice, no. 281. Online: <http:www.euractiv.com/en/enlargement/state-aid-new-member-states/article (accessed 2 September 2007).

Lejour, A. M. and de Mooij, R. A. (2005), 'Turkish Delight: Does Turkey's Accession to the EU Bring Economic Benefits?', *Kyklos*, 58(1): 87–120.

Lejour, A. M., de Mooij, R. A. and Capel, C. H. (2004), 'Assessing the Economic Implications of Turkish Accession to the EU', Netherlands Bureau for Economic Policy Analysis, CPB Document, 56.

Levinsohn, J. (1993), 'Testing the Imports-as-Market-Discipline Hypothesis', *Journal of International Economics*, 35: 1–22.

Liel, A. (2001), *Turkey in the Middle East: Oil, Islam and Politics*, Boulder, CO, and London: Lynne Rienner.

Littoz-Monnet, A. and Villanueva Penas, B. (2005), 'Turkey and the European Union: The Implications of a Specific Enlargement', RRI/KIIB papers, Brussels: Royal Institute of International Relations. Online: <http:www.irri-kiib.be/papers/050404Turquie-ALM-BVP.pdf> (accessed 2 September 2007).

Lohrman, A.-M. (2002), 'A Dynamic Analysis of Turkey's Trade with the European Union', *Russian and East European Finance and Trade*, 38(2): 44–58.

Loizides, N. G. (2002), 'Greek–Turkish Dilemmas and the Cyprus EU Accession Process', *Security Dialogue*, 33(4): 429–44.

Long, David (1997), 'The Why and How of EU Enlargement', Working Paper 16, Institute of International Relations, University of British Colombia.

Lorentzen, J. and Møllgaard, P. (2002), 'Competition Compliance: Limits to Competition Policy Harmonization in EU Enlargement', University of Copenhagen, Centre for Industrial Economics.

Lundell, M., Lampietti, J., Pertev R., Pohlmeier, L., Akder, H., Ocek, E. and Jha, S. (2004), *Turkey: A Review of the Impact of the Reform of Agricultural Sector Subsidization*, Washington: World Bank.

McLaren, L. M. (2000), 'Turkey's Eventual Membership of the EU: Turkish Elite Perspectives on the Issue', *Journal of Common Market Studies*, 38(1): 117–29.

Mãné-Estrada, A. (2006), 'European Energy Security: Towards the Creation of the Geo-Energy Space, *Energy Policy*, 34(18): 3773–86.

Martin, P., Midgley, E. and Teitelbaum, M. (2002), 'Best Practice Options: Turkey', *International Migration*, 40(3): 119–31.

Matthews, O. (2006), 'Who Lost Turkey?', *Newsweek*, 11 December.

Mercenier, J. and Yeldan, E. (1997), 'On Turkey's Trade Policy: Is a Customs Union with Europe Enough?', *European Economic Review*, 41: 871–80.

Missiroli, A. (2002), 'EU–NATO Cooperation in Crisis Management: No Turkish Delight for ESDP', *Security Dialogue*, 33(1): 9–26.

Mousseau, D. Y. (2006), 'Turkey and the EU: The Importance of the Markets', *Survival*, 48(3): 97–108.

Müftüler-Bac, M. (1996), 'Turkey's Predicament in the Post-Cold War Era', *Futures*, 28(3): 255–68.

—— (2004), 'The New Face of Turkey: The Domestic and Foreign Policy Implications of November 2002 Elections', *East European Quarterly*, 37(4): 421–38.

—— (2005), 'The Institutional and Theoretical Implications of the Enlargement on Turkey's Accession to the European Union', in Jean-Claude Vérez (ed.), *D'un élargissement à l'autre: La Turquie et les autres candidats*, Paris: l'Harmattan, 149–161.

Murphy, A. B. (2004), 'Turkey's Place in the Europe of the 21st Century', *Eurasian Geography and Economics*, 45(8): 583–7.

Muus P. and van Dam, E.W. (1996), 'Comparative Research on International Migration and International Migration Policy: Migration from the Maghreb and Turkey to the European Union, and from Mexico, Guatemala and El Salvador to the United States', Centre for Migration Research, University of Amsterdam, Luxemburg: Office for Official Publications of the European Communities.

NATO (North Atlantic Treaty Organization) (2004), 'Istanbul Cooperation Initiative'. Online: <http://www.nato.int/docu/comm/2004/06-istanbul/docu-cooperation.htm> (accessed 2 September 2007).

Nichols, T., Sugur, N. and Demir, E. (2002), 'Beyond Cheap Labour: Trade Unions and Development in the Turkish Metal Industry', *Sociological Review* 50 (1): 23–47.

OECD (Organization for Economic Cooperation and Development) (2006a), 'Assessment and Recommendations – Turkey'. Online: <http://www.oecd.org/document/21/0,2340,en_2649_201185_37492245_1_1_1_1,00.html.> (accessed 2 September 2007).

—— (2006b), 'Database'. Online: <http://www.new.sourceoecd.org/rpsv/statistic/s3_about.htm?jnlissn=16081153> (accessed 2 September 2007).

Öğütçü, M. (1995), 'Eurasian Energy Prospects and Politics. Need for a Longer-term Western Strategy', *Futures*, 27(1): 37–63.

Oğuzlu, T. H. (2003), 'An Analysis of Turkey's Prospective Membership in the European Union from a Security Perspective', *Security Dialogue*, 34(3): 285–99.

Okkerse, L. and Termote, A. (2004), 'Hoe Vreemd is Vreemd op de Arbeidsmarkt? Over de Allochtone Arbeidskrachten in België', Dienst Statistiek en Economische Informatie, Statistische Studie No. 11.

Önis, Z. (2000), 'Luxembourg, Helsinki and Beyond: Towards an Interpretation of Recent Turkey–EU Relations', *Government and Opposition*, 35(4): 463–83.

—— (2004), 'Diverse but Converging Paths to European Union Membership: Poland and Turkey in Comparative Perspective', *East European Politics and Societies*, 18(3): 481–512.

—— (2006), 'Varieties and Crises of Neoliberal Globalization: Argentina, Turkey and the IMF', *Third World Quarterly*, 27(2): 239–63.

Önis, Z. and Yilmaz, S. (2005), 'The Turkey–EU–US Triangle in Perspective: Transformation or Continuity?', *Middle East Journal*, 59(2): 265–84.

Oskam, A., Longworth, N. and Vilchez, I.M. (2005a), 'Consequences for the EU-27 of Enlargement to Turkey', in A. M. Burrell and A. J. Oskam (eds), *Turkey in the European Union:Implications for Agriculture, Food and Structural Policy*, Wallingford and Cambridge, MA: CABI, 218–49.

Oskam, A., Longworth, N. and Yildiz, A. (2005b), 'Turkey's Economy and Regional Income Distribution', in A. M. Burrell and A. J. Oskam (eds), *Turkey in the European Union: Implications for Agriculture, Food and Structural Policy*, Wallingford and Cambridge, MA: CABI, 9–25.

Oskam, A., Burrell, A., Temel, T., van Berkum, S., Longworth, N. and Vilchez, I. M. (2004), 'Turkey in the European Union: Consequences for Agriculture, Food, Rural Areas and Structural Policy', Report Commissioned by the Dutch Ministry of Agriculture, Nature and Food Quality (Executive Summary), Wageningen University.

Özbudun, E. (1998), 'Constitution Making and Democratic Consolidation in Turkey', in M. Heper, A. Kazancigil and B. A. Rockman (eds), *Institutions and Democratic State-craft*, Boulder, CO: Westview Press, 227–43.

Özcan, M. (2005), 'Turkey's Possible Influences on the Internal Security of the European Union: The Issue of Illegal Migration', in S. Laçiner, M. Özcan and I. Bal (eds), *European Union with Turkey: The Possible Impact of Turkey's Membership on the European Union*, Ankara: ISRO, 87–134.

Özdemir, D. (2004), 'Integratietheorie en het nut van het vredesdividend', in R. T. Griffiths and D. Özdemir (eds), *Turkije in Europa: Turkije en het lidmaatschap van de Europese Unie*, Utrecht: Lemma, 139–51.

Özel, S. (2004), 'Der Lange Weg nach Europa: Die Saga von den Beziehungen der Türkei zur EU', *Internationale Politik*, 59(11/12): 115–24.

Park, W. H. (2005), 'The Security Dimensions of Turkey–EU Relations', in M. Lake (ed.), *The EU and Turkey: A Glittering Prize or a Milestone?*, London: Federal Trust for Education and Research, 127–40.

Patton, M. J. (2006), 'The Economic Policies of Turkey's AKP Government: Rabbits from a Hat?', *Middle East Journal*, 60(3), 513–36.

Phillips, D. L. (2004), 'Turkey's Dream of Accession', *Foreign Affairs*, 83(5): 86–97.

Piracha, M. and Vickerman, R. (2001), 'Immigration, Labour Mobility and EU Enlargement'. Online: <http://www.kent.ac.uk/economics/research/1europe/RIIAChapter-final.pdf> (accessed 2 September 2007).

Polat, N. (2006), 'Identity Politics and the Domestic Context of Turkey's European Union Accession', *Government and Opposition*, 41(4): 512–33.

Przewieslik, W. (2005), 'Ist die Türkei Reif für die EU?', *Merkur-Deutsche Zeitschrift für Europäisches Denken*, 59(1): 14–27.

Rehn, O. (2005a), 'EU and Turkey together on the Same Journey'. Online: <http://www.europa-eu-un.org/articles/en/article_5110_en.htm> (accessed 2 September 2007).

Rehn, O. (2005b), 'Accession Negotiations with Turkey: Fulfilling the Criteria', European Economic and Social Committee EU–Turkey JCC, Brussels, 28 November.

—— (2006a), 'Building a New Consensus on Enlargement: How to Match the Strategic Interest and Functioning Capacity of the EU?', European Policy Center, Brussels, 19 May.

—— (2006b), 'Reforms in Turkey: In the First Place it is the Interest of the Turkish Citizens', EP Debate on Turkey, Strasbourg, 26 September.

—— (2006c), 'Europe's Next Frontiers', Lecture at the Finnish Institute of International Affairs, Helsinki, 27 October.

—— (2006d), 'Debate on Enlargement in the European Parliament', Strasbourg, 13 December.

Republic of Turkey, Ministry of Culture and Tourism (1923), 'Atatürk declares on Agriculture'. Online: <http://www.kultur.gov.tr/EN/BelgeGoster.aspx?17A16AE30572D313A C8287D72AD903BECCFE6697666DD6A3> (accessed 2 September 2007).

Republic of Turkey, Ministry of Culture and Tourism (2003), 'Seventh Reform Package'. Online: <http://www.civilitasresearch.org/publications/view_article.cfm?article_id=47)> (accessed 2 September 2007).

Republic of Turkey, Prime Ministry, State Planning Organization (2003). Online: <http://www.regional-studies-assoc.ac.uk/events/aalborg05/bilen.pdf> (accessed 2 September 2007).

Republic of Turkey, Prime Ministry, State Planning Organization (n.d.), 'Executive Summary of the Turkish National Action Programme for the Adoption of the Acquis'. Online: <http://www.secipro.net/doc_meetings/20030619113710611.doc> (accessed 2 September 2007).

Rill, B. (2006), *Kemal Atatürk: Een Biografie*, Roeselare: Roularta.

Roberts, J. (2004), The Turkish Gate: Energy Transit and Security Issues, *Turkish Policy Quarterly*, 3(4). Online: <http://www.esiweb.org/pdf/esi_turkey_tpq_id_13.pdf> (accessed 2 September 2007).

Rochtus, D. (2002), 'De Kemalistische Staat op de Proefstand', in Dirk Rochtus, Gerrit De Vylder and Veli Yüksel (eds), *Turkije: Springstof voor de Europese Unie?*, Antwerpen and Apeldoorn: Garant, 163–87.

Rouleau, E. (2000), 'Turkey's Dream of Democracy', *Foreign Affairs*, 79(6): 100–14.

Rumford, C. (2002), 'Placing Democratization within the Global Frame: Sociological Approaches to Universalism and Democratic Contestation in Contemporary Turkey', *Sociological Review*, 50(2): 258–77.

—— (2003), 'Resisting Globalization? Turkey–EU Relations and Human and Political Rights in the Context of Cosmopolitan Democratization', *International Sociology*, 18(2): 379–94.

Sayek, S. and Selover, D. D. (2002), 'International Interdependence and Business Cycle Transmission between Turkey and the European Union', *Southern Economic Journal*, 69(2): 206–38.

Scandizzo, P. L. (1998), 'Growth, Trade and Agriculture: An Investigative Survey', Rome: FAO Economic and Social Development Paper, 143.

SIPRI (Stockholm International Peace Research Institute) (2007), 'SIPRI Yearbook 2007: Armaments, Disarmament and International Security'. Online: <http://www.sipri.org/contents/milap/milex/mex_trends.html> (accessed 2 September 2007).

Somer, M. (2005), 'Failures of the Discourse of Ethnicity: Turkey, Kurds and the Emerging Iraq', *Security Dialogue*, 36(1): 109–28.

Sozen, S. and Shaw, I. (2003), 'Turkey and the European Union: Modernizing a Traditional State?', *Social Policy & Administration*, 37(2): 108–20.

Stern, N. (1996), *Growth Theories, Old and New and the Role of Agriculture in Economic Development*, Rome: FAO.

Suárez de Vivero, J. L. and Rodriguez Mateos, J. C. (2006), 'Maritime Europe and EU Enlargement: A Geopolitical Perspective', *Marine Policy*, 30(2): 167–72.

Sugden, J. (2003), 'Leverage in Theory and Practice: Human Rights and Turkey's EU Candidacy', *Turkish Studies*, 4(1): 241–64.

Swinnen, J. F. M. (2004), 'Eastern Enlargement of the EU and its Implications for Agriculture and Agricultural Policies', *Food Economics*, 1(1): 5–11.

Swinnen, J. F. M. and Rozelle S. (2006), *From Marx and Mao to the Market: The Economics and Politics of Agricultural Transition*, New York: Oxford University Press.

Talmon, S. (2001), 'The Cyprus Question before the European Court of Justice', *European Journal of International Law*, 12(4): 727–50. Online: <http://www.jura.uni-duesseldorf.de/RAVE/ends/endsv/v16/v162.htm> (accessed 2 September 2007).

Taniyici, S. (2003), 'Transformation of Political Islam in Turkey: Islamist Welfare Party's Pro-EU Turn', *Party Politics*, 9(4): 463–83.

Tank, P. (2001), 'Turkey as a Special Case for the EU: Will the Generals Retreat from Politics?', *Security Dialogue*, 32(2): 217–30.

Tekin, A. (2005), 'Future of Turkey–EU Relations: A Civilization Discourse', *Futures*, 37: 287–302.

Temel, T. (2005), 'Expected Consequences for Turkey of EU Entry in 2015', in A. M. Burrell and A. J. Oskam (eds), *Turkey in the European Union: Implications for Agriculture, Food and Structural Policy*, Wallingford and Cambridge, MA: CABI, 251–77.

Theisen, H. (2004), 'Überdehnung oder Überwindung? Europas Kulturelle Grenzen', *Osteuropa*, 54(3): 34–46.

Tibi, B. (1998), 'Die Postkemalistische Türkei: Zwischen EU und Pantürkischem Islamismus', *Internationale Politik*, 53(1): 1–8.

Tocci, N. (2001), 'Turkey and the European Union: Reversing Vicious Circles in Turkey's Political Economy', *Russian and East European Finance and Trade*, 37(4): 5–38.

Togan, S. (2000), 'Effects of a Turkey–European Union Customs Union and Prospects for the Future', *Russian and East European Finance and Trade*, 36(4): 5–25.

—— (2001), 'The Turkish Economy and the European Economies in Transition', in S. Togan and V. N. Balasubramanyam, *Turkey and Central and Eastern European Countries in Transition*, Basingstoke and New York: Palgrave, 7–49.

—— (2004), 'Economic Aspects of the Accession of Turkey to the European Union', *Intereconomics: Review of European Economic Policy,* 39: 300–3.

Transparency International (2005), 'Corruption Perceptions Index'. Online: <http://www.transparency.org/news_room/in_focus/cpi_2005> (accessed 2 September 2007).

Traser, J. (2005), Report on the Free Movement of Workers in the EU-25: Who's Afraid of EU Enlargement', Brussels: European Citizen Action Service. Online: <http://www.ecas.org/file_uploads/1182.pdf (accessed 2 September 2007).

Tüsiad (2003), 'Turkey News: 18–24 March 2003'. Online: <http://www.tusiad.us/specific_page.cfm?CONTENT_ID=330> (accessed 2 September 2007).

Tüsiad and Yased (2004), 'Foreign Direct Investments. Attractiveness of Turkey: A Comparative Analysis'. Online: <http:www.tusiad.us/Content/uploaded/turkey-foreign-direct-investlent-attractiveness.pdf> (accessed 2 September 2007).

Üçer, E. (2006), 'Turkey's Accession to the European Union', *Futures*, 38: 197–211.

Uğur, M. (1999), *The European Union and Turkey: An Anchor/Credibility Dilemma*, Aldershot, Brookfield, Singapore and Sidney: Ashgate.

—— (2004), 'Economic Mismanagement and Turkey's Troubled Relations with the EU. Is there a Link?', in M. Uğur and N. Canefe (eds), *Turkey and European Integration: Accession Projects and Issues*, London and New York: Routledge, 75–99.

Ülgen, S. and Zahariadis, Y. (2004), 'The Future of Turkish–EU Trade Relations: Deepening versus Widening', EU–Turkey Working Papers, 5.

UN (United Nations) (2005), 'Human Development Index (2005)'. Online: <http://www.answers.com/topic/list-of-countries-by-human-development-index> (accessed 2 September 2007).

—— (n.d.) Charter of the United Nations. Online: <http://www.un.org/aboutun/charter/> (accessed 2 September 2007).

UNIDO (United Nations Industrial Development Organization) (1995), *Policies for Competition and Competitiveness: The Case of Industry in Turkey*, Vienna: United Nations Industrial Development Organization.

US Department of State (2004), *Country Reports on Human Rights Practices 2004: Turkey*. Washington: Bureau of Democracy, Human Rights, and Labor. Online: <http://www.state.gov/g/drl/rls/hrrpt/2004/41713.htm> (accessed 2 September 2007).

Van de Meerssche, P. (2006), *Internationale Politiek. Deel II: 1945–2005*, Leuven: Acco.

Vandenbussche, H. and Zanardi, M. (2006), 'The Global Chilling Effects of Antidumping Proliferation', LICOS Discussion Paper, 167/2006.

Vergil, H. (2002), 'Exchange Rate Volatility in Turkey and its Effects on Trade Flows', *Journal of Economic and Social Research*, 4(1): 83–99.

Waxman, D. (1998), 'Turkey's Identity Crisis: Domestic Discord and Foreign Policy', Series on Conflict Studies, Washington: Research Institute for the Study of Conflict and Terrorism, 1–26.

Wetenschappelijke Raad voor het Regeringsbeleid (2004), *De Europese Unie, Turkije en Islam*, Amsterdam: Amsterdam University Press.

Weymouth, L. (2006), 'Whatever Is Necessary', *Newsweek*, 9 October.

Wilkens, K. A. (1998), *Turkey Today: Troubled Ally's Search for Identity*, New York: Foreign Policy Association.

Wimmel, A. (2005), 'Transnationale Diskurse in der Europäischen Medienöffentlichkeit: Die Debatte zum EU-Beitritt der Türkei', *Politische Vierteljahresschrift*, 46(3): 459–83.

World Bank (2005a), 'Gini Coefficients'. Online: <http://www.answers.com/topic/list-of-countries-by-income-equality> (accessed 2 September 2007).

—— (2005b), 'World Development Indicators 2005'. Online: <http://www.publications.worldbank.org/WDI/> (accessed 2 September 2007).

—— (2006a), 'Turkey: Country Economic Memorandum: Promoting Sustained Growth and Convergence with the European Union'. Online: <http://www.worldbank.org.tr/wbsite/external/countries/ecaext/turkeyextn/> (accessed 2 September 2007).

—— (2006b), 'World Development Indicators 2006'. Online: <http://www.web.worldbank.org/wbsite/external/datastatistics> (accessed 2 September 2007).

World Economic Forum (2006), 'Global Competitiveness Index'. Online: <http://www.weforum.org/pdf/Global_Competitiveness_Reports/Reports/gcr_2006/top50.pdf> (accessed 2 September 2007).

WTO (World Trade Organization) (2001), 'Overview of Developments in the International Trading Environment', *Annual Report by the Director-General*. Online: <http://www.wto.org/english/res_e/booksp_e/annual_report_dg2001_e.pdf> (accessed 2 September 2007).

Yasar, B. S. (2006), 'An Overview of Anti-Dumping Practices in the World and in the Framework of EU–Turkey Relations', LICOS Discussion Paper, 174/2006.

Yavuz, H. M. and Khan, M. R. (2004), 'Turkey and Europe: Will East Meet West?', *Current History*: 389–93.

Yesilada, B. A. (2002), 'Turkey's Candidacy for EU Membership', *Middle East Journal*, 56(1): 94–111.

Yildiz, K. (2005), *The Kurds in Turkey: EU Accession and Human Rights*, London; Ann Arbor, MI: Pluto Press.

Yilmaz, B. (2002), 'Turkey's Competitiveness in the European Union: A Comparison with Greece, Portugal, Spain and the EU/12/15', *Russian and East European Finance and Trade*, 38(3): 54–72.

Young, H. and Rees, N. (2005), 'EU Voting Behavior in the UN General Assembly, 1990–2002: The EU's Europeanizing Tendencies', *Irish Studies in International Affairs*, 16: 193–207.

Zürcher, E. J. (1997), *Turkey. A Modern History*, London and New York: I. B. Tauris.

Index

corruption 13, 15, 16, 19, 170; anti-corruption measures 159–61; control 84, 142; foreign direct investment (FDI) 92; government 160; political 151, 153; prevents privatization 67

Corruption Perceptions Index (CPI) 159

Council of Europe 21; Civil Law Conventions on Corruption 160; Copenhagen 151; democracy 151

Council of Higher Education 153

Council of Ministers 22, 28, 39; decision making body 23; decision making powers 32; legislation 40; National Security Council (NSC) 155; voting 30, 41

Council of State 14

coup: 1913 (January) 2; 1960 (May) 8, 10, 25, 153; 1970 12; 1980 13, 29; 1997 15; 2007 (April) 17

Court of Accounts 14, 151

Court of Auditors 160

Court of Cassation (Supreme Court of Appeals) 14, 164

Court of Human Rights 21

crisis: economic 13, 57–8; European Economic Community (EEC) 26; financial 15; identity 188; oil 13; political 12, 20, 25; Suez 22

culture 4, 38; development 5; diversity 169; identity 145; rights 162

current account: deficit 64–5

customs union 22, 25, 26, 31, 47, 97–9; agreements 123; compliance 103; effects on trade 87; foreign direct investment (FDI) 78, 80; free trade 50; progress 149; revised 171; Turkey 34, 35

Cyprus 16, 34, xvii; accession 37, 39, 42; bilateral relations 171, 174, 176–80, 182; influence in EU 139; missiles 135; not recognized by Turkey 48; occupation by Turkey 131, 176; offered EU membership 36; relations with Turkey 31, 149; Turkey invades 28; Turkey threatens 38; voting within EU 42

Czech Republic 33

Dardanelles 1, 176

de Mooij, R.A. 103, 125, 161

defence: budget 22; European Rapid Reaction Force 40

Defence and Co-operation Agreement: USA and Turkey 140

Delors, Jacques (President, European Commission) 30

Demirel, Süleyman 11, 12, 19, 133; becomes President 15

democracy xviii; Birkelbach Report 23; Central and Eastern European Countries (CEEC) 33; liberalization 170; Modern Turkey 3; multi-party 6, 7, 18, 151, 157; parliamentary 10, 151; political systems 9, 151; reforms 13, 59; restored 19, 28, 29; secular 155; shift of policy areas 32; in Turkey 24, 25, 27, 30, 131

Democratic Left Party 16

Democratic Party (DP) 7, 8, 15, 151; coup 153; removed 8–9

demographics 113, 115

Denktas, Rauf (Northern Cyprus) 177, 195n6

deregulation: competition 150; financial sector 72

d'Estaing, Valéry Giscard: opposes Turkish accession 149

devaluation 8, 17, 56; expected 57

development 10; agriculture 83; aid from EEC 24; cultural 5; economic 8, 28, 54–5, 146; human 50, 52, 54; Organization for Economic Co-operation and Development (OECD) 26; regional 123; social 54–5, 146; socio-economic 5

Dink, Hrant 194n11

diplomacy 3, 130; Eastern European 133

discrimination: of migrants 111; of women 5

domestic industrial structure 72; concentrated 67–8

domestic production: protectionism 99

earthquakes 38, 57, 174

Ecevit, Bülent 11, 12, 15, 58; as Prime Minister 16

economic: activity 124; boom 11; co-operation 10; corruption 160; crisis 13, 56, 57–8, 71; crisis 1929 5–6; criteria 185, xvii; development 28, 54, 126, 146; difficulties 148; equality 52–3; freedom 69; growth 15, 23, 55–60, 65, 76–7; history 55–8; integration 29, 30, 150, 155, 185; interests 4; interference 69; key indicators 54–5; liberalization 58, 170; misery 20; partners 24; policy 6, 24; power 154; recovery 20, 60; reforms 59, 157, xvii; rights 162; stability 49; theory 68, 81, 95; transformation 73, 130

Economic Congress of İzmir (1923) 5

214   *Index*

economic problems: Turkish accession to
    EU xvii
Economist, The 184
economy: agriculture 118; international
    91; state control 6; Turkey 182; weak 33
education 7, 17, 74–5, 144–9; investment
    114; minorities 169; religious 8, 11, 14;
    spending 73
EEC (European Economic Community)
    xvi; membership transition 24
elections 5; 1965 11; 1973 12; 1983 14;
    1987 14; 1999 16; 2002 16; Eastern
    European 31; European Council 32;
    multi-party 7; of the President 17; vote
    rigging 8
electoral system 10, 151; coalition 160;
    reforms 14
employment 9; access 113; agriculture 83;
    France 23; rights 35; service industries
    83; social policy 108–10; of women 60
employment rates 60
EMU (Economic and Monetary Union) 29,
    30, 32, 93–5; Copenhagen criteria 49
energy supplies 133, 136, 181
enlargement 24, 36, 40, 41, 47; agriculture
    121; benefits 185; benefits to Turkey
    187–8; budget 181; capacity 180;
    Central and Eastern European Countries
    (CEEC) 34; negotiations 26, 32; service
    provision 105
enterprise: restructuring 84–5
equality 1; economic 52–3; opportunities
    108; social 52–3
Erbakan, Necmettin 13, 15; as Prime
    Minister 16
Erdoğan, Recep Tayyip 16–18, 19, 177;
    international relations 135
Erim, Nihat 12
Erkin, Feridun Cemal (Minister Foreign
    Affairs, Turkey) 25
Erzan, R. 116
EU 16; absorption capacity 180–2; budget
    33, 125, 127, 180; co-operation 65;
    Common Agricultural Policy (CAP)
    187; Common External Tariff 122;
    Convention Against Torture 162;
    Convention on Human Rights 162;
    convergence 74, 93, 110, 121; decision
    making 39; employment regulations
    60; enlargement xvii–xviii; functional
    capacity 180; history 20; integration
    181; Internal Market Programme 103;
    markets 72–91; negotiations 18; policies

181; pressures Turkey 153; problems
    with Turkey 58; regional policy 123–4;
    restructuring 36; soft power 185; tension
    with Turkey 140; trading partner 85
EU membership 14, 16–17, 55, xviii;
    application by Turkey 59–60, 182;
    benefits to Turkey 156, 187–8; Central
    and Eastern European Countries (CEEC)
    148; EMU (Economic and Monetary
    Union) 95; movement of workers 112;
    Turkey 131, 136, 148, 155; Turkish
    citizens 145; USA supports Turkey 140
Eurobarometer Opinion Polls 114–15, 186
European: citizenship 32; defence 40;
    integration 20; laws 72; states 4
European Assembly 22
European Atomic Energy Community
    (EAEC) 22–3, 25
European Bank for Restructuring and
    Development (EBRD) 66
European Central Bank 95
European Coal and Steel Community
    (ECSC) 21–2, 25
European Commission 22, 28, 116,
    xvi–xvii; composition 39; *Progress
    Report 2006* xviii; proposals 23; reform
    package 150
European Convention on Human Rights:
    Convention on the Protection of Human
    Rights and Fundamental Freedoms 157
European Council 28, 36, xvi–xvii;
    Brussels (December 2004) 43, 176;
    Cannes (June 1995) 34; Copenhagen
    (December 2002) 42, 139; Copenhagen
    (June 1993) 33, 42, 171; December
    2004 45; Dublin (June 1990) 32;
    EMU (Economic and Monetary
    Union) 93; Essen (October 1994) 34;
    Fontainebleau (June 1984) 29; Hanover
    (June 1988) 30; Helsinki (1999) 38,
    41, 43; human rights 161; Lisbon 34;
    Luxembourg (December 1997) 37;
    Milan (June 1985) 29; Nice (December
    2000) 39; right of appeal 44; Strasbourg
    (December 1988) 30
European Court: of Human Rights 30, 162; of
    Justice 22, 101, 104–5, 110–12, 178, 188
European Defence and Security Policy
    (EDSP) 138, 140–1
European Defence Community (EDC) 22
European Economic Area (EEA) 32
European Economic Community (EEC)
    22–3, 24, 25; enlargement 26

CPSIA information can be obtained
at www.ICGtesting.com
Printed in the USA
BVHW04*0949261018
530490BV00018B/125/P